The Kingdom of God, the Black Pentecostal Church, and Empowerment

THE SPIRIT AND SOCIETY: PUBLIC THEOLOGY

Within the field of religious studies, Black Public Theology has been variously defined, often not connected to Christian faith. This series approaches Black Public Theology from the perspective of lived Christianity, including Spirit-inspired public engagement in Black contexts. Authors and contributors seek to connect Christian belief with the rest of Black lived experience that is those modes of life and existence which occur outside of the typical conception of the worship space.

The series includes select monographs by scholars within or sympathetic to the Black Pentecostal/Charismatic movement. Additionally, the compendium presents critical reflections on social challenges that disproportionately affect Black communities and the respective prophetic responses of Spirit-inspired ministries and organizations.

This peer-reviewed compilation has contributions from scholar-practitioners in the global African Diaspora as well as on the continent of Africa. The series will feature a range of disciplinary approaches including constructive theology, history, sociology, and philosophy. Drawing upon quality research, the works are a useful contribution to public theological discourse written with academic and faith-based readership in mind.

The Kingdom of God, the Black Pentecostal Church, and Empowerment

How the Power of the Holy Spirit Can Liberate the Black Community

DANA CARSON

Foreword by Trevor Grizzle

CASCADE *Books* • Eugene, Oregon

THE KINGDOM OF GOD, THE BLACK PENTECOSTAL CHURCH, AND EMPOWERMENT
How the Power of the Holy Spirit Can Liberate the Black Community

The Spirit and Society: Public Theology

Cascade Books
An Imprint of Wipf and Stock Publishers
199 W. 8th Ave., Suite 3
Eugene, OR 97401

www.wipfandstock.com

PAPERBACK ISBN: 979-8-3852-2411-1
HARDCOVER ISBN: 979-8-3852-2412-8
EBOOK ISBN: 979-8-3852-2413-5

Cataloguing-in-Publication data:

Names: Carson, Dana, author.

Title: The kingdom of God, the Black Pentecostal church, and empowerment : how the power of the Holy Spirit can liberate the Black community / Dana Carson.

Description: Eugene, OR: Cascade Books, 2026 | Series: The Spirit and Society: Public Theology. | Includes bibliographical references and index.

Identifiers: ISBN 979-8-3852-2411-1 (paperback) | ISBN 979-8-3852-2412-8 (hardcover) | ISBN 979-8-3852-2413-5 (ebook)

Subjects: LCSH: African American churches. | Pentecostal churches—Doctrines. | Kingdom of God.

Classification: BR563.N4 C356 2026 (print) | BR563.N4 (ebook)

For information, please address correspondence to:
Dana Carson Kingdom Ministries
7401 Gulf Freeway, Houston, TX 77017
Website: www.DrDanaCarson.org
Email: info@DrDanaCarson.com
All biblical quotations are from the New King James Version unless otherwise noted.

This book is dedicated to two of my spiritual fathers, who I consider two of the greatest Pentecostal pioneers and innovators impacting Pentecostalism worldwide—Apostle Richard D. Henton, founding pastor of Monument of Faith Church in Chicago, and Apostle Earl Wayne Wilcots, founding pastor of Bible Days Revival Church in Houston. Thank you for your labor in the Lord and your encouragement and support for me as a spiritual son. You made a difference in your lifetimes, and I truly miss you both!

Contents

Acknowledgments

THIS BOOK COULD NOT have come to life without the dedication, support, and expertise of so many people.

First and foremost, I want to acknowledge my wife and friend, Rachelle Dianne Carson, my Baruch! Knitted to me in the flesh and the spirit—I could not do what I do without her. As my chief editor, thank you for your insights, patience, and guidance through each stage of this journey. Your keen eye and thoughtful feedback have brought clarity and depth to this book. I am deeply grateful to the editorial team—Min. April Smith, Katrin Hunt, and Dr. Shannon Cormier have been by my side from the first draft to the final edits. Your expertise, eyes for detail, and tenacity have brought us to this point—you are all invaluable.

I am grateful to my wonderful children, Dana II and his wife Monet, John Anthony and his daughter Jaide, to Angel Naomi, Marielle Alli, and Devon Jarrod family—thank you for your unending sacrifice of me as your father for the betterment of others.

Thank you to my staff, who contributed directly or indirectly to bringing this book and others to readers around the world. Finally, thank you to everyone who has read my work, offered encouragement, or inspired ideas in conversations. I owe this book to all of you.

With heartfelt gratitude,
Dana Carson, MBA, DMin, PhD

Foreword

For a theology to be relevant and useful, it must be contextual; it must mirror the face, speak the language, and address the needs and most pressing concerns of its target audience. For this reason, probably in some way, all theology claims some degree of contextuality. The very title, *The Kingdom of God, the Black Pentecostal Church, and Empowerment: How the Power of the Holy Spirit Can Liberate the Black Community*, leaves no one in doubt as to what Dr. Carson's purpose and goal is.

For various reasons, Black communities in America have historically faced unique issues and challenges. African Americans have always turned to the Black church as a refuge in hard times. Afro-Pentecostal/Charismatic churches play a significant role in serving marginalized people in African American communities and as change agents. The author comes to the topic not as an ivory tower spectator, but as one steeped in the life of the community and as a scholar. Dr. Carson is one of the premier church leaders in America, with more than forty years of pastoral experience and a ministry with global reach and impact. A scholar, he has multiple degrees from some of the leading universities in the nation. He is the founder and president of Kingdom Theological Seminary and the R.O.C.K. Church in Houston, Texas. Carson's vision and passion for the Black Pentecostal Church is palpable and infectious. He has studied kingdom theology in all its variegated forms and adopted it as the maxim for the church and the seminary.

A bifurcated view has long prevailed in traditional Christianity regarding the work of the Holy Spirit in the world. The Spirit's work has largely been seen as spiritual and ecclesial, confining his role to the church. The work of redeeming and restoring society is left to human agency. Tracing the historical roots of the Pentecostal/Charismatic/Neo-Pentecostal church back to Azusa and further back to Africa, in his book,

Carson shows that the Spirit's empowerment has been at the forefront of social and spiritual advancements in the Black Pentecostal and Charismatic church in America.

A phenomenon of the African American church and a marvel of historic Afro-Pentecostalism has been its ability to meld social activism and preach a social gospel without losing the fire of the Holy Spirit. This was the vision and enduring legacy of William J. Seymour, the global spearhead of Pentecostalism, who spawned the Azusa Street Revival of 1906 with the belief that the blood of Christ had washed away the color line, relativizing and marginalizing racism—if not eliminating it altogether. It is from this tradition of Spirit empowerment and social engagement that Carson's theology sallies.

This ability to hold in tension the church's call to salvation and sanctification with the social mandate of impacting society with the gospel was epitomized in the late Leonard Lovett. A clergyman and academic, he was able to straddle the domains of church and academy, and synthesize theology and ethics, love and justice, and personal and social salvation. The transformative impact of the gospel of the kingdom on society is the driving passion of Carson's book.

Afro-Pentecostalism has never shied away from confronting personal and social sin in ways that bring deliverance or a state of psychological and social liberation to victimized Black people. A constellation of Pentecostal scholars have both written about or have been engaged in such ministry in some of the hardest areas in the country. The following come to mind: Bishop O. T. Jones Jr., Cheryl Townsend Gilkes, David Daniels, Alonzo Johnson, Cheryl Sanders, Eugene Rivers, and Estrelda Alexander. The Black Pentecostal church is known not only for standing against individual and systemic sin but also for embracing the sinner, feeding the poor, and giving the outcast a place at the table without regard to race, gender, or station in life. Carson takes this further by helping to provide the training, skills, and resources by which people can become empowered and self-sustaining.

The foundational premise of the series which features this book, The Spirit and Society: Public Theology, is to show how the gospel of the kingdom of God "lifted an oppressed people, the Jews," with a promise to do the same for all socially and economically marginalized people wherever they may be found. Unlike Black, liberation, and feminist theologies that seek to bring about social, political, and economic change through revolution, Carson envisions liberation, renewal, and transformation through a "kingdom theology of community and economic empowerment" for disadvantaged communities.

Approach the book with an open mind, ready to explore the renewed roles of the Black Pentecostal church Carson has set forth. Church leaders, members, clergy, laity, scholars—all will find its kingdom approach to social and political problems refreshing. Use it as a guide in your journey toward community building that reflects kingdom values that are life-changing and world-impacting.

Trevor Grizzle, PhD

Preface

I'M A SIXTY-FIVE-YEAR-OLD AFRICAN American from Chicago, in the Englewood District, one of the highest crime areas in the country. Black men have a very low probability of making it out of Englewood, due to inadequate education, sub-par economic opportunities (planned classism or caste system), and low access to quality health care. As I reflect on how I was both failing and falling in a country that boasts about being the land of opportunity, I vividly remember growing up in this environment as though it was yesterday. I was a high school dropout who eventually finished my high school education during the summer across the street from the Robert Taylor Homes, known as the projects, in an extremely high crime area. After failing two courses, I dropped out of Gage Park High School in my senior year. Dawson Skills Center offered an evening educational program I was able to attend so that I could complete the one missing credit I needed to graduate.

Very few people believed in me outside of my parents, my childhood pastor, Rev. Robert Skinner Sr., and a few distant adults. Thinking about the mean and dangerous streets of the South Side in the Englewood District, as an ignorant teenage boy, I realize that I was protected from ultimate failure because of the strict tutelage of my parents and my participation in my Black Bapti-costal church, Greater Pleasant Valley Missionary Baptist Church. I was not raised in an academic environment. My parents were former sharecroppers from Mississippi with an eighth- and ninth-grade education, who relocated to Chicago in the Great Migration when Southern blacks were looking for better opportunities in the North. My parents believed in hard work; both of them were factory workers. My father was employed by Lindberg Lane (a model toy company), and my mother worked for Union Special (a sewing machine company).

My life started behind the projects until my parents purchased an apartment building on the other side of the projects. It was amazing as I think about it—former sharecroppers bought property in an all-white neighborhood. In 1973, my new neighborhood experienced white flight, which is the opposite of reverse gentrification—when property values go down as whites move out and Blacks move in. We used to be the only Black family on the block, but over the course of two years, all the white families moved out. They sold their properties at a higher value to Blacks who wanted to be in mixed neighborhoods but didn't know that there would be a white flight and depreciation in property value.

Growing up on the South Side of Chicago taught me a lot about the streets and survival due to how fast-paced, untrustworthy, and devious the culture was in the hood. I experienced a lot of death, crime, gang violence, and drugs in my neighborhood, which helped to shape my worldview and expectations. The most positive things in our neighborhoods, which helped some of us, were schools, sports programs, and churches. What helped to shape my life the most was my little Baptist church. Even though I didn't have a relationship with Christ, the church was a major social influence in my life. As I got older, though, I often wondered how we had so many churches yet so much social, civil, and economic unrest. In any event, I found my social circle there and gained some musical skills.

Once I finished at Dawson, W. W. Jackson helped get me into the HBCU Wiley College in Marshall, Texas, known today as Wiley University. After I finished my BA, I relocated to Chicago to live with my parents until I could get a job and get on my feet. I wasn't having much luck in Chicago finding a professional job. No one seemed to have heard of Wiley College, so I worked a commission-based job with Atlanta Life Insurance, a Black-owned company. It wasn't competitive with larger companies but was popular in the Black community for awhile. Eventually, I moved back to Texas for graduate school at the now Texas A&M University-Commerce and completed my master's in counseling and guidance in 1985. So I was twenty-four years old with a master's degree and no direction.

I became an auditor for the State of Texas, a political job that one of my former professors, the late Dr. Telly H. Miller, assisted me in securing. But it wasn't long before God came knocking at my door with the call to ministry. I left my professional career and began a church on December 5, 1986, with nine people in a house. Then God told me to go to seminary at Oral Roberts University; it's a wonderful story I hope you can hear one day. But this was the beginning of my spiritual life, which revolutionized my future and mentality. In the end, it was my church background that served as the substratum of my ability to hear the voice of God and enter the realm of the church. In particular, it was the Black church that prepared me unconsciously for that which was to come. I owe eight degrees and a mega ministry to the empowerment of the Black church. In fact, I owe my life achievements to God and his church in the Black community because it preserved, protected, and perpetuated my success and existence.

"Thank God for the Church!"

Dana Carson, MBA, DMin, PhD

Introduction

In this book, I will explore and examine how the kingdom theology of the Black church can empower Black communities. I will examine the evolution of the Black Pentecostal/Charismatic/Neo-Pentecostal church and its function in Black community empowerment. The book will discuss how Pentecostal/Charismatic churches must move beyond traditional glossolalic speech, or "tongues," as an end goal and move toward a new kingdom-minded model that empowers individuals and communities. This book will also examine both the interpretation and the function of the Person of the Holy Spirit concerning the Black Pentecostal church experience and Black community empowerment. It will establish that Jesus' understanding and experience with the Holy Spirit was responsible for lifting the oppressed and empowering the individual from a kingdom perspective.

The book will discuss the kingdom of God by exploring the traditional views of the kingdom of God and how a renewal approach by the Black Pentecostal/Charismatic/Neo-Pentecostal church can be more impactful in the economic transformation of people of color. It will compare black liberation theology and the liberation theology of the kingdom of God. The emphasis will be the development of a "kingdom theology of community and economic empowerment" for disadvantaged communities worldwide, with a non-classist methodology. The book will discuss how the kingdom ministry of Jesus served as a model of kingdom liberation that addressed racism, sexism, and classism, and how a renewal theology of the kingdom of God can liberate the oppressed and impact the forgotten inner-city and ghetto colonies, not just in America but worldwide. However, the book's foundational premise will be the examination of the gospel of the kingdom of God and how it lifted an oppressed people, the Jews, to a place of empowerment. The kingdom is not just an eschatological expectation but a present reality, transforming lives and communities everywhere it is preached.

1

The Black Church and the Pathway to Pentecostalism

I WANT TO BEGIN by defining my understanding of the Black church. It has traditionally been the strength of the Black community. C. Eric Lincoln said, "There is no disjunction between the black church and the black community, and the church is the spiritual face of the black community."[1] However, the traditional, mainline churches have lost the appeal they once had. Historically, the Black preacher, predominantly male, was one of the greatest role models of the community. But for several decades, young adult African American males have uprooted themselves from the traditional church.[2] The most popular mainline churches in the Black community were the Baptist churches, Methodist churches, and then Holiness/Pentecostal churches such as the Church of God in Christ (COGIC) and Pentecostal Assemblies of the World (PAW). So, in this chapter, I want to examine the Black church and its Pentecostal/Charismatic experience.

There is both a rich and a dark history in the development of the so-called Black church. Thus, when I discuss the term "Black church," I do so with spiritual and theological reluctance, due to my understanding that there is only *one* church—the kingdom-minded church of Jesus Christ (Matthew 16:17–19). So how did we begin labeling the church as the Black church and the white church? When we consider the history of

1. Lincoln and Mamiya, *Black Church in the African American Experience*, 199.

2. Carson, "How Independent Churches in Select Areas Are Reaching Young Adult African American Males Between the Ages 14–35," 5.

the church movement in the US, the Society of the Promulgation of the Gospel in Foreign Parts, and the Church of England in 1701, we understand how the concept of the Black church evolved from the context of slavery. As one who appreciates my heritage and history, I understand that it was birthed in a context of oppression, inequality, and social and economic rejection.

The term "Black church" was created due to the term "white church," where Blacks were not welcome to participate based on their race. However, the history of the so-called church demonstrates the resilience, tenacity, and strength of Black and Brown people around the world. Often, when we discuss the Black church, it is looked at through the lens of diminishing equity or from a distorted perspective. The "Black church" always stands consciously or unconsciously beside the concept of a white church in a deficit position. Thus, it is necessary to examine briefly the origin and development of the Black church and its historical significance.

Much has been written and said about the reasons why Black males no longer participate in great numbers in the mainline Christian church. One of the main issues is the seldom-addressed topic of the Black presence in the development of the Christian church and the presence of Blacks in the Bible in general. Some pastors, theologians, and sociologists have noted the effects that a European presentation of Christianity has had on Blacks, Black males in particular. Because of the solely European presentation of the gospel and biblical literature, many contemporary Blacks have had a difficult time relating to the Bible. Thus, more contemporary literature deals with the Black presence in the Bible. With this in mind, African contributions to Christianity will be explored with a focus on its impact on modern-day Christianity.

AFRICAN CONTRIBUTIONS TO CHRISTIANITY

There has been much conjecture about Africa's impact on Christianity. The book *Blacks Who Died for Jesus*, by Mark Hyman, is a credible work that gives a succinct presentation of Blacks who have made a significant contribution to the Christian faith, beginning with the life of Christ.[3] The continent of Africa has always played a major role in the development of Christianity and Judaism. Many commentators believe that the garden

3. Hyman, *Blacks Who Died for Jesus.*

of Eden may have been located in Africa due to the rivers listed in the Genesis account. Moses, the great Hebrew deliverer, was groomed in Africa (Egypt) and married to an African woman from Ethiopia. He received counsel from his Ethiopian father-in-law, Jethro. Thus, without exhausting the Older Testament significance of Africa, it is indisputable that Africa played an extensive role in the development of Older Testament history.

The Gospel of Matthew records that after the birth of Christ, his parents fled to Egypt in Africa for safety because King Herod, the district governor under the Romans, was hunting the infant Jesus down. In fact, this is the first account connecting the continent of Africa with the Newer Testament story. Nothing more is discussed about this episode in the life of Jesus. The African theme emerges again at the end of the life of Jesus. Lamin Sanneh states that the oldest known Gospel of the Newer Testament, the Gospel of Mark, which is largely based on the eyewitness account of the apostle Peter, records the trial of Jesus. As he was led to the place of crucifixion, they met a man called Simon from Cyrene, who was compelled to carry the cross behind Jesus. Cyrene was a Roman province in the African country of Libya. Sanneh also suggests that Africa became one of the most important outposts of the broader mission to the gentile world.[4]

The next important event of the Christian church that hints at the presence of Africans is the Day of Pentecost, as recorded in Acts. This account mentions people present from both Egypt and Cyrene, "where the disciples received their collective commissioning to undertake Christian mission."[5] The book of Acts records that among the Christians who spread Christian teachings were people from Cyrene. They were instrumental in establishing the church in Antioch, where the disciples were first named "Christians."[6]

The book of Acts records elsewhere the baptism of an important government official who was a chancellor for the Ethiopian palace. He is described as being in the service of Candace, the queen. A eunuch, this Ethiopian dignitary was on his way to Jerusalem to perform duties connected with worship to Yahweh. Sanneh states, "According to a tradition preserved by the church historian Eusebius, writing in the early fourth century, the name of this 'Ethiopian' official was Judich." Sanneh believes

4. Sanneh, *Whose Religion Is Christianity?*, 36.

5. Sanneh, *Whose Religion Is Christianity?*, 14.

6. Acts 11:19–20, 26.

that this man was from the kingdom of Meroe and says that we can never know the impact Philip had on Meroe personally. However, history records that Meroe grew to be a prosperous and flourishing Christian kingdom in the Upper Nile Valley, lasting several centuries.[7]

Sanneh cites Apollos from Alexandria in Egypt as another significant first-century Christian from Africa who helped spread the gospel to Europe and Asia. The Scriptures record that he was a gifted man who was further instructed in the gospel message by Priscilla and Aquila, for he had only heard the preaching of John the Baptist. Eusebius espoused a traditional belief that John Mark, the Gospel writer, established churches in Africa and is the founder of the oldest Christian church in the world, the Coptic church in Ethiopia, which is in Africa. To this day, the Coptic church considers Mark its founder. According to Sanneh, history also records that the apostle Thomas performed Christian work in Egypt on his way to India.[8]

The first through sixth centuries marked another consequential era of African contributions to Christianity. Alexandria in Egypt was among the strongest Christian centers in the second and third centuries. Sanneh notes that the famous catechetical school, presided over by people like Clement of Alexandria (150–215), was located there.[9] Origen, known by some as the father of systematic theology, was a product of the school in Alexandria. The first several centuries of Christianity was a crucial era for Christianity as it fought for existence and definition. Christianity exists as an orthodox belief today because of the contributions of Africans like Athanasius, who almost single-handedly saved the Christian church from the Arian heresy. He argued for the divinity of Christ, stating that he was *homoousia* or of the same substance as the Father.

The North African Tertullian was responsible for providing leadership and scholarship to the church. He is regarded as the father of Latin Christianity because he developed a Latin vocabulary for Christian theology. Tertullian was also the first to coin the term "Trinity." Tertullian witnessed the persecution of many Christians and spoke the famous words, "The blood of the martyrs is the seed of the church."[10]

Other prominent African contributors to the early church include St. Augustine, who helped shape the church's Trinitarian theology, among

7. Sanneh, *West African Christianity*, 3.

8. Sanneh, *Whose Religion Is Christianity?*, 43.

9. Sanneh, *Whose Religion Is Christianity?*, 14–15.

10. Labanca, "Blood of the Martyrs is Still Seed for the Church."

many other contributions, and the revered bishop of Carthage, Cyprian. These African figures were vital to establishing the Christian church and doctrine against all forms of heresy. Sanneh states that, from the centralized administration of the empire under Rome and the personal contributions of individual Africans, the early church struck firm roots in African soil.[11] The Coptic Church still exists today, in an Islamic context, and gives claim to more than five million members while suffering as a minority religion.

Africa, then, has never been a total stranger to Christianity, though, beginning in the seventh century, the church suffered major setbacks due to the rise of Islam. The Muslim armies spread quickly over Egypt and North Africa. Thus, for 700 to 800 years, Islam spread throughout Africa. In Africa, Christianity was no longer a popular religion until the missionary movement in the fifteenth century. It has been thought by many that the transatlantic slave trade marked the first encounter Africans had with Christianity; this will be discussed later. While this was true for some, it was not true for all. It was more likely that some captured slaves had their own brand of Christianity. Thus, when we consider the Black church and its history and historical roots, especially as it relates to the Pentecostal/Charismatic worship styles of the so-called Black church, we must consider the impact of African religion.

AFRICAN RELIGION

African religious worship is essential to Black Christian worship since many of the practices of Black Christians have their foundation in African religious traditions. Gayraud Wilmore shows that African religions know nothing of a rigid demarcation between the natural and the supernatural. All life is permeated with forces or powers in some relationship to human weal or woe.[12] African scholars such as Gabriel M. Setiloane, Malcolm J. McVeigh, John S. Mbiti, and Harry Sawyerr have examined the traditional religious beliefs of Africans and show that the African concept of God is monotheistic.[13] Muzorewa E. Bolaji Idowu finds that although God is one, various communities may have different names for

11. Sanneh, *West African Christianity*, 1.

12. Wilmore, *Black Religion and Black Radicalism*.

13. Setiloane, *African Theology*; McVeigh, *God in Africa*; Mbiti, *African Religions and Philosophy*; Sawyerr, *Creative Evangelism*.

God.[14] Therefore, the many names of God need not imply polytheistic practices in African religion; it is the same God whose self-revelation occurs throughout the world. This interpretation is supported by Malcolm J. McVeigh, who says that the God of African traditional religion and Christianity is, in fact, the same. The God who reveals himself fully in Jesus Christ is none other than the one who has made himself known to African religious experience.[15]

Gwinyai H. Muzorewa says, "African theologians share the view that God is the original source and the beginning of all things." He also contends that this one God is a just God. Thus, justice, as an attribute of God, is an important theme in African theology. For Muzorewa, "Africans believe, while God is invisible, His acts are tangible."[16] He argues that in this understanding there lies a potential doctrine of pneumatology.

Another important concept in African religion is the concept of ancestral spirits. Sawyerr observes that "the presence of the dead is assumed and invoked when the life of the tribe is threatened with disaster."[17] Thus, because of this common belief in African religion, strong credence lies in the reality of the spirit world. Some African theologians maintain that Africans believe "the spiritual is just as important and consequential as the physical."[18] McVeigh writes that African attention is centered on the ancestors, who are looked up to as the guardians of individuals, families, and the community as a whole.[19] Those in the flesh constantly seek communion with the departed.

Ancestrology sheds light on the doctrine of sin for traditional African religions. Muzorewa explains the cleansing rite for the deceased. He states that the ancestor goes through an installation process called "chenura." This process refers to the exoneration of the would-be ancestor's sins, even inadvertent ones, by the forgiving community. That rite allows the now "ancestor" to commune with the saints who have previously died and to fellowship with God spiritually.[20] Thus, when ancestors are invoked or mentioned, they are viewed as righteous and incapable of committing wrong, and they are existentially to regulate the morality of

14. Idowu, *African Traditional Religion*, 35–36.

15. McVeigh, *God in Africa*, 81.

16. Sawyerr and Parratt, *Origins and Development of African Theology*, 10.

17. Sawyerr and Parratt, *Origins and Development of African Theology*, 12.

18. Mbiti, *African Religions and Philosophy*, 14.

19. McVeigh, *God in Africa*, 103.

20. Muzorewa, *Origins and Development of African Theology*, 13.

the community. Indeed, the ancestors are believed to watch over their own families.

Another important theme in traditional African religion is the concept of good and evil. African religion spends a great deal of time and energy analyzing the causes and effects of good and evil. Geoffrey Parrinder notes that "some scholars believe that evil may be attributed to the ancestors."[21] Other scholars disagree with Parrinder, contending that evil has other forces as its agents, be they human, spiritual, or natural forces. One thing for certain is that evil is a reality in African religion, even though it is not clear where it originates. However, according to Muzorewa, "In African thought, the agent of evil itself is not basically evil; it becomes evil as it causes evil to happen."[22]

A final important belief in traditional African belief is the concept of humanity. Muzorewa states that this concept largely determines all other African cosmological concepts. Most African scholars agree that humanity is defined in the context of community. "All that goes into the making of man is incorporated in the complex unity of the tribe, outside of which all others are strangers and inferior, if not enemies."[23] Tribal involvement is key to the understanding of the human in Africa. Thus, Muzorewa states that African humanity is primarily defined by a sense of belonging, serving one's own folk, and kinship. For the African, it is not enough to be a human being; unless one shares a sense of community, one can easily turn out to be an enemy.[24]

Mercy Oduyoye observes that Africans recognize life as life in community. We can truly know ourselves if we remain true to our community, past and present. The concept of individual success or failure is secondary. The ethnic group, the village, and the locality are crucial in one's estimation of oneself.[25] Our nature is a two-way relation: with God and with our fellow human beings. In certain tribes in Africa, every piece of property is referred to as "ours" as opposed to "mine." Parents are referred to as "ours" versus "my." Thus, Africans understand themselves in the context of community, or at least family. Mbiti writes, "The existence of the individual is the existence of the corporate."[26] He also says, "Nature

21. Parrinder, *African Traditional Religion*, 60.

22. Muzorewa, *Origins and Development of African Theology*, 13.

23. "Supreme Being in African Traditional Religion And Christianity."

24. Citing Ndubuisi-Nwuzor, "Survey of African Christology."

25. Oduyoye, *Hearing and Knowing*, 132–35.

26. Mbiti, *African Religions and Philosophy*, 14.

brings the child into the world, but society creates the child into a social being, a corporate person."[27]

As mentioned earlier, African religion involved the whole person; thus, so did African worship. African worship involved playing musical instruments, chanting, shouting, and dancing, all of which are akin to Pentecostal/Charismatic worship styles. African worshipers worshiped to please their gods; thus, it was intense and sincere. It must be remembered that Africans practiced Christianity in the first six centuries of the church. Mbiti writes that Christianity in Africa is so old that it can rightly be described as an Indigenous, traditional, and African religion.[28] Long before the start of Islam in the seventh century, Christianity was well established all over North Africa, Egypt, parts of the Sudan, and Ethiopia. As stated earlier, it was a dynamic form of Christianity, producing great scholars and theologians like Tertullian, Origen, Clement of Alexandria, and Augustine.[29] Mbiti writes that Africans made a great contribution to Christendom through scholarship, participation in church councils, defense of the faith, movements like monasticism, theology, the translation and preservation of the Scriptures, martyrdom, the famous catechetical school of Alexandria, liturgy, and in the midst of heresies and controversies.[30]

The rise of Islam, as mentioned earlier, caused a great reduction in the number of Christian churches, leaving only the churches in Egypt and Ethiopia. Christians remained in all of the above-mentioned places in Africa but were few in number. For Christians in those areas to openly confess, their faith could have cost them their lives. C. Eric Lincoln writes that Africa knew the Hebrew nation in its infancy—from Abraham even—and the civilizations of Africa were ancient even then.[31] It is sometimes necessary to remind Christians in the West that Egypt is in Africa, that Egyptians are Africans, and that no one in ancient Egypt had the clairvoyance to exclude the Black Africans from history in trying to accommodate the wish theories of our latter-day historians.

African religion played a significant role in the establishment of the Christian church. Over time, practices and beliefs that were anti-Christian developed in Africa. But Africans always maintained their belief in

27. Mbiti, *African Religions and Philosophy*, 14.

28. Mbiti, *African Religions and Philosophy*, 229.

29. Oden, *How Africa Shaped the Christian Mind*, 20–25.

30. Mbiti, *African Religions and Philosophy*, 229–30.

31. Lincoln, *Race, Religion, and the Continuing American Dilemma*, 15.

one supreme creator, God. Albert J. Raboteau indicates that European travelers frequently identified African gods with demons or devils and accused Africans of devil worship. Or they mistook the image of the god for the god himself and called them fetish worshipers. However, the representation of the gods as fetishes is a mistake.[32]

Africans would dance before these gods. Typically, the dance would be performed with the accompaniment of songs and music, and the steps would be revelatory of their gods. Music and dance were so essential to West African religion that theirs are sometimes referred to as "dance religions." Bryan Edwards notes that the "obeah" man or sorcerer practiced negative spiritual medicine. The "myalman" counteracted with positive spiritual medicine, which came through dancing and possession trances, sometimes referred to as "Jamaican Cumina," an ancestral cult.[33]

Wilmore says that "the Medicine man in African societies was a source of help and healing for the community." Mbiti speaks of him as "the greatest gift" to the community and as "both doctor and pastor."[34] Wilmore suggests that it is this person who often emerged as the slave preacher, the religious leader of the Black community, without the appointment of the white slave masters.[35]

As we examine African religious practices, we will see that some worship beliefs and styles resemble patterns of Black Pentecostal and Charismatic worship styles and practices, which we will explore in more detail. The Black church and its worship styles and practices, from both a non-Pentecostal and Pentecostal or Spirit-filled perspective, not only have their roots in African religious practices but also in antebellum slavery. While a short exploration of Blacks and slavery will be surveyed as we discuss the Black church, it is essential to briefly visit the participation of Blacks in Christianity during the transatlantic slave trade.

Slavery was a very telling time as it relates to Blacks and Christianity because religion was a point of irritation for slave owners. Before laws were established in the late seventeenth century, owners were concerned about the proselytization of slaves and argued against their baptism because some laws prohibited Christians from enslaving other Christians. Thus, slave conversions were feared. In response, in 1667, a law introduced

32. Raboteau, *Slave Religion*, 84.

33. Edwards, *History, Civil and Commercial, of the British Colonies in the West Indies*, 85–87.

34. Mbiti, *African Religions and Philosophy*, 170.

35. Wilmore, *Black Religion and Black Radicalism*, 19.

by the Virginia assembly concluded that baptism does not change the status of a person's bondage or freedom. Morgan Godwyn argued that the Christian faith made slaves better workers and helped to promote security against rebellion and fidelity to the slave master.[36] Columbus Salley and Ronald Behm recorded "that the Church of England accepted the position stated by Morgan Godwyn in 1680 that Christianity and slavery are fully compatible."[37] However, they also stated that Christianity was a major barrier to be hurdled on the way to chattel slavery since Christians could not be held as slaves. Thus, this issue was governmentally settled in 1729 according to English law. The Attorney General and Solicitor-General gave their formal opinions that baptism could not alter the temporal condition of a slave within the British kingdoms.

The eighteenth century represented one of the most critical periods in the destruction and dehumanization of Black people in America. Salley and Behm state, "The process of slave 'dehumanization' from the moment of capture to the moment of purchase parallels the concentration camp experiences of World War II." The eighteenth century was the era of "programming."[38] This was the epoch in which Blacks were totally subjugated and taught distrust for one another, engendering self-hatred and apparent trust for their masters. This period marks the era of extreme merchandising of Blacks. Among Christians, the Black Christian was taught that there was a distinction between the Black Christian and the white Christian, a distinction that still impacts the ideology of the Black church and the Black community today.

The seventeenth century ended with laws prohibiting interracial marriages (1691) and laws allowing slaves to be baptized Christians. John Boles says, "After 1700, the laws against blacks hardened dramatically, and roughly after that date, it is accurate to speak of the Chesapeake as a chattel slave society where blacks had few rights protected by laws."[39] It is astonishing that a society that had such a cruel system of slavery and racism could have such a desire to practice a belief in the Christian God and Jesus Christ, whose ministry marked "the acceptable year of the Lord" (Luke 4:19).[40] In the Older Testament, the acceptable year of

36. Godwyn, *Negro's and Indians Advocate, Suing for Their Admission into the Church*, 4–6.

37. Salley and Behm, *What Color Is Your God?*, 27.

38. Salley and Behm, *What Color Is Your God?*, 13.

39. Boles, *Black Southerners, 1619–1869*, 25.

40. Luke 40:19.

the Lord is called "the year of Jubilee." This was a time when all property was returned to its rightful owner, no labor was done in the fields, and all slaves were released. The year of Jubilee followed seven years of Sabbaths, which was the fiftieth year. Yet, the eighteenth century began with Blacks basically having no rights in the Americas. Then, at the turn of the century, the Church of England (Anglican) began its missionary campaign, under the auspices of the Society of the Promulgation of the Gospel in Foreign Parts (SPG).

THE RISE OF THE BLACK CHURCH

The SPG was a missionary arm of the Anglican Church. It was formed in 1701 to minister to the colonists of America and also instruct the Native Americans and Negroes. The bishop of London headed the SPG. It published tracts and sermons and sent out missionaries and catechists, financed through funds sought after in England. Its first intention was to evangelize the white settlers; however, it also made attempts to evangelize slaves.

Though the Church of England had a strong desire to evangelize the colonies, the slave masters, as mentioned earlier, objected to the proselytization of slaves. The slave owners still had reservations about the baptism of slaves even after colonial assemblies had declared that it did not change the legal or personal status of the slave. Raboteau cites several reasons for the objections, but the tension was primarily due to economic issues and religious instruction. Because of the catechetical process, a slave would have to receive religious instruction before baptism. Raboteau writes, "The plantation work schedule gave the slave little leisure for religious instruction."[41] Raboteau further discusses how the SPG in London received letters from clergy in South Carolina complaining about the intense labor practices of the slave masters. Their complaint stated that the slaves did not have a day to worship. The slave master allotted individual plots for the slave to plant for themselves to avoid being responsible for feeding and clothing them. They were allowed to clear ground and plant for their families on Sunday; hence, the clergy were unhappy. Raboteau claims that even when slaves were not forced to work on the Sabbath, finding time for religious instruction was problematic since the minister had enough work from the white folk on his hands.

41. Raboteau, *Slave Religion*, 99.

Moreover, the slaves frequently used whatever leisure time they had for visiting, dancing, and merriment activities, which seemed to the missionary to be profanations of the Lord's Day.

Albert Raboteau also mentions that the slave masters objected to slave conversion because they believed that Africans were too "brutish" to be instructed. He postulated that this objection, in part, was due to the linguistic and cultural barriers that existed between African-born ("Guinea") slaves and English colonials.[42] This represented a significant challenge even for the missionaries who directed their attention to American-born slaves, who had some kind of facility in English. Raboteau cites a Virginia House of Burgesses' reply to Col. Francis Nicholson, governor of Virginia, who was instructed by London to recommend to the Virginia Assembly that it pass laws ensuring that negroes and Native Americans would be educated in the Christian faith. The House's response to this request was that American-born negroes should generally be baptized and trained in the Christian faith. However, negroes who are imported —because of their supposed gross bestiality, rudeness of their manners, the variety and strangeness of their languages, and the weakness and shallowness of their minds—were thought impossible to catechize.[43] In addition, he says that some planters went as far as to say that Africans were incapable of instruction.

Raboteau also writes that the danger beneath the arguments for slave conversion, which many masters feared, was the egalitarianism implicit in Christianity. The most serious obstacle to the missionaries' access to the slaves was the slaveholder's dim awareness that a Christian slave would have some claim to fellowship, a claim that threatened the security of the master-slave hierarchy. Even after other fears had been removed by legislation or by argument, unease with the concept of spiritual equality between master and slave caused slave owners to reject the idea of Christianizing their slaves.[44] Another complaint of the planters was that Christianity would make the slaves "saucy" since they would begin to think of themselves as equal to white folks. Some even articulated that they would never come to the Holy Table while slaves were received there. Slave owners often expressed fears that Christianity would make their slaves not only proud but ungovernable and even rebellious.

42. Raboteau, *Slave Religion*, 100.

43. Raboteau, *Slave Religion*, 102.

44. Raboteau, *Slave Religion*, 103.

C. Eric Lincoln lists three objections to the evangelizing of slaves by white Protestant Americans:

(1) the hearing of the gospel required time that could otherwise be economically productive;

(2) slaves gathered together in a religious assembly might become conscious of their own strength and plot insurrections under the cover of religious instructions;

(3) there was a long-standing English tradition that once a slave became a Christian, he could no longer be held as a slave.[45]

Lincoln also notes that the white slave holders feared that the Christian slave might forget their place in the scheme of things and see themselves as spiritual equals, as it related to spiritual matters. He reports that one slave-owning mistress became quite agitated with the possibility of seeing one of her slaves in heaven. Some called negroes "black dogs" and adamantly proclaimed that it was impossible for them to share the same eschatological fate as white people.

These concerns posed a great dilemma for the SPG. It felt compelled to evangelize both the slave masters and slaves; however, it could not have access to the slaves because of the fears of the slave masters. The SPG met strong resistance from the New England colonies and the Southern planters. In the South, English missionaries were considered meddlers. Thus, the missionaries had to devise a scheme that would allow them to appeal to the logic of slave masters. Raboteau states that in response to these concerns by the SPG, "almost every apologist for the evangelization of the slaves felt obliged to prove that Christianity would actually make better slaves." The bishop of London wrote in a letter to the slave masters that Christianity would not cause the slaves to be less responsive to their obligations. Quite the contrary, it would cause them to perform a better job because they would conduct duties not only from a fear of men but from a sense of duty to God and the belief and expectation of a future accounting.[46] They appealed to the profit motives of the slave owners by pointing out that converted slaves "do better for their masters' profit than

45. Lincoln and Mamiya, *Black Church in the African American Experience*, 9.

46. SPG, quoted in Humphreys, *Historical Account of the Incorporated Society for the Propagation of the Gospel in Foreign Parts*, 332; cited in Raboteau, *Slave Religion*, 101–2.

formerly, for they are taught to serve out of Christian love and duty."[47] The SPG was eventually allowed to do work among the slaves, but only after the legal issue of holding Christians as slaves was settled to the satisfaction of the slaveholders and after the firm assurance that Blacks would not be taught principles that would be inimical to their status as slaves.[48]

Because of slavery and its oppressive system, the church in London allowed itself to be moved to develop a doctrine of accommodation that acquiesced to the institution of slavery. This marked the period when Scripture was grossly misinterpreted and taken out of context to support the institution of slavery. Raboteau notes that one passage of Scripture that was often quoted independent of a proper exegesis was Paul's admonition that "every man abide in the condition wherein he is called with great indifference of mind" (1 Corinthians 7:20).[49] Thus, the clergypersons of London produced an attractive theology for America that was used for slave control. Raboteau also notes that in 1724, the church in London prepared an attractive financial proposition for the slave masters if they made available their slaves for a conversion experience. Raboteau notes that "This offer would allow a tax break for allowing Indians, negroes, and mulatto children to engage in Christian education."[50]

It must be mentioned that while the bulk of slave owners opposed the conversions of slaves, some did not oppose evangelizing activities among Blacks. Raboteau mentions that religious leaders, such as George Fox in 1657 and William Edmundson in 1676, instructed the Quakers to educate their slaves. Fox, in a tract entitled "Gospel Family Order," reminded slaveholding Quakers that "Christ died for all . . . tawnies and for blacks as well as for you that are called whites." Fox also exhorted them not only to instruct the slaves but also that slaves should be released after a considerable term of years and with some compensation for their labor. Edmundson argued along the same lines, refuting the treatment of slaves and the mental oppression that they had to undergo, which was a direct contradiction to truth.[51]

But history records that the oppressive system of racism prevailed, and the church of London gave over to the triumphant thought of the

47. Humphreys, *Historical Account of the SPG*, 332; cited in Raboteau, *Slave Religion*, 101.

48. Frazier, *Negro Church in America*, 7–8.

49. Raboteau, *Slave Religion*, 137; 1 Corinthians 7:20.

50. Raboteau, *Slave Religion*, 128–30.

51. Raboteau, *Slave Religion*, 110.

day. Thus, white slave theology was developed and perpetuated for centuries as the will of God for whites and Blacks and would forever plague the ideology of the white church and the Black church. It was a theology that supported a caste system, promoting classism, sexism, and racism, all in the name of Christianity.

Chancellor Williams writes that the Christian doctrine was based on the premise that God himself, being white, had cursed the Blacks and made them the "servants of man"—man being the white man, for was he not made in the "image of God"? To worship God, in effect, was to worship the white man. Williams also explains that scores of these little psychological gimmicks were "embedded in cultural thought and had more devastating effects upon blacks than armed forces." Isaac Olaleye postulates that the "early New England Calvinist distorted Calvin's theory of predestination, saying that blacks were un-elect of God, and predestined to be slaves."[52]

While there was much debate surrounding the conversion rights of slaves, C. Eric Lincoln says that "the theologians never did resolve the question of souls to everyone's satisfaction, but the 'people' issue was settled finally by a political agreement between the North and the South that a slave was equal to three-fifths of a man."[53] The issue of race and religion during this period became the seedbed for future religious thought in America. This so-called Christian doctrine served as a vicious weapon in the hands of white oppressors to control the thoughts, desires, and futures of Blacks and was used through the institution of the church. Lincoln writes, "The Christianization of slavery meant, first of all, the sanctification of the practice of slave-holding as having biblical precedent and spiritual merit."[54] It implied the approval, even the favor, of God, for saving the African from a life of savagery. It meant the implementation of a curse on the "sons of Ham," who were destined forever to be "hewers of wood and drawers of water."[55]

On the other side of the rationale for slavery was the belief that the enslavement of the "lesser breeds" was an inevitable and necessary step toward the fulfillment of the white race's "manifest destiny," a destiny that somehow converted the Black man's labor into the white man's burden.

52. Williams, *Destruction of Black Civilization*, 285–87; Felder, "Impact of Christianity on the Black Race," 330–31.

53. Lincoln, *Race, Religion, and the Continuing American Dilemma*, 25.

54. Lincoln, *Race, Religion, and the Continuing American Dilemma*, 24.

55. Genesis 9:25–27; Joshua 9:21, 23, 27.

During the process of the Christianization of slaves, the Roman Catholic Church discovered that those who were brought into the church became less troublesome. Similarly, Lincoln writes concerning the practices of the Puritan pastor Cotton Mather. He explains that Mather was a New England pastor who was the foremost advocate for the raising of heathen Blacks through the instrumentality of the Christian church. Mather wrote an essay in 1706 entitled "The Negro Christianized," which addressed Boston slave masters and extolled the benefits of slave conversions. The address included such statements as:

> Consider the incomparable benefits of enslaving your negroes . . . [They] would rise to immediate felicity, while having no earthly benefits. They remain your slaves but become the children of God. They only enjoy the small allowance of justice you see fit; they become your vassals and, with total submission, wait upon you, yet the angels of God take them under their guardianship. Masters, you will be happy eternally, for in the future, they will exist in the Heavenly City, forever blessing the gracious God for the day when He first made them your servants.

Mather would hold Sunday evening religious meetings with the slaves in his home, with the chief aim of making exemplary servants. He organized the "Society of Negroes." In this Society, Mather developed a table of Ten Commandments that demanded the obedience of the slave, respect and fidelity to his master, as well as patience and contentment with his own condition as God-willed and God-ordained. His reward would be a mansion in heaven where he would be the companion of angels in a glorious paradise.[56]

Osofsky gives a brief synopsis of a sermon preached to a Maryland slave congregation in 1743:

> I now come to lay before you your duties to your masters and mistresses on earth. And for this, you have one general rule you ought always to carry in your minds: and that is,—to do all service for them as if you did it for God Himself.—Poor creatures! You little consider, when you are idle and neglectful of your master's business—when you steal and waste and hurt any of their substance,—when you are saucy and impudent,—when you are telling them lies, and deceiving them,—or when you prove stubborn or sullen and will not do the work . . . [These]

56. Mather, *Negro Christianized*, 5–6; discussed in Lincoln, *Race, Religion, and the Continuing American Dilemma*, 24–25.

> are faults against God Himself who hath set your masters and mistresses over you, in His own stead . . . Servants, be obedient to them that are your masters according to the flesh with fear and trembling, in singleness of your heart as unto Christ.[57]

Thus, the Black man had no personal existential significance aside from existing for the success of the white race.

E. Franklin Frazier remarks that the church of the period taught that "Black men were expected to accept their lot in this world and if they were obedient and honest and truthful they would be rewarded in the world after death."[58] Laws were established that prohibited Black males from having any authority or say-so concerning their family and so with a mother in regard to her child. The slave was disenfranchised from their culture and not allowed to be integrated into his new world, so that many Blacks believed it was their lot to serve the white man. Franklin records the 1743 speech of a negro preacher being used by the master to communicate the following words:

> God will reward me, and indeed I have good reason to be content and thankful; and I sometimes think more so than if I was free and ever so rich and great; for then I might be tempted to love and serve myself more than God . . . But now I can't help knowing my duty. I am to serve God in that state in which He placed me. I am to do what my master orders me.[59]

Hans Baer and Merrill Singer write that Christianity was utilized to accomplish five functions:

(1) It provided an ideological rationale for the enslavement of Africans and the social cohesion of white society.

(2) It was part of the deculturation process that the slaves were subjected to after arriving in the Americas.

(3) It had the effect of subduing and pacifying the slaves.

(4) It helped enhance the profitability of the slaves by ensuring their willingness to work hard under adverse conditions.

(5) It created uniformity among people of diverse cultural backgrounds.[60]

57. Mather, *Negro Christianized*, cited in Pillsbury, "Church as It Is," 45.

58. E. Franklin Frazier, quoted in White, "Reactions to Oppression," 214.

59. Quoted in Raboteau, *Slave Religion*, 136.

60. Baer and Singer, *African-American Religion in the Twentieth Century*, 17.

Peter Paris postulates that slavery established a societal condition wherein Blacks inherited at birth a status that excluded them from all of the privileges usually associated with being human. Boles states, "Black denigration elevated the lowest white to a level above the most talented slave into a pseudo fraternity of white equals."[61]

Slaves and their unborn progeny constituted part of their owner's total property assets—with no freedom, no liberty, no rights. In short, the logic of the system was based on the proposition that Blacks were not fully a part of the human race, a view that frequently sought legitimation in both science and religion. Tom Skinner notes that in the early eighteenth century, healthy male slaves were sold for $600 and healthy females for $300. If a slave master purchased one of each, he could eventually build a substantial workforce. Skinner also observes that there was no legal institution of marriage among the slaves. Marriage among the slaves was simply living together with the permission of the slave master, but no marriage certificate was given. The couple lived with the potential threat of permanent separation at the slave blocks. The slave masters practiced studding as they would with any other profit-producing animal. This process involved a healthy male slave impregnating healthy female slaves to breed healthy children as his sole job. When one woman became pregnant, he was then moved to another quarter. Skinner contends that one healthy black male could sire a hundred children in ten years.[62] However, he was not allowed to be a parent to any of them. Neither were slave women permitted to raise their children past the milk stage. Parenthetically, one cannot help wondering if these early practices play a part in the current reality of fatherless children and negligent mothers in urban communities today.

While the eighteenth century marked the era in which Christianity was used to subjugate Blacks, it was also the era of influx. This period recorded the largest number of slave imports in any century. America was no longer getting slaves primarily from the West Indies but had now entered into the direct market, traveling across the Atlantic and purchasing their own slaves. Thus, there was a tremendous increase in the number of slaves brought to America. August Meier and Elliott Rudwick report "that with the increase of numbers of negroes, fear of lawlessness and insurrection rose, leading to the passage of stringent slave codes regulating their

61. Boles, *Black Southerners*, 5.

62. Tom Skinner, quoted in Carson, *Five Watersheds of History and Theology*, 106.

activity." In 1739 and 1740, insurrectionary plots had been discovered in South Carolina, which led to laws restricting unsupervised slave gatherings and a prohibition of the sales of liquor to Blacks.[63] Lerone Bennett says that in 1710, there were 50,000 negroes, but by the signing of the Declaration of Independence, there were more than 500,000. By the time of the Civil War, the little seed of twenty in Jamestown had grown to four million.[64]

Salley and Behm note that any subsequent intellectual or psychological response of Black people to the institution of slavery would, by definition, be a response to a "Christianity that was inextricably united with the oppressive forces of white dominance."[65] Early in the Black experience with "Christianity," the image developed that Christianity is synonymous with whiteness, which is synonymous with oppression. Having studied the role of the Christian churches in defending the institution of slavery, they cite J. Oliver Buswell III, who divided the historic scriptural justifications for slavery alleged by proslavery clerics and lay people into four groups:

(1) general assertions that the institution was natural, "ordained of God," and of benefit to the enslaved;

(2) examples of slavery described or alluded to in the Bible, chiefly in the Older Testament;

(3) instructions regarding the behavior of slaves and masters, chiefly in the Newer Testament; and

(4) underlying the whole structure of the defense system were the supposed teachings regarding the negro race, chiefly based upon elaborations on the story of Ham and the curse of Noah.[66]

On the other hand, Blacks/negroes who grasped for identity and hope found them in the Christian faith, but not according to the interpretation of their white slave masters. Gayraud Wilmore writes that even though they adopted the outward appearance of Christian conversion, they took from it only what proved efficacious for easing the burden of their captivity and gave little attention to the rest. They were aware that

63. Meier and Rudwick, *From Plantation to Ghetto*, 19.

64. Lerone Bennett, quoted in Carson, *Five Watersheds of History and Theology*, 105–6.

65. Salley and Behm, *What Color Is Your God?*, 13–14.

66. Salley and Behm, *What Color Is Your God?*, 18.

the God who demanded their devotion and from whom came the Spirit that infused their secret meetings and possessed their souls and bodies in the ecstasy of worship was not the God of the slave master with his whip and gun. He was also not the God of the plantation preacher with his segregated services and injunctions to servility and blind obedience.[67]

During this period, we can see the beginning stages of what St. Augustine might have referred to as an instance of the "invisible church," evolving from the negro church to what we discuss now as the Black church. The slaves learned how to think about God not with a restrictive, limiting theology but as a deliverer and a God of justice. Frazier observes that the negro slave found in Christianity a new orientation toward the world at large, and in doing so, he adapted the Christian religion to his psychological and social needs.[68] One of the best sources of information on how the negro adapted Christianity to his peculiar psychological and social needs is to be found in that great body of sacred folk music known as the "negro spirituals." Frazier concludes that the theology of the slaves can largely be seen in the spirituals. They demonstrate that the slaves received the Christian faith as a coping mechanism and, thus, an authentic experience for them. He contends that after the organized, orchestrated religious meeting of the slave master, the slaves would steal away into wooded areas and practice their own form of Christianity. It is amazing to reflect upon the invisible church and the church in the bush—church services held in secret that involved the full man—spirit, soul, and body. The negroes would sing and dance until their souls and spirits were free even though their bodies were not.

Raboteau, in his analysis of the "invisible institution," says that while there was the institutional Black church composed of free negroes, there existed on the plantation at night another church of negroes. "In the secrecy of the quarters or the seclusion of the brush arbors ('hush harbors'), the slaves made Christianity truly their own."[69] Thus, he further states that the religion of the slaves was both institutional and noninstitutional, visible and invisible, formally organized and spontaneously adapted. Regular Sunday worship in the local church was paralleled by illicit, or at least informal, prayer meetings on weeknights in the slave cabins or in surrounding woods. Preachers licensed by the church and hired by the master were supplemented by slave preachers licensed only by the Spirit.

67. Wilmore, *Black Religion and Black Radicalism*, 27–28.

68. Frazier, *Negro Church in America*, 16.

69. Raboteau, *Slave Religion*, 212–13.

Raboteau goes on to explain how the slaves called a meeting at night during the day, saying that the Blacks would sing that day the spiritual song, "Steal Away to Jesus."[70] This meant that they would be having worship that evening. Attending these meetings involved great risk. Every attendee ran the risk of being flogged and labeled a troublemaker. However, the liberality of expression was so important for the slaves in their worship experience that they were willing to take the chance. Though risky, they were not uncalculated risks, for they took every possible measure to ensure that they would not get caught. In many instances, they met and had church in a circle and placed a pot of water to absorb the sound. When they met in homes, they would place iron pots in the middle of the floor to absorb the sound of singing, shouting, dancing, preaching, and praying, worship styles that resembled African religious sessions as well as the modern Black church, and in particular, modern Black Pentecostal church worship styles. It's noteworthy that the worship style and patterns of Black Pentecostalism already existed, though the Pentecostal church had not been born or acknowledged during this time.

On some occasions, masters would allow slaves to worship independently of them in their cabins. Raboteau records the testimony of a white lady who attended a slave prayer meeting. Despite her criticism that the prayer that was offered was meaningless, Mary Boykin Chestnut could not dispute the intensity that moved her deeply. She said this about the meeting:

> Jim Nelson, the driver . . . was asked to lead in prayer. He became wildly excited, on his knees, facing us with his eyes shut. He clapped his hands at the end of every sentence, and his voice rose to the pitch of a shriek, yet was strangely clear and musical, occasionally in a plaintive minor key that went to your heart. Sometimes, it rang out like a trumpet. I wept bitterly . . . The Negroes sobbed and shouted and swayed backward and forward, some with aprons to their eyes, most of them clapping their hands and responding in shrill tones: "Yes God!" "Jesus!" "Savior!" "Bless de Lord, amen," etc. It was a little too exciting for me. I would very much have liked to shout, too. Jim Nelson, when he rose from his knees, trembled and shook as one in a palsy, and from his eyes, you could see the ecstasy had not left him yet. He could not stand at all and sank back on his bench.[71]

70. Raboteau, *Slave Religion*, 212–13.

71. Chesnut, *Diary from Dixie*, 191–92.

Frazier calls this the "invisible church," or the negro church of the plantation. "The Negro preacher played an important role in the invisible church," according to Frazier. "The Negro preacher was 'called' to his office and, through his personal qualities, achieved a position of dominance."[72]

The call of the negro preacher was attributed to a religious experience that was an indication that God had chosen him as a spiritual leader. Frazier notes that Frederick Douglass claimed that among the slaves, the preacher was one of their notables. He further discusses that the prestige of the preacher was heightened if the preacher received a license from the Baptist or Methodist church. The qualification of the preacher was the following: he must possess some knowledge of the Bible, which must be combined with the ability to articulate this knowledge. This was normally done through preaching rather than teaching; it was through the telling of stories that the gospel message was communicated. Thus, the preacher had to be able to tell the story. The slave preacher also must be able to sing, for a part of preaching was the ability to sing spiritual or sacred songs. These dynamics created an atmosphere of moaning, shouts, holy dancing, and ecstatic forms of worship, now exhibited in the modern Black.

This form of worship essentially entered the open form of religious expression during the Great Awakening, which began in the New England area and spread to the West and the South. *The Concise Columbia Encyclopedia* defines the Great Awakening as "a series of religious revivals that swept over the American colonies about the middle of the 18th century, beginning in the 1720s, when Theodore Frelinghuysen and Gilbert Tennent made local stirrings in New Jersey."[73] The movement was continued (1734) in New England by Jonathan Edwards. It was spread by a tour (1739–1741) of George Whitefield and reached the South with the preaching (1748–1759) of Samuel Davis. The Great Awakening led to bitter doctrinal disputes but also resulted in missionary work among the Indians and the founding of new educational institutions. It encouraged a democratic spirit in religion.[74] The Great Awakening was considered to be one of the greatest religious revivals of American history. This movement emphasized the doctrine of becoming "born again" or "regeneration," which involved the moving of the Spirit. This movement was marked by physical expression. It involved singing, lively preaching, confessing sins,

72. Frazier, *Negro Church in America*, 20–21.

73. *Concise Columbia Encyclopedia*, "Great Awakening," 361.

74. *Concise Columbia Encyclopedia*, "Great Awakening."

etc. The First Great Awakening occurred in the 1730s to 1770s, and the Second Great Awakening in 1790–1840. From this movement, evangelical theology was developed.

In my estimation, the Great Awakenings are the foundation of the Black Pentecostal church—its worship style and theology. Lincoln and Mamiya write that both of these Awakenings had a significant impact on the religious life of Blacks in that "The Christianity that was spread among slaves during the First and Second Great Awakenings was an evangelical Christianity that stressed personal conversion through a deep regenerating experience, being 'born again.'"[75] They record that the First Great Awakening marked the beginning of Blacks' involvement in the Baptist church. The first Black Baptist church, Silver Bluff Baptist Church (Jackson, South Carolina), was founded by George Liele, who became a Christian due to the First Great Awakening. Wesley Roberts writes that the 1740s Great Awakening, with its enthusiastic preaching and emotional meetings, resulted in a great harvest of Black converts, most of whom were slaves.[76] Perhaps the most significant impact of the First Great Awakening was that it served to cause greater discomfort in the religious life of the slaves since physical freedom did not accompany spiritual freedom.

The informal services of the Baptists and, later, the Methodists attracted the most Blacks—as did early Methodism's antislavery stance. The evangelism of Blacks was high on the list for both the Methodists and the Baptists and, on a minimal level, for the Presbyterians. By 1786, Blacks made up about 10 percent of the Methodist Church.[77] The Great Awakenings represented what Carter G. Woodson said was the "Dawn of the New Day" in the religious development of negroes.[78] E. Franklin Frazier postulates that the largest numbers of Negroes in the South were attracted to the revivals conducted by the Baptists and Methodists. Black participation grew as a result of the Awakenings. Still, segregated seating was typical; the area reserved for blacks was usually called the "Negro Pew" or the "African Corner." Such discrimination motivated Blacks, where possible, to organize their own churches, though white leaders actively opposed that.[79] Liele's church and later Richard Allen's formation

75. Lincoln and Mamiya, *Black Church in the African American Experience*, 5.

76. Roberts, "Rejecting the Negro Pew."

77. Roberts, "Rejecting the Negro Pew," referencing 1786 membership statistics.

78. Woodson, *History of the Negro Church*, 103–4.

79. Frazier, *Negro Church in America*, 7–9.

of the African Methodist Episcopal Church are examples of this. African American religious life was further formed during the Second Great Awakening.

The Quakers, another white denomination of the era, were very vocal about their opposition to slavery, though some owned slaves. They distributed anti-slavery tracts and conducted open anti-slavery rallies. These drives sought to abolish the institution of slavery among the Quakers, desiring that it would have overreaching effects. Salley Jr. and Behm note that "by 1800, American Quakers had virtually ceased to be slaveholders."[80] They also stated that the Methodists had a record of antislavery action. The Methodist church required its traveling preachers to release their slaves in a 1780 Baltimore Conference meeting. In this meeting, they established that slavery was against the laws of God, humanity, and nature, and hurtful to society, contrary to the dictates of conscience and pure religion.

Frazier explains that these highly emotional revival services were appealing to Blacks. He also notes, though, that it was not until after the American Revolution that large masses of the negro population became converts and joined the Methodist and Baptist churches.[81] During the closing years of the eighteenth century, the religious revivals in Kentucky and Tennessee tended to reinforce the forms of conversion that characterized the Methodist revivals and were used in some places by the Baptists and Presbyterians. Franklin argues that Blacks were drawn to the Baptist and Methodist churches, not because they were reminiscent of African religion, but because they appealed more to the poor than the Anglican church. He contends that they were more attracted to these denominations because their preachers lacked the formal education that ministers had in the Anglican Church. Thus they had a greater appeal "to the poor, and the ignorant and the outcast."[82]

Lincoln records that this period of the First Great Awakening marked the intentional efforts of whites to evangelize Blacks, and it was also the time when Blacks were allowed involvement. He posits that serious efforts to proselytize Blacks did not bear fruit until 1740, even though during the colonial period unsuccessful attempts were made. When negroes attended "the white man's church during the colonial period, they were assigned a place, a place of contempt and indignity intended

80. Salley and Behm, *What Color Is Your God?*, 44.

81. Frazier, *Negro Church in America*, 7.

82. Franklin, *From Slavery to Freedom*, 246.

to reinforce the place assigned to them in the secular world." Lincoln notes that in 1743, a school was established in Charleston, South Carolina, organized to train Blacks in missionary work. Thus, Blacks were given religious attention. This period actually marked the epoch of Black preachers. Lincoln records "that large numbers of blacks, slave and free, were accepted into the Baptist and Methodist communions."[83] He also mentions that "John Wesley himself baptized the first black Methodist in 1758 and, in 1766, the first Methodist congregation to be established in America included on its rolls, a black woman."[84]

The Second Great Awakening had the most significant impact on Blacks, according to Lincoln and Mamiya. The Christian experience was barely available to Black interest before that revival movement swept the American frontier. The spiritual romance of the camp meetings of the Awakening stirred the religious imagination of the Black diaspora. It brought thousands of displaced African Americans and their descendants into meaningful Christian communion for the first time. They also note that the Second Great Awakening allowed for the freedom to use "the spiritual as a distinctive form of black worship," which formed the basis for the Pentecostal tradition because of the emphasis on "perfectionism" and secured the technique of church revivals in the African American religious experience.[85] The early Pentecostal tradition of "perfectionism" grew out of the nineteenth-century Wesleyan Holiness movement, deeply influenced by John Wesley's doctrine of Christian perfection (entire sanctification—being freed from the power of willful sin and perfected in love). This movement provided Blacks with the necessary coping mechanism needed for emotional and psychological survival.

Wilmore writes that for the slave, reverence toward God was, first of all, the joyous affirmation of God's presence and providence. Once the Spirit came near, many Blacks opened themselves to it with a vivaciousness and abandon that was expressed most satisfactorily in song and dance. The secular and the sacred met and embraced each other in the bodily celebration of the homologous unity of all things—the holy and the profane, good and evil, the beautiful and the dreadful. To give oneself up with shouts of joy and "singing feet" to this wholeness of being, to the ecstatic celebration of one's creaturehood, and to experience that

83. Lincoln, *Black Church Since Frazier*, 14–15.

84. Lincoln, *Black Church Since Frazier*, 16.

85. Lincoln and Mamiya, *Black Church in the African American Experience*, 9–11.

creaturehood taken up and possessed by God in a new state of consciousness, was to imbibe the most restorative medicine available to the slave.[86]

Wilmore also contends that the dominant motif of slave religion was the affirmation of joy, and sometimes this joy was expressed in apparently carnal pleasure.[87] He discusses how this was an area of disgust and bewilderment for the white missionaries. They had an extremely difficult time understanding how the slaves could handle sacred things with lighthearted humor. They often labeled the joyous atmosphere of the slaves as one of stupidity and one that needed refinement. The white preachers labored arduously to get the slaves to relegate their religious behavior to a quiet, ethereal expression of the soul governed by fear and trembling. The white preachers conceded that the shouts of Saturday night over a bottle of spirits were "suspiciously" like the shouts of Sunday morning. This social indoctrination is one of the ideologies of the contemporary church that causes disdain for the so-called Black church worship experience, even though white Pentecostal and Spirit-filled churches attempt to adopt this style of worship.

Baer and Singer write that camp meetings constituted high points in the religious life of the slaves.[88] When the intensity of their religious fervor proved to be offensive to whites, the slaves removed themselves to a more secluded spot where they could express themselves more fully and freely. This sensitivity is still present; when whites attend a Black worship service, Blacks try to make it more intelligent and less fiery due to the discomfort of whites and their preferred worship styles. E. Franklin Frazier labeled this experience of private worship as the "invisible church." This is the environment where Blacks had private prayer meetings, sang songs, shouted, and even married. Wilmore states that slave religion was partly a clandestine protest against the hypocrisy of a system that expected Blacks to be virtuous and obedient to those who themselves lived lives of indolence and immorality in full view of the ones they purported to serve as examples.[89]

Mary Berry and John Blassingame discuss the unique characteristics of slave religion and their connection to Africa.[90] They contend that the slaves' religious beliefs differed from those of his master in several

86. Wilmore, *Black Religion and Black Radicalism*, 66.

87. Wilmore, *Black Religion and Black Radicalism*, 46.

88. Baer and Singer, *African-American Religion in the Twentieth Century*, 18.

89. Wilmore, *Black Religion and Black Radicalism*, 47–48.

90. Berry and Blassingame, *Long Memory*, 41–45.

ways. First, most Black Christians believed in conjurors. Second, many of the death and burial customs differed from those of whites, with funerals held long after burials and graves being decorated with articles belonging to the deceased. Third, music was more important in Black than white churches and had a more complicated rhythmic structure. Although the first slaves learned of Christianity from white missionaries, they quickly fused it with West African beliefs and created their own religion. The frenzied shouting frequently noted by whites was, for example, a variant of African spirit possession. Other adapted African characteristics were the ring shout, the call-and-response pattern of sermons, prayers, and songs, the unrestrained joy, and the predilection for the total physical and emotional expression of the Spirit of God.

The preaching of the Second Great Awakening was exceptionally intriguing for the slaves because it personified some of the worship characteristics of African religion. E. Franklin Frazier writes that "the field hands were especially attracted by the Methodist and Baptist missionaries who, in their revival meetings, preached a simple doctrine of salvation through conversion in which a highly emotional experience was of primary importance."[91] Raboteau postulates that the powerful emotionalism, ecstatic behavior, and congregational response of the revivals were amenable to the African religious heritage of the slaves, and forms of African dance and song remained in the shout and spirituals of Afro-American converts to evangelical Protestantism.[92] In addition, the slaves' rich heritage of folk belief and expression was not destroyed but augmented by conversion. Franklin noted that the spiritual or religious folk songs grew out of the independent religious meetings of Blacks while they secretly worshiped without the surveillance of whites.[93] As much as they could, whites carefully guarded the religious gatherings of the Blacks to prevent the occasions for conspiracies and revolts. Thus, when the slaves got a chance, they would "steal away" for independent worship experiences.

Frazier surmises that in the preaching in the camp meetings and revivals of the Second Great Awakening, Blacks found hope and a prospect of escape from their earthly woes in the fiery message of salvation. Also, they found an opportunity for emotional release in these groups because

91. Frazier, *Negro Church in America*, 10–11.

92. Raboteau, *Slave Religion*, 66–67.

93. Franklin, *From Slavery to Freedom*, 206.

of the emphasis placed on feeling as a sign of conversion. This type of religious experience allowed slaves who harbored repressed feelings "to let loose." Frazier contends that this kind of emotional experience created an opportunity for an ephemeral sense of social solidarity for the displaced Blacks.[94] For a period, these revival meetings brought Blacks into union with their fellow man and broke the barriers that isolated Blacks morally from whites. The Awakening movements provided relevance for Black worshipers and an opportunity to express and feel their worship experience. I like to think of them as Baptists and Methodists waiting to manifest their Pentecostalism.

Baer and Singer state that "the First Awakening emphasized spiritual equality rather than racial equality, as indicated by Whitefield's affirmation of slavery in a private letter to John Wesley in 1751."[95] Yet, they write that the Second Great Awakening had an even more profound impact on African American religiosity than the First. The New Light Presbyterians, the Separate Baptists, and the Methodists spread the evangelical message to the new southwestern frontier. The camp meetings proved to be highly effective in increasing slave conversions. Indeed, "The Presbyterians launched the camp meetings that became the focus of the Second Great Awakening and was quickly adopted by other evangelical denominations and finally became a distinctly 'Methodist institution.'"[96] They stated that the Methodist church, in its conference meetings between 1780 and 1784, condemned the institution of slavery on the grounds of being contrary to the gospel.

Baer and Singer note that the anti-slavery stance of the Methodist Church came from its founder, John Wesley. Wesley insisted that believers should fight against the slave trade until it was totally eradicated. The Methodist Church asked "that its members would free their slaves, and in their conference, called for the excommunication of any member who purchased or sold a slave."[97] Yet, in the test of time, branches of the Methodist Church began to fold under social pressure and continue to support the institution of slavery. This phenomenon resembles the dilemma the modern-day United Methodist Church faced recently in its internal rift regarding same-sex marriage and clergy; initially, it stood against it, but subsequently caved in to the social pressures of the day. Thus, several

94. Frazier, *Negro Church in America*, 11.

95. Baer and Singer, *African-American Religion in the Twentieth Century*, 23.

96. Raboteau, *Slave Religion*, 132.

97. Baer and Singer, *African-American Religion in the Twentieth Century*, 17.

conservative Methodist denominations in America have broken away from the central United Methodist Church.

To add to the pressure of slavery was Eli Whitney's invention of the cotton gin, which served as a catalyst for an increase in slaves. According to Meier and Rudwick, the cotton gin was "a simple device for separating the seeds from the lint, making the production of the short-staple cotton highly remunerative."[98] This invention increased the potential uses of cotton and required more to be processed. Cotton cultivation soon began to spread, and more slaves were imported to keep up with the demands. Once again, the church buckled when choosing between evangelism and economics. Though many of the churches repositioned themselves on race issues, slaves were still embracing the message of the Second Great Awakening.

Raboteau states that the religious effects of the Second Great Awakening touched the young people. He states that children between the ages of eight and thirteen were present preaching and praying. The inclusion of Blacks grew at a rapid rate. The Methodist Church recorded 1,890 Black members in 1786, increasing to 11,682 in 1790. In 1797, Black membership stood at 12,215.[99] Raboteau says that this figure represented one-fourth of the total membership of the Methodist Church. He states that it is speculated that Blacks represented about one-fourth of the membership of the Baptist church. The number of Blacks in the Baptist church at the close of the eighteenth century was estimated between 18,000 and 19,000. Raboteau attributes the growth of both denominations to the fervor of the Great Awakening. He records that the "first separate black church in the South and the North belonged to the Baptist church founded between 1773 and 1775 in Silver Bluff, South Carolina, across the Savannah River from Georgia." This church became the mother of several Baptist missions. Thus, the First and Second Great Awakenings catapulted the beginning of the independent Black church.[100]

This period attracted many negroes to the revivals, which led to conversion. Raboteau gives several reasons for this appeal, one being that "the Evangelical religion spread by revivalists initiated a religious renaissance in the South as a somnolent religious consciousness was awakened by revivalist preachers."[101] The revival was also a means of church extension

98. Meier and Rudwick, *From Plantation to Ghetto*, 19.

99. Raboteau, *Slave Religion*, 137–38.

100. Raboteau, *Slave Religion*, 132–33.

101. Raboteau, *Slave Religion*, 132.

for Presbyterians, and particularly Methodists and Baptists. The mobility of the circuit rider and the local autonomy of the Baptist preacher were suited to the needs and conditions of the rural South.[102] There was an individualistic emphasis to revivalism that had an intense concentration on inward conversion, which fostered an inclusiveness that could border on egalitarianism. The evangelical preachers preached to racially mixed congregations.

The constant emphasis on the conversion experience rather than the process of religious instruction made Christianity more accessible to illiterate slaves and slaveholders alike. For the most part, the Anglican Church primarily taught the slaves the Ten Commandments, the Apostles' Creed, and the Lord's Prayer. However, the revivalist preacher helped them to feel the weight of sin, to imagine the threats of hell, and to accept Christ only as Savior.[103] The revivalists tended to minimize complex explanations of doctrine. The enthusiasm of the camp meeting, though it seemed excessive to some churchmen, triggered by the personal, emotional appeal of the preacher, ignited a common response of the membership. Indeed, "the plain doctrine and heavy emotion of revivalist sermons appealed as much to the black as to the white farmer." Raboteau notes that the Baptists and Methodists did not insist on a well-educated clergy. A converted heart and a gifted tongue were more important than the amount of theological training received.[104] If a converted slave showed talent for exhorting, he exhorted, and not only to Black audiences. The tendency of evangelical religion to level the souls of all persons before God became manifest when awakened Blacks reached unconverted whites.

The turn of the century and the Second Great Awakening marked a change in the religious position and condition of Blacks. Raboteau explains that the revivalist impulse of the Great Awakening broke out anew on the frontier in 1800.[105] The Great Western Revival, inaugurated by the Gaspar River and Cane Ridge camp meetings in Kentucky, embraced Blacks, who eagerly participated in the tumultuous exercises that became characteristic of frontier revivalism. During this era, Blacks began to preach to and even pastor whites. C. Eric Lincoln records that, in 1801, a black named Lemuel Haynes pastored an all-white congregation in

102. Raboteau, *Slave Religion*, 136.

103. Raboteau, *Slave Religion*, 137.

104. Raboteau, *Slave Religion*, 136.

105. Raboteau, *Slave Religion*, 139.

Hartford, Connecticut, and William Lemon was called to pastor a white church in Gloucester, Virginia. Lincoln states that late in the eighteenth century, Blacks traveled with white Methodist preachers under the title "exhorters," and people came to hear the Black preachers.[106]

Raboteau states that Black preachers in either all-white or racially mixed congregations could be free or enslaved. Most of the established, independent Black churches in the eighteenth and nineteenth centuries were founded by *free* Black preachers, not enslaved ones. Some of the Black preachers were so effective and moved whites to such an extent that the congregation would purchase their freedom, provide housing, and receive them as their pastor. These men, once freed, had the legal standing and organizational capacity to charter churches, purchase property, and incorporate congregations—steps that enslaved people could not legally take.

While the preaching of Blacks proved to be so inspiring that some white congregations sought their gift, some states passed laws prohibiting Blacks from being licensed or ordained. Under these laws, their gifts and ministries were restricted. They were not allowed to preach outside the presence of their white slave master. In many states, their duties were restricted to funerals and marriages. The Methodist Church got around this law by establishing the licensed office of "exhorter." Exhorters were lay preachers allowed to preach and discipline Black members within a certain locale.

The visible Black church was born in this era. Raboteau records that where small Black churches were tolerated, they sprang up during this period under the leadership of negroes. But whites did not support this practice, so Black churches often met in secret. Because of the influx of Black converts, many Baptist and Methodist churches were considered interracial but segregated congregations. They were allowed to coinhabit a facility but not a brotherhood. Negroes were not afforded the same privileges as white members, which included the right to vote, receive sacraments, and participate in open seating. Raboteau suggests that it was not uncommon for Blacks to outnumber whites in a worship service.[107] And when the Black population became too great in number, oftentimes a separate service was designed for them, or whites withdrew, leaving the Blacks to form their own services. He further explains that even before

106. Lincoln, *Black Church Since Frazier*, 23–24.

107. Raboteau, *Slave Religion*, 139.

the nineteenth century, a few African Baptist churches were formed. These churches were considered independent "to the extent that they called their own pastors and officers, joined local Baptist associations with white churches, and sent black delegates to association meetings." However, "by the 1820s, black churches were under the supervision of white pastors."[108] Raboteau claims that this took place until the beginning of the Civil War, reasoning that the white preacher was providing slaves with too much knowledge, in the eyes of slave masters.

Lincoln records that, by 1816, there were 42,000 Blacks in the Methodist Church alone, and 30,000 of these were Southern slaves. By the time the Methodist church split over the issue of slavery in 1844, its Black membership was up to 150,000. He further suggests that there were probably as many Blacks in the Baptist church; however, it cannot be substantiated because of the lack of data. He goes on to note that few Blacks could be counted among the Congregationalists, the Episcopalians, the Presbyterians, or Lutherans. However, Presbyterians and particularly the Congregationalists rivaled the Methodists in their concern for the education of Black people. Considering its power and scope, the Roman Catholic Church in America does not appear to have been a factor of marked significance in either the Christianization or the education of African Americans; its principal ministry was confined to ethnics of European descent.[109]

The Civil War was a time of transition for the Christian church. Tension existed within denominations, especially between their Southern and Northern congregations. While the Northern church somewhat supported the freedom of slaves, the Southern branches of denominations resented this, leading them to not change their views about slavery. Though the North was more open to the ideas of Reconstruction after the Civil War, racism was still a problem in society. Whites found social equality for Blacks practically inconceivable, and many believed that because of the Black person's (supposedly) innate inferiority, he would forever remain in the lower ranks of society. Indeed, some of the abolitionists themselves were ambivalent on the question of negro equality. They discussed other issues surrounding Reconstruction, saying "that the resistance of the South was forceful and fast, and that slavery had been destroyed, but the 'southern mind' found other ways to perpetuate

108. Raboteau, *Slave Religion*, 139.

109. Lincoln, *Black Church Since Frazier*, 25–26.

many of its assumed benefits." They further elaborated that Southerners knew that if they could prevent Blacks from having access to the skills and capital necessary to function freely, they would remain subjugated.[110]

Salley and Behm postulate that white dominance was maintained over Black freedom by creating a series of "Black Codes." They say that these codes were put in place to give a false sense of freedom by legalizing Black marriages, allowing them to own and dispose of property, and to sue and be sued. However, these laws were established to keep the Black "exactly what he was as long as possible: a propertyless rural laborer under strict controls, without political right, and with inferior legal rights."[111] Former slaves had a very difficult time adjusting to their new so-called freedom, for they had been groomed for the plantation and now had to deal with a "plantation mentality."[112]

Reconstruction marked a new political era for Blacks that would have a tremendous impact on the so-called Black church, marking the rejection of President Andrew Johnson's inadequate plans for Reconstruction during the early months of his administration. Salley Jr. and Behm credit a measure of the political success of Blacks to some of the white radical Republicans who favored "political equality" and assistance for Blacks.[113] They note that through the efforts of these radical Republicans, the Fourteenth and Fifteenth Amendments to the Constitution were approved, the Freedmen's Bureau was created and supported, and governments of the Southern states temporarily gave the former slaves political equality. Yet, because of the resistant attitudes of the whites, political and civil rights were unstable and threatened. The Freedmen's Bureau, established to provide emergency relief, schools, and protection for former slaves, was disbanded in 1869, shortly after it began. The federal troops were no longer present in the South, and the South was a long way from accepting the equality of Blacks. Thus, white Southerners, who had an abnormal passion for the continued subjugation of Blacks, were very active during this time, rolling back the rights and offices previously granted. There were many white groups established to ensure that Blacks would not progress. One group in particular was the Ku Klux Klan, a volunteer organization committed to promoting white supremacy by any means necessary. Many of their practices were illegal, but they felt

110. Hackett, *Religion and American Culture*, 320.

111. Litwack, *Been in the Storm So Long*, 277.

112. Salley and Behm, *What Color Is Your God?*, 121–22.

113. Salley Jr. and Behm, *Negro Suffrage in South Carolina*, 4.

religiously and morally justified. They sought to have total control over the negro and to drive him and his fellows from power and establishment. The KKK was responsible for lynchings, terrorism, and vicious murders.

Lynching became the new philosophy for dealing with white race frustration and issues. J. C. Furnas notices that the KKK was made up of poor white or small white farmers who had been taught to have a distaste for Blacks.[114] These Southern lynching mobs would make their rounds while freely passing the bottle, resulting in intoxication. Phillips claims that mobsters who were angry because of a crime that a Black committed would sometimes burn him alive on the spot of the crime or lynch him.[115] This practice was accompanied by inviting Blacks to come and watch to strike fear in their hearts so that they would never violate the law, space, or practices of the white people. The few whites who tried to sympathize and advocate on behalf of Blacks were attacked for their position. Thus the Reconstruction period gradually came to an end because of the repeal of legislation and the relaxation of restraints.

Eventually, the system of segregation was legalized, and the South held the belief that the system of race relations should be left up to it. Salley Jr. and Behm posit that "blacks had been reduced to economic and political powerlessness in a society about to enter the fullness of an industrial age."[116] They claim that the latter decades of the nineteenth century and the early years of the twentieth were marked by great white violence against Blacks. The law stood helpless and ineffective while thousands of Black men and women were brutally murdered and terrorized. They further express that not only was the South engaged in this activity, but "the North had violent anti-black riots."[117] Blacks were "equal" citizens but did not receive equal protection under the law.

Salley Jr, and Behm say that Christianity played a major role in the perpetuation of this oppressive mindset. Hence, the churches in the North felt a need to offer support for Reconstruction efforts, and churches in the South felt a need to support the Southern way of life. The three major denominations—Baptist, Methodist, and Presbyterian—experienced dissension after the war and could not reunite. According to Salley Jr. and Behm, the Southern churches developed a religious style and temperament that was nostalgic and defensive, serving only to widen

114. Furnas, *Road to Harper's Ferry*, 325.

115. Phillips, *American Negro Slavery*, 344.

116. Salley Jr. and Behm, *Negro Suffrage in South Carolina*, 7

117. Salley Jr. and Behm, *Negro Suffrage in South Carolina*, 10.

the gap between themselves and Northern churches. They stated, "More central than the schisms was the fact that the white southern churches continued black subservience in the name of God."[118] They further record that the white Protestant church, a major Southern social institution, was one of the first groups in the South to segregate after the Civil War and affirm racism as a valid ethos for race relations in the South. They argue that Protestantism "helped pave the way for the capitulation to racism at the turn of the century."[119]

During this era, the church could have offered solace for a displaced and abused people, but instead it chose to perpetuate social injustice. Though Northerners made some support efforts, it was not enough to diminish the hostile treatment of the racist South. In the wake of such attitudes and rejection came a strong desire for independent Black churches among the freed negroes.

THE INDEPENDENT BLACK CHURCH

The independent Black church was not a creation of Reconstruction. It was developed during slavery by freed negroes. This era's first and primary independent church was the African Methodist Episcopal Church, founded by Richard Allen and Absalom Jones. E. Franklin Frazier writes that Richard Allen was the most famous negro preacher in the North because of the role he played in the organization of an independent negro church organization.[120] Allen was born into slavery in Philadelphia but was sold to a planter in Delaware. He was brought up under the influence of Methodist preachers and converted in 1777. Frazier reports that Allen was allowed to conduct prayer meetings and preach in the house of his master, whom he also converted.

Consequently, Allen and his brother were allowed to purchase their freedom for $2,000 because their master became convinced that slavery was morally wrong. After Allen's freedom, he worked odd jobs and continued to be extremely religious until he became a preacher in 1780. Bishop Francis Asbury (Methodist) allowed Allen to travel with white preachers. While on one of his trips to Philadelphia, Allen recognized the need for negroes in religious leadership and organization and

118. Salley Jr. and Behm, *Negro Suffrage in South Carolina*, 14

119. Salley Jr. and Behm, *Negro Suffrage in South Carolina*, 15.

120. Frazier, *Negro Church in America*, 36.

proposed that a separate church for negroes be established. The catalyst for this change was the fact that the concerns of negroes were not being addressed and that racist practices were being exercised.

The movement for a separate Black church grew out of racist practices at the St. George Methodist Episcopal Church of Philadelphia, Pennsylvania, in particular, the seating of Blacks in the gallery. It was at this church that one of the most humiliating acts was committed towards Allen and Jones. Allen and Jones attended a worship service, and while they were kneeling in prayer at the altar, Allen, Jones, and another member were dragged from the front of the church to the rear. The so-called "churchmen" at St. George commented that "niggers" were not allowed at the altar. After this experience, Allen and Jones left the church and, together with other negro members, founded the Free African Society.

This experience served as the impetus for organizing the African Methodist Episcopal Church. Unfortunately, after Allen and Jones formed the Free African Society, they disagreed on the worship pattern of the church. Allen sought to perpetuate the worship style of the Methodist Church, contending that this was the style to which the Blacks were accustomed. Regrettably, the assimilation mentality of Blacks existed when Blacks were seeking independence and empowerment. Their only model was the white model, which was considered the "right" model. As a result of the differences between Allen and Jones, they started different churches. Jones wanted to adopt the worship pattern of the Protestant Episcopal Church. Allen organized the Bethel Church and dedicated its building in Philadelphia in 1794.

Allen's movement spread to other cities and other churches were established. However, it was not until a delegation from the different churches met in 1816 that the movement was named the African Methodist Episcopal Church (AME). Allen was elected bishop, and the "Book of Discipline," which contained the articles of religion used by the Wesleyans, was adopted. The foundational theology and practices of the Black church, in terms of its theological disposition, were adopted from white churches. This epoch of history led to the establishment of the AME Zion Church and Independent Baptist churches, which were formed in Southern states like Maryland, Virginia, Georgia, and Kentucky, and Northern cities like Boston, New York, and Philadelphia. Other denominational churches, such as the Pentecostal churches, were formed much later.

The nineteenth century was a period that created a sense of independence amongst Black people and churches. Franklin says that "this era represented a merger of the 'invisible institution' of the negro church, which had taken root among the slaves, and the institutional church, which had grown up among the negroes who were free before the Civil War."[121] Baer and Singer briefly record and outline certain criteria for being considered an independent Black church. They quote Clifford Sernett, who wrote, "If a particular congregation was composed primarily of free negroes, had title to its place of worship, a black pastor, and could conduct its business affairs without harassment, it can be called independent."[122] They further discuss that in order to be called independent, the churches had to be able to exercise a certain measure of autonomy or self-regulation.

They say most of the churches in the South conformed to laws requiring them to affiliate with white-controlled religious bodies. However, many known Black churches never joined any association. Baer and Singer argue that independent Black churches provided the following for their members:

(1) an arena for the formation, maintenance, and expression of African American culture;

(2) a social support network for participants, ranging from formal structures such as mutual aid and burial societies to informal ones that allowed for camaraderie and recreation;

(3) a set of honorable titles and awards not achievable in the larger society;

(4) and a context for the acquisition and practice of leadership and organizing skills that sometimes were transferred to social activism in the larger society.[123]

Finally, Baer and Singer contend that separate Black Baptist churches were an outgrowth of the First and Second Great Awakenings and that more Blacks were attracted to the Baptist churches than any other church, including the Methodist.[124] Growing up on the South Side of Chicago, it was clear to me that the majority of the Black community that attended church went to Baptist churches. However, their churches displayed

121. Franklin, *From Slavery to Freedom*, 244.

122. Sernett, *Black Religion and American Evangelicalism*, 113, quoted in Baer and Singer, *African-American Religion in the Twentieth Century*, 28.

123. Baer and Singer, *African-American Religion in the Twentieth Century*, 30.

124. Baer and Singer, *African-American Religion in the Twentieth Century*, 31.

Pentecostal worship behavior such as dancing, shouting, and speaking in tongues. While dancing and shouting are more reflective of African religious practices, many Black Baptist churches would have episodes of people speaking in tongues. However, it wasn't a part of their doctrinal teachings.

We can see that the Black church was slowly developing into an empowering institution that would impact Black people and the Black community. Frazier remarks that many societies were formed after the Civil War by free negroes who aided and assisted Blacks in their struggle for liberation.[125] Many organizations formed to empower Blacks had their foundation in the Black church. He gives many examples of these organizations, but one, in particular, was the first Temple and Tabernacle of the Knights and Daughters of Tabor, in Independence, Missouri, under the leadership of Reverend Moses Dickson (founded in 1871). Rev. Dickson formerly organized a secret society, the Knights of Liberty. Having fought in the Civil War, he disbanded the 50,000-member organization to form his new organization after the war's end.[126]

This newly founded society aimed to spread Christian religion and education. The members were counseled to purchase real estate, avoid intemperance, and cultivate true manhood. By the close of the nineteenth century, his organization claimed nearly 200,000 members in eighteen jurisdictions, scattered from Maine to California and from the Great Lakes to the Gulf of Mexico. These kinds of movements reveal how relevant and empowering the Black church has been in its evolution. The Black church was more than just strictly a religious organization; it taught independence and economic freedom. According to Frazier, the Black church is perhaps solely responsible for the education and the economic liberation of Blacks.[127] The church was leading the way in the life of the Black community after Reconstruction, and the church represented the people on educational, economic, and political fronts.

At the same time, Salley and Behm write that the Black church, from the Civil War until World War I, can be described as "the accommodative church."[128] The preachers in these churches oriented their members to white denominationalism in society. As Black ministers had played the

125. Frazier, *Negro Church in America*, 35.

126. Lincoln and Mamiya, *Black Church in the African American Experience*, 175–76.

127. Frazier, *Negro Church in America*, 36.

128. Salley and Behm, *What Color Is Your God?*, 56–57.

role of mediator before the Civil War, they continued during this period. In terms of race relations, the Black churches' primary function was to accommodate their members to their subordinate status in white society. Salley and Behm argue that in these churches, the negro preacher in a white-dominated church was easily controlled, and if he was difficult, he would be threatened. One of the ways that the preacher was used was to perpetuate an "otherworldly" message that had no existential value. Black minds were turned from the oppression and exploitation of this present world towards a world of the future, a world to come. This kind of message was smiled upon and encouraged by the white church. Often, churches whose messages centered on the other world would tend to receive favors from the white church. Salley and Behm state that "at best, the black church was a mere extension of white-racist ideology wrapped in black skins."[129] They claim that the practices of these churches eventually led to the accusation that the Black church served as a vehicle of white control.

They further suggest that even when education was impressed upon Blacks, it focused on industrial and manual skills, thus grooming Blacks for a subordinate role in society. Tom Skinner notes that the "South Carolina legislature forbade black people to work in any capacity except farming and menial service without special license."[130] The Reconstruction era represented tremendous challenges for Blacks, for it presented thousands of uneducated, unemployed Blacks to the American society with nowhere to go, not even the church. Meier and Rudwick discuss the challenges of the so-called free slaves and conjecture that the elite negroes sought civil and political rights.[131] Still, the ex-slaves desired, most of all, land of their own to cultivate and the opportunity to acquire an education. What's amazing about these two desires is that they still exist today after the evolution of civil rights and the Black church.

Meier and Rudwick further explicate the challenges faced by Blacks during the Reconstruction period, among them the desire to acquire land in the face of government and white opposition and a general unwillingness to sell it to Blacks.[132] Even though this attitude existed, some ex-slaves managed to purchase farms. Landowner laws were quite restrictive in the South, though they were more relaxed in the North. In the South,

129. Salley and Behm, *What Color Is Your God?*, 55.

130. Skinner, *Black and Free*, 78.

131. Meier and Rudwick, *From Plantation to Ghetto*, 105.

132. Meier and Rudwick, *From Plantation to Ghetto*, 106.

the landowner laws helped to replace the institution of slavery. It was a more technological approach to the practice of slavery. Meier and Rudwick postulate that the Black Codes adopted in the South allowed whites to maintain power over Blacks through social control by fixing the negro "in a subordinate place in the social order," providing "a manageable and inexpensive labor force."[133]

This system included vagrant laws that held if a negro was unemployed and did not possess a permanent address, he was declared delinquent. He then would be arrested and fined, and if he could not pay, he had to contract his labor until his debt was paid. Meier and Rudwick also discuss the other labor-intensive plan of the South, the institution of sharecropping.[134] This system emerged from the previously mentioned labor contract system present in the vagrant law. It began during the Civil War and the early Reconstruction years. Sharecropping was the act of negroes entering a contractual agreement with a plantation owner, whereby rather than working for a wage, the freedman rented a plot of land and paid the plantation owner a certain proportion of the cotton crop. While this seemed to be attractive externally, history records that the negro never got ahead in this system. The system had hidden costs, so at best, the negro learned how to live from paycheck to paycheck. Hidden costs would include lodging, taxes, and farm equipment rental. Additional psychological costs included low self-esteem, low self-worth, and humiliation. Thus, when all the work was done, the only one who made a substantial profit was the plantation owner, who had once again received the benefits of slavery through a clandestine system of social and economic oppression.

Skinner argues that the Emancipation Proclamation of 1865 declared the freedom of Black people, describing what the Black man was not—a slave. But it did not define him as a man.[135] Because Blacks were not respected as human, the women were raped, the men murdered and castrated, and the schools burned down by this "Christianized," intellectual, and highly domestic culture that criticized the morality and mores of Blacks. Skinner observes that "between 1877 and 1925, thousands of black people were lynched, their women raped, their children beaten, and their homes burned. They were disenfranchised and relegated to

133. Meier and Rudwick, *From Plantation to Ghetto*, 109.

134. Meier and Rudwick, *From Plantation to Ghetto*, 110

135. Skinner, *Black and Free*, 74.

fourth-class citizenship. During that time, virtually no white person was arrested, tried, or convicted for a crime against a black man."[136]

Blacks needed a nation where they could live in peace and dignity. Indeed, it was apparent that they would never be given the opportunity on American soil. Thus, the Black church became one of a limited number of "alternative" nations. The Black church now faced the great challenge of assisting a large urban community with limited economic opportunity and a theology that looked forward primarily to afterlife rewards rather than the reality of life in the here and now. God had broken their physical chains, but now the Black church would have the challenge of delivering Blacks from their mental chains. This was not an easy task when one considers the conditioning process that Blacks and whites underwent in both the antebellum and postbellum periods of American history.

Theodore Wilson chronicles the arguments white slaveholders held—that their slaves were the best-treated laborers in the world, especially when compared to the peasant workers in Europe.[137] He also writes of the remarks that W. E. B. Du Bois made in response to this uninformed ethos. Du Bois stated that slavery had profound psychological effects on Blacks because of the enforced feelings of inferiority that were daily forced upon the minds of Blacks, as they had to address the white slaveholders as masters. The system created a sense of helplessness. One could not defend his family or his manhood.

Wilson further explains the acts that created psychological effects upon Blacks, saying that there was the enduring ritual of race etiquette, reinforced by the masters at every turn, which stipulated that proper behavior and conduct for Blacks involved bowing when meeting the master, standing and showing great humility in his presence, accepting floggings from the master's children, and approaching the mansion in the most self-effacing, humble, and beseeching manner.[138] Most planters employed floggings and other modes of physical punishment to ensure ritualistic obedience and deference to plantation rules. Slaves were frequently flogged, punished, or disciplined for failing to complete assigned tasks, running away, learning to read, bickering or fighting with whites or with other slaves, stealing, drunkenness, working too slowly, impertinence, asking to be sold, claiming their freedom, and damaging tools or household articles.

136. Skinner, *Black and Free*, 75.

137. Wilson, *Black Codes of the South*, 7.

138. Wilson, *Black Codes of the South*, 17.

The issue of whether or not the negro was affected permanently by the institution of slavery has been debated back and forth by liberals and racists while never coming to a conclusion that has appeased both sides. Peter Paris states:

> The history of African Americans begins with the Transatlantic Slave Trade, which lasted for more than three and one-half centuries. Through its cruel design, millions of Africans were extracted from their homeland as chattel to furnish a labor market. No person of African descent in America has escaped the enduring stigma of that period. Every freed slave was continually vulnerable to the ubiquitous threat of being forced back into slavery by the arbitrary whims of unscrupulous persons.[139]

The twentieth century, on the surface, did not offer Blacks many different alternatives than those of the last century. To continue the practice of racial oppression, documents were written to validate the inferior status of Blacks. Some of these books were published by religious presses, which disclosed the ideologies of the Christian church of the twentieth century. Franklin posits that to justify a racist system, "the demagogues, who were supported by the white propertied classes, engaged for 25 years in a campaign to prove that the negro was subhuman, morally degenerate, and intellectually incapable of being educated."[140]

Early in the twentieth century, books were published seeking to establish the inferiority status and intellectual inabilities of blacks, with the support of many Christian churches. These books sought to perpetuate the racist caste system goals of the white population through the medium of the church once again. We saw first colonizers using the Bible in the Congo (1441) to subjugate Blacks and reduce them to an inferior culture. Then we saw the Bible used to make docile and obedient slaves in the mid-seventeenth century. The perpetuation of this practice leads us into the twentieth century. Isaac O. Olaleye writes that the Bible was used in 1900 to prove the inferior status of blacks.[141] In 1900, Charles Carroll released *The Negro: A Beast or In The Image of God?*, with a religious publisher of the time—the American Book and Bible House.[142] Olaleye reports that Carroll's book contained "biblical" and "scientific" data

139. Paris, *Social Teaching of the Black Churches*, 1.

140. Franklin, *From Slavery to Freedom*, 255.

141. Olaleye, *Crisis of Mission in the African American Church*, 22–23.

142. Carroll, *Negro*.

proving that the negro was not a part of the human race. The author also stated that scientific research confirms that the negro has the characteristics of apes and monkeys and is simian in nature. He asserted "that the negro and the lower apes and four-footed animals all belong to one kind of flesh, the flesh of beasts." Olaleye records the sad effect of such literature when he writes that *The Negro: A Beast or In the Image of God?* was hailed as "the reasoner of the age," "the revelator of the century!," "the Bible as it is!" and the true accounting of "the negro and his relation to the human family!" Such attitudes have prevailed well into the present. Olaleye recounts the content of a news interview on the CBS Evening News on February 15, 1990. He reports that a white Afrikaner from South Africa said that Blacks were not human, and "if they come close to me, I'll blow their faces into pieces." This comment was made as they discussed the potential of integrating South African society now that Black leader Nelson Mandela was released.[143]

E. Franklin Frazier writes that while politicians and newspapers were forming public opinions and personal attitudes, Carroll's book appeared.[144] Frazier states the publisher says in the preface of the book "that if this book were considered intelligently and prayerfully, then it will be to the minds of the American people like unto the voice of God from the clouds appealing to Paul on his way to Damascus." So that the American people might be convinced of the scientific nature of the biblical truths presented in this book, the author includes pictures of God and an idealized picture of a white man to prove that white people were made in the image of God, as stated in the Bible, and a caricature of the negro showing that he could not have been made in the image of God.[145]

The book had a wide circulation, especially among white churchgoers. It helped to fix in white minds that the negro was not a descendant of Adam and Eve, "but simply a beast without a soul," which Carroll argued in the last chapter of his book.[146] Frazier asserts that not only did this book give religious sanctions to the belief of the inferiority of the negro, but it also caused this negative image of negroes to be engraved in every public edifice, railroad station, courthouse, and theaters with signs that pointed to different entrances and exits for Blacks, as well as separate

143. Olaleye, *Crisis of Mission in the African American Church*, 22–25.

144. Frazier, *Negro Church in America*, 35.

145. Frazier, *Negro Church in America*, 35–36.

146. Frazier, *Negro Church in America*, 36.

facilities that served Blacks.[147] Indeed, in every representation of the negro in the period, the Black man was pictured as a gorilla dressed up like a man. Many newspapers in the South would not carry the picture of a Black unless he had committed a crime.

Frazier also mentions that the vilification of the negro continued into the next decade with so-called "new" discoveries on the negro by self-proclaimed authorities. Doctoral dissertations were published that claimed to contain scientific proof that negroes were "as destitute of morals as any of the lower animals." Also, at the beginning of World War I, these authorities on the negro published a work that claimed that the negro was instinctively criminal. In 1915, an army surgeon assured the American people that many animals below man manifest a far greater amount of real affection in their lovemaking than do negroes, and that it is very rare that we see two negroes kiss each other.[148] Thus, as Franklin angrily contends, as a result of the campaign by whites to prove that negroes were subhuman and unfit for human association, the masses of Blacks found their niche and refuge in the Black church. The Black church served as a place where they could sing, express themselves, and look forward to another world. Blacks who migrated North soon discovered that they were considered subhuman there as well. Frazier notes that the church was the chief center of the negro social life in both the cities and the rural areas. It provided the chief means for self-expression and erected a shelter against a hostile white world.

Though the church acted as a place of refuge for Blacks in an angry and hostile white world, Salley Jr. and Behm observe that "all too often, the black church reinforced a plantation mentality that established 'whiteness' as the standard of fellowship with God and laid the basis for black exclusion in worldly matters."[149] In addition, highly esteemed white Christian preachers and evangelists such as Dwight L. Moody and Billy Sunday, when traveling to the South, held segregated meetings. The white church had a long history of supporting the American system of racism, doing so on the grounds of biblical interpretation. But we are now well aware that the concept of race is a social construct, not a biological one, created in the sixteenth century. It was used to justify the enslavement of Africans in colonial America. Thus, the Black church can place its birth

147. Frazier, *Negro Church in America*, 37–38.

148. Frazier, *Negro Church in America*, 37.

149. Salley Jr. and Behm, *Negro Suffrage in South Carolina*, 16.

and its history on the refusal of the white church to embrace Black Christians as fellow Christians in an egalitarian system of brotherhood.

The 1900s would be the century in which the relevance of the Christian church would be largely determined, and other major organizations and institutions would be organized. It would represent broadly the shift from the negro church to the Black church. While Reconstruction grappled with the merger of the "invisible institution" or the negro church and the independent, institutional church of the free negroes, the twentieth century presents the Black church, as defined by Blacks who were now refusing to be labeled negroes. The negro church was now ready for liberation and redefinition.

THE BLACK CHURCH

C. Eric Lincoln writes that the negro church that Frazier wrote about no longer exists. Lincoln contends that the negro church had to die to be reborn—having come to the conclusion that "'negro' and 'Christian' were irreconcilable categories."[150] Out of the death of the negro church came the bold, strident, and self-conscious Black church. Lincoln argues that the Black church and the negro church are not synonymous, nor is the Black church simply the negro church radicalized. Lincoln contends that the negro church died because the practices and philosophies that governed, structured, and conditioned it are not relevant practices that contemporary Blacks who represent the future of religion can attest to or affirm. Hence, the Black church is a departure from the critical norms that made the negro church what it was. The negro church died in the moral and ethical holocaust of the Black struggle for self-determination because the call to Christian responsibility is, in fact, first and foremost, a call to human dignity and, therefore, logically inconsistent with the limitations of negro-ness. A man cannot serve God and mammon; neither can he be both in the image of God and not in God's image. Yet, the negro church that died lives on in the Black church born of its loins, flesh of its flesh, for there are no disjunctions in religion.

The Black church represents a new self-perception for the Black community that varies from the historical white definition. Indeed, the Black community is portrayed as emerging, freed, and having the potential for a great future. The Black church gives a fresh outlook on how

150. Lincoln, *Black Church Since Frazier*, 39.

humanity should see God, which is not according to the Eurocentric perspective of the past. One of the significant events that raised fundamental issues for the Black church was the civil rights movement of the sixties. While it was politically motivated, it had strong implications for the existence of the Black church and American Christianity. The civil rights movement of Montgomery, Alabama (and beyond) led by Black clergy, spoke loudly to the American people, especially the American church.

In fact, the early twentieth century marked the beginning of the preacher/politician. Many of the preachers in the Black church in the early 1900s represented Blacks in the political, educational, and spiritual arena. Lincoln writes, "The black church was born out of the travail of slavery and oppression."[151] He contends that the black church has historically been a symbol of liberation. This can be seen overtly in Dr. Martin Luther King Jr.'s Montgomery Improvement Association, a movement formed from the churches of Alabama that redefined the Black church's responsibility as an agent of social change. This formation was not without resistance from white racists. Consequently, Black churches were bombed, and both children and adults died. This violent reaction was due to the Black church's demands for equal opportunity and equal rights.

Lincoln says that the white community, by bombing the 16th Street Baptist Church in Birmingham, taking the lives of four little girls attending Sunday school, sent a message to the Black church.[152] The message, signed in the blood of children, was that the Black church should not participate in the freedom movement for Blacks. However, these white racist attempts were unsuccessful, and the Black church became more involved in the quest for social change. Lincoln suggests that "the black church, as a self-conscious, self-assertive, inner-directed institution, was born, as the black church, not the negro church reborn, neither is it the white church replicated." He argues that the white church is the principal reason for the Black church, "for just as the white church permitted and tolerated the negro church, it made the black church necessary for a new generation of black people who refused to be negroes and who are not impressed by whatever it means to be white."[153]

Historically, white Christians had great difficulties fellowshipping with black Christians. Lincoln writes, "Wherever white Christians and black Christians had come in contact with each other in America, black

151. Lincoln, *Black Church Since Frazier*, 16.

152. Lincoln, *Black Church Since Frazier*, 214.

153. Lincoln and Mamiya, *Black Church in the African American Experience*, 12.

Christians had been demeaned by the white man's presumption of racial superiority."[154] Black Christians have a sense of dignity and self-respect in the Black church that they could never imagine having in white churches, since the Black church created its own literature, established its own publishing houses, elected its own bishops and other administrators, founded its own colleges and seminaries, and developed its own unique style of worship.

Because Black individuals themselves have frequently been unsure of their identity, and because the Black church is itself a creature of the countercurrents of American racial proclivities, the Black church has not always been without ambivalence in its understanding of what it is and why. At times, it has seen itself as a less perfect counterpart of the white church, striving for parity in perfection.[155] This self-demeaning undervaluation made some negro churches more white in their ritual behavior and more white in their social attitudes than many of the white churches they sought to emulate. The Black church was maligned for being "black—a nigger institution." The Black church has struggled at times with its own role, sometimes relegating it to emotionalism and music. Outsiders tend to see the Black church as maladministered, but Lincoln argues that this is inevitable based on their Blackness. They would always be seen as negative while not being given equal access to the "niceties of life."

The Black church is a powerful institution that Lincoln ascribes as having no disjunction between it and the community. He declares, "The black church is the spiritual face of the black community."[156] The Black church has always served as an empowerment source for the Black community. The Black church was a symbol of identity and prestige. The pastor gained respect from their church (the pastor was given a personal office) and the denomination. There was no other single movement or event that would have lasting effects upon the role of the Black church as Dr. King's Montgomery movement and the Southern Christian Leadership Conference (SCLC) of 1957. Dr. King's commitment to nonviolence became the philosophy of the SCLC. Lincoln conjectures that the nonviolent resistance movement was both instructive and embarrassing to the white American religious establishment. It was the perfect example of fundamental Christian ethics being put into practice. But the

154. Lincoln, *Black Church Since Frazier*, 15.

155. Lincoln and Mamiya, *Black Church in the African American Experience*, 11.

156. Lincoln, *Black Church Since Frazier*, 1.

practitioners were Black, and their strategy of returning love for evil and nonviolent response in the face of indescribable violence was directed essentially at white Christians.

Lincoln points out that a few white ministers spoke in support of King and the SCLC and promptly lost their pulpits.[157] Some whites and many Blacks lost their lives in this struggle for civil rights. Many Black clergy leaders emerged, especially out of the Baptist church, such as Wyatt Walker, Fred Shuttlesworth, Ralph Abernathy, and Leon H. Sullivan. These men deeply engaged the power of the Black church for social change and civil rights. However, some spoke in opposition, including the president of the National Convention, Joseph Jackson, who contended that it was not the place of the Black church to engage in these civil pursuits. Jackson regarded King as a provocateur and an ultimate menace to the Black people and the clergy profession. He and others argued that change should come by exemplary conduct, which comes through preaching the gospel and saving the flock for Jesus. Nonetheless, Peter Paris writes that "the black churches, under the norm of the black Christian tradition, are characterized by their common quest for human freedom and justice, that is, the equality of all persons under God."[158]

Paris observes that the Black church has continuously been conflicted in moral thought between loyalty to Christ and their loyalty to race.[159] Paris suggests that between serving the needs of the race and serving the Lord of the church, on the one hand, Black churches have been race institutions, always working in the interest of the race by preaching freedom, civil rights, temperance, and industry. On the other hand, the churches have been religious institutions with a strong sense of obligation to be faithful to the Redeemer, whom they worshiped as the source of ultimate truth and whose eschatological vision they employed as their criterion for social criticism.

As mentioned earlier, the term "Black" church carries within it a psychological implication of self-pride. Paris discusses some of the effects of the term "Black" as it relates to the empowerment of the church and community:

157. Lincoln, *Black Church Since Frazier*, 215.

158. Paris, *Social Teaching of the Black Churches*, 3.

159. Paris, *Social Teaching of the Black Churches*, 4.

(1) the term "Black" has become universally accepted by African Americans as their preferred name for the race, and such former terms as "negro" and "colored" have been retired to the dustbins of history;

(2) a new sense of pride in Black identity, African heritage, and Afro-American history;

(3) a significant psychological and cultural decrease in the race's sense of inferiority;

(4) an increased capacity for the pursuit of racial self-interest;

(5) and a growing appreciation of racial, ethnic, and cultural pluralism as harmonious with racially integrated society.[160]

Historically, the Black church has been the bulwark of the community. It was the institution from which entrepreneurial businesses were birthed and nurtured. Major Black colleges were started in the basements of Black churches, such as Morehouse and Spelman Colleges and Fisk and Howard Universities. Lincoln and Mamiya note that much of Black culture was forged in the heart of black religion and the Black church.[161] A demise of the Black religious tradition would have profound implications for the preservation of Black culture.[162]

Paris states, in conclusion, that at one time, Black churches were viewed (especially by whites) as otherworldly and escapist institutions, reflecting the despair of the Black community and/or manifesting themselves as poor replicas of white churches. The revisionist Black scholarship of the past two decades has helped change that misconception. As a result, Black churches are no longer viewed primarily as defective institutions merely because they differ from white churches. Also, increasingly, they are no longer being understood simply as social institutions with political and psychological import but as religious institutions.

C. Eric Lincoln and Lawrence H. Mamiya have written extensively on the Black church experience, providing denominational insights about all the major Black church movements. In their work, they define the Black church. They write, "We use the term 'black church' as do other scholars and much of the general public as a kind of sociological and theological shorthand reference to the pluralism of black Christian

160. Paris, *Social Teaching of the Black Churches*, 117–18.

161. Newbigin, *Gospel in a Pluralistic Society*, 188.

162. Carson, "How Independent Churches in Select Areas Are Reaching Young Adult African American Males," 90.

churches in the United States."[163] In general usage, any Black Christian person is included in "the Black church" if they are a member of a Black congregation.[164] Lincoln and Mamiya calculate that there are seven major Black denominations and a small scattering of other Christian groups that make up the body of Black Christians. They state that 80 percent of all Black Christians belong to the seven major denominations.[165]

Lincoln and Mamiya list the models of the Black church from the work of Hart Nelsen and Anne Kusener Nelsen, *The Black Church in the Sixties.*[166]

1.	The Assimilation Model	The essence of this view is the belief in the necessity of the demise of the Black church for the public good of Blacks. The Black church is seen as a stumbling block to assimilation in the American mainstream. The assimilation model also views the Black church as anti-intellectual and authoritarian. This model is found in the views and studies of E. Franklin Frazier.
2.	The Isolation Model	The Black church is characterized by "involuntary isolation," which is due to the predominantly lower-class status of the Black community. Isolation from civic affairs and mass apathy are the results of racial segregation in ghettos. Thus, Black religion is viewed as being primarily lower class and otherworldly. The isolation model is found in the work of Anthony Drum and Charles Silberman.
3.	The Compensatory Model	The Black church's main attraction is to give large masses of people the opportunity for power, control, applause, and acclaim within the group, which they do not receive in the larger society, as St. Clair Drake and Horace Cayton asserted in *Black Metropolis*. This view is also related to Gunnar Myrdal's perspective in *An American Dilemma*, which holds that the Black community is essentially pathological and Black culture is a "distorted development" of general American culture, so Black people compensate for this lack of acclaim and lack of access to mainstream society in their own institutions.

163. Lincoln and Mamiya, *Black Church in the African American Experience*, 1.

164. Lincoln and Mamiya, *Black Church in the African American Experience*, 1.

165. Nelsen and Nelsen, *Black Church in the Sixties*, 5–6.

166. Lincoln and Mamiya, *Black Church in the African American Experience*, 1.

4.	Ethnic Community–Prophetic Model	This model is a more positive interpretation of the Black church. It emphasizes the significance of the Black church "as a base for building a sense of ethnic identity and a community of interest among its members." It also accentuates the potential of the Black church or its minister to be a "prophet to a corrupt white Christian nation."[167]
5.	Dialectical Model	There are six pairs of dialectical polars, which are: The dialectic between priestly and prophetic functions. The dialectic between otherworldly vs. this-worldly. The dialectic between universalism and particularism. The dialectic between the communal and the private. The dialectic between charismatic vs. bureaucratic. The dialectic between resistance vs. accommodation.

The Nelsens caution that these models are not an exhaustive list. For instance, they note that other dialectic polarities could include sexual politics (male-female) or liberation theology (oppressor-oppressed).[168]

The Black church has a legacy of struggling for equality on hostile turf. As a result, it has emerged as the only institution in the Black community with the mental, economic, and spiritual stamina to withstand the challenges of oppression to an abused people. The Black church has been a vital force in economics, education, and politics, and a constant voice against racism, classism, and sexism.

WESLEYANS, HOLINESS, AND THE PENTECOSTAL CHURCHES

When considering comprehensively the social context in which Africans were thrust in the Americas, the Black church certainly played a significant role. Throughout the historical development of the Black church, it has displayed worship forms and styles of Pentecostalism before the formal launching of the Pentecostal/Charismatic church movements of the twentieth century. I contend that the organic expression of worship of people of color resembles that of Pentecostal worship because it is akin to African religious worship styles and patterns. Could it be that God

167. Nelsen and Nelsen, *Black Church in the Sixties*, 8.

168. Nelsen and Nelsen, *Black Church in the Sixties*, 14–15.

used the Black church to create the foundation for the evolution of the Pentecostal church, which was to come in the twentieth century?

Pentecostalism is a renewalist religious movement within Christianity that places special emphasis on the direct personal experience of God through the baptism of the Holy Spirit. Church historian Curtis Ward proposes the existence of an unbroken Pentecostal lineage from the early church to the present, with glossolalia and gifts following. However, early Pentecostals considered the movement a latter-day restoration of the church's apostolic power. Most historians of Pentecostalism hold that the movement emerged from late nineteenth-century radical evangelical revival movements in America and Great Britain.[169]

The modern Pentecostal church has its unofficial roots in the eighteenth-century Wesleyan movement, which gave birth to the Holiness church, which later gave birth to the Pentecostal church. Vinson Synan states, "John Wesley, the indomitable founder of Methodism, was also the spiritual and intellectual father of the modern holiness and Pentecostal movements, which have issued from Methodism within the last century."[170] John Wesley is credited by the modern Pentecostal movement because of his holiness doctrine, which served as the infrastructure of the Pentecostal movement. Wesley's lifespan extended throughout much of the eighteenth century, which he greatly affected. He lived during challenging racial and religious battles from 1703 to 1791.

James S. Thomas stated that in mid-eighteenth-century England and America, slavery represented one of the most evil systems Wesley encountered. When John and Charles Wesley founded the Holy Club in 1729, slavery was over 100 years old. Thomas sees that John Wesley had a difficult time with the concept of slavery and concluded that its practice could not be tolerated. Thomas notes that Wesley recorded his thoughts about slavery in a tract and was quoted saying, "O burst thou all their chains in sunder: Thou Saviour of all, make them free, that they may be free indeed."[171] Thomas maintains that while some could argue that Wesley was referring to spiritual freedom, it would not have been consistent with Wesley's overall stance on the issue of slavery. In fact, in a letter written by Wesley in 1791 to William Wilberforce, who was also fighting to abolish slavery in England, he wrote:

169. Synan, *Holiness-Pentecostal Tradition*, 1–3.

170. Synan, *Holiness-Pentecostal Tradition*, 13.

171. Wesley, *Thoughts Upon Slavery*.

> [U]nless the divine power has raised you up to be as Athanasius contramundum, I see not how you can go through your glorious enterprise in opposing that execrable villainy, which is the scandal of religion, of England, and of human nature. Unless God has raised you up for this very thing, you will be worn out by the opposition of men and devils. But if God be for you, who can be against you? Are all of them together stronger than God? Oh, be not weary of well doing! Go on, in the name of God and in the power of his might, till even American slavery (the vilest that ever saw the sun) shall vanish away before it. Reading this morning, a tract wrote by a poor African, I was particularly struck by that circumstance that a man who has a black skin, being wronged or outraged by a white man, can have no redress; it being a "law" in all our colonies that the oath of a black against a white goes for nothing. What villainy is this? That he who has guided you from your youth up may continue to strengthen you in this and all things, is the prayer of, dear sir, Your affectionate servant.[172]

Wesley was born during great controversies and would later publicly address some of America's religious and social ills.

He was educated in the Anglo-Catholic tradition rather than the continental Reformed Protestant tradition. Methodism, with its strong Arminian base, was a reaction against the extreme Calvinist position of the day. Calvinism promulgated that only the elect could be saved and that it was impossible to know for sure if you were one of the elect. Methodism assured that anyone could find salvation, and through the "conversion experience," one could know for sure that they were saved. Synan writes, "Methodist theology placed great emphasis on this conscious religious experience."[173] Wesley, the son of an Anglican clergyman, began his ministry at the age of twenty-five after completing his Oxford education. After taking Anglican orders, he sought to define his convictions by reading such authors as Jeremy Taylor, Thomas à Kempis, and William Law. These men's works greatly affected his life and helped shape his theology. Having read these works that primarily focused upon the life of Christ and the believers' responsibility to ethical and moral holiness, Wesley began his own personal pilgrimage.

172. John Wesley, Letter to William Wilberforce, February 24, 1791, 350–51.

173. Synan, *Holiness-Pentecostal Tradition*, 2.

Synan reports, "The remainder of Wesley's life was spent in the pursuit of the holiness of heart and life that Taylor, Kempis, and Law upheld in their works."[174] Most of Methodism was shaped by Wesley's initial convictions for personal holiness. To pursue his own holiness, a young Wesley traveled to Georgia as a missionary to the Indians and colonists. Synan reports that when Wesley returned to England in February of 1738, he wrote, "I went to America to convert the Indians; but oh, who shall convert me?"[175] As Wesley's holiness pilgrimage continued, he was to meet many people who would greatly affect and influence his life. Wesley was influenced by a Moravian Pietist from Germany, Count Zinzendorf, and by Martin Luther, just to name two.

Wesley's encounter with Zinzendorf revealed that he did not share his position of a second perfecting experience of divine grace. Wesley believed in the second work of the Spirit in the life of the believer, which differed from the traditional belief that one was perfected at conversion. Indeed, by 1740, Wesley's ideas on theology were fairly well cast in the permanent mold that would shape the Methodist movement, which would serve as a pre-Pentecostal theology that was to come.

Succinctly stated, they involved two separate phases of experience for the believer: the first, conversion, or justification, and the second, Christian perfection, or sanctification. In the first experience, the penitent was forgiven for his actual sins of commission, becoming a Christian but retaining a residue of sin within. This remaining inbred sin was the result of Adam's fall and had to be dealt with by a second blessing. This experience purified the believer of inward sin and gave him "perfect love" toward God and the human.[176] Synan contends that Wesley never taught sinless perfection but a perfection of motives and desires and that sinless perfection would come only after death.

This quest for holiness became the theme of Methodism, and fiery expressions accompanied it. In the endeavor to seek this second blessing of sanctification, Methodist worshipers were characterized as panting and groaning for pardon, while others were beseeching God with tears to cleanse them thoroughly of their sins. One observer wrote, "Some would be seized with a trembling, and in a few moments, drop on the floor as if they were dead; while others were embracing each other with streaming

174. Synan, *Holiness-Pentecostal Tradition*, 3.

175. Synan, *Holiness-Pentecostal Tradition*, 14.

176. Synan, *Holiness-Pentecostal Tradition*, 16–17.

eyes, and all were lost in wonder, love, and praise."[177] It was said that shouting could be heard from miles around that would take place in the camp meetings of early Methodism. These expressions of worship greatly resemble the worship behavior of Pentecostal churches, though devoid of the gifts of the Spirit and speaking in glossolalic speech.

Virginia and Kentucky became key locations in the Methodist movement. In the 1700s, the Virginia area experienced great growth, and in the 1800s, the Kentucky area did as well—each marked revivalism in the Methodist Episcopal church. While the emotions mentioned previously marked the 1700s expressions of the Methodists' second blessing encounter, in the 1800s, they were slightly different. This later encounter with the second blessing included falling, jerking, barking like dogs, falling into trances, the "holy laugh," and wild dances like David did before the ark of the Lord. These two revivals in Methodism mark significant eras.

The 1700s marked Wesley's initial quest for holiness and the doctrine of second blessing/perfected love for God and man. This was before Reconstruction, so it had great meaning. Slavery was the way of America, and racial hatred for Blacks was the accepted norm for society and the church. Hence, Wesley's emphasis on holiness and how it was characterized in practical terms of love was revolutionary for the times. However, the thrust for holiness was lost during and after the Civil War and Reconstruction. Synan postulates that long before 1858, the Southern churches had largely abandoned the quest for holiness in theory and practice.[178] From about 1830 until the outbreak of war, Southern theological energies were directed toward supporting and defending the institution of slavery. A study of the literature of the Methodist Episcopal Church South before the war shows that perfectionism was barely discernible.

Reconstruction marked a major challenge to the fires of Methodism, which had been extinguished during the war. This challenge to Methodism set the groundwork for the Pentecostal church through the Holiness movement. After Reconstruction, churches experienced the challenge of established religion by Darwinism, socialism, higher criticism, and the social gospel. There was also an environment of loose morals that began tearing away at the church. Synan reports, "No denomination felt the

177. Synan, *Holiness-Pentecostal Tradition*, 9.

178. Synan, *Holiness-Pentecostal Tradition*, 20.

winds of change more than the Methodist church."[179] The language of the Methodist church would quickly become obsolete if something did not happen. It was antiquated to speak of the mourners' bench, penitent believers, and camp meetings. Thus, the Holiness movement was launched by the Methodists.

The Methodist Church again launched camp meetings to stir persons' hearts to God. These camp meetings were pioneered by the Reverend William B. Osborn of the New Jersey Methodist Conference, and the Reverend John S. Inskip, pastor of the Green Street Methodist Episcopal Church. They implemented the camp meetings while Mrs. Harriet E. Drake of Wilkes-Barre, Pennsylvania, agreed to finance half of the cost of the camp meetings. Thus, a call to sanctification became the central message of the meetings, a quest for holiness.

In 1867, the modern holiness crusade began. Synan writes, "This may properly be considered the beginning of the modern Holiness movement in the United States."[180] This quest for holiness, called the National Camp Meeting for the Promotion of Holiness, was an unqualified success. These camp meetings had tremendous success, and many claimed to have experienced sanctification in the meetings. The meetings progressed because of the ecumenical claims of the movement, which involved Presbyterians, Baptists, and Congregationalists. But, as Synan observes, "In spite of the great popularity of the doctrine of holiness after 1867, controversy over it began to be felt in the Methodist church during the 1880's."[181] This controversy was believed to be partly due to the interdenominational appeal of the movement while being primarily led and supported by Methodists.

The controversy ended in 1885, when the Reverend Atticus Greene Haygood, a Methodist minister from Georgia, began to attack the holiness doctrine on the grounds that it was a "do-it-yourself" salvation. He began preaching a doctrine emphasizing growth in grace vs. instantaneous holiness. This started the break of Methodism from the Holiness movement. As the Methodist Episcopal Church continued to teach a second blessing of gradual sanctification, the Holiness movement and the Methodist Episcopal Church grew further apart. Synan writes, "As the controversy deepened, defenders of holiness became less loyal to the church, and the

179. Synan, *Holiness-Pentecostal Tradition*, 23.

180. Synan, *Holiness-Pentecostal Tradition*, 26.

181. Synan, *Holiness-Pentecostal Tradition*, 34.

defenders of the church became less loyal to the doctrine of holiness."[182] Out of this division between Methodism and holiness, scores of holiness denominations began, particularly in the Midwest and the South. Synan indicates, "The most radical of these groups was the 'Fire-Baptized Holiness Church,' which began in Iowa in 1895 and was organized into a denomination in South Carolina in 1898."[183] The Holiness church saw itself not as a redeeming agent of society but as one who was called to reject it. Synan explains, "In the holiness system of values, the greatest 'social sins' were not poverty, inequality, or unequal distribution of wealth, but rather the evil effects of the theater, ball games, dancing, lipstick, cigarettes, and liquor."[184] Thus, the theological position of the Holiness church was predicated upon the twofold work of the Spirit that took place in conversion, also called "regeneration," and sanctification, distinct in time and content from conversion, and also called the "baptism in the Holy Spirit" or "second blessing." This was known as the "Wesleyan understanding of sanctification," where sanctification occurred "at a definite, fixed time."

The Holiness movement served as the transition between the Methodist movement and the Pentecostal movement. Many who participated in the twentieth-century Pentecostal movement came from either the Methodist or Holiness churches. Baer and Singer suggest that "the terms 'Holiness' and 'Pentecostal' often are used to refer to many conversionist sects, but various scholars attempt to differentiate between them on historical, doctrinal, and sociological grounds."[185] Many of the twentieth-century Holiness churches eventually dropped "holiness" from their name and labeled themselves "Pentecostal." While the Fire-Baptized Holiness church was a thriving church, no name was as popular as the Church of God. Synan reports, "Between 1880 and 1923, no less than two hundred groups adopted some version of that name to designate their church."[186]

From this revived understanding of Wesleyan thought, the Holiness church sought to see entire sanctification as a second blessing. In contrast, the Methodist church continued its understanding of sanctification as a gradual grace process. These churches provided the infrastructure of the Pentecostal movement. Thus, the close of the nineteenth century

182. Synan, *Holiness-Pentecostal Tradition*, 39.

183. Synan, *Holiness-Pentecostal Tradition*, 42.

184. Synan, *Holiness-Pentecostal Tradition*, 47.

185. Baer and Singer, *African American Religion*, 101.

186. Synan, *Holiness-Pentecostal Tradition*, 68.

marked a crucial period in the life of the church, especially as it relates to Pentecostalism. In America, the Methodist and Holiness churches were separated, and both needed a fresh move of the Spirit. Across the Atlantic, in Scotland, however, a fresh move was coming that was important to Pentecostalism.

2

The Evolution of the Black Pentecostal/ Charismatic Church

THE FIRST-CENTURY CHURCH— THE MODEL PENTECOSTAL CHURCH

PENTECOSTALS COMMONLY REFER BACK to the first-century church as the foundation for the Pentecostal experience. Their theological position is formulated from the books of Joel and Isaiah, the Gospels, the Pauline epistles, and the book of Acts. Howard Ervin, a Pentecostal scholar, writes about Pentecostalism from a theological premise, stating that "the purpose of Pentecost is unmistakably world evangelism."[1] Ervin describes the basic theological position of the Pentecostal church and contends that the Pentecostal experience was characterized by glossolalic speech. Thus, he outlines the book of Acts based on experiences he believes confirm that glossolalic speech accompanied an infilling with the Spirit, commonly referred to as the baptism in the Holy Spirit. He notes the following passages:

- The Disciples' Pentecost: Acts 2:1–4
- The Jewish Pentecost: Acts 4:31
- The Samaritan Pentecost: Acts 8:14–17
- The Ethiopian Eunuch's Pentecost: Acts 8:38–39
- Paul's Pentecost: Acts 9:17

1. Ervin, *Spirit Baptism*, 19.

- The Roman Pentecost: Acts 10:44
- The Ephesian Pentecost: Acts 19:1–6[2]

Thus he says that Jews, Samaritans, and Romans; Saul, a persecuting Pharisee; an Ethiopian eunuch; and twelve disciples of John the baptizer all called on the name of the Lord Jesus, and all were saved. Moreover, after their conversion, each received the baptism in the Holy Spirit as a birthright, for the promised gift of the Holy Spirit was "to all that are far off, everyone whom the Lord our God calls to Him." Whether stated or implied, it is a fair conclusion from the biblical evidence that tongues were the "external and indubitable proof" of their baptism in the Holy Spirit.[3]

THREADS OF PENTECOSTALISM

After the first century, the early church's Pentecostal experience was no longer the norm. It was not until 155 AD that Pentecostal experiences, rooted in Montanism, were recorded. Harvey Cox notes that tongue-speaking had been reinstituted under the leadership of Montanus, who led a vigorous Christian movement in the latter half of the second century. He taught Christian doctrine while being assisted by two prophetesses, Priscilla and Maximilla, who were believed to have experienced trances and spoken in tongues.[4]

Cox continues to posit that, on the surface at least, the Montanist movement bears a striking similarity to early Pentecostalism, which also combined women prophets with trance and tongues and end-time eschatology. Cox further conjectures that the movement continued in some places for five centuries and spawned many successors. The Montanist movement practiced prophetic speech and stern living. Paul Tillich even argued that the ethical principles that existed in the Montanist movement assisted in the fervor of the Christian church. Later, however, the Christian church resisted the Montanist movement, which contributed to its growing moral, spiritual, and disciplinary laxity.[5] Although there have been other reports of the Pentecostal experience among some during this

2. Ervin, *Spirit Baptism*, 68–80.
3. Ervin, *Spirit Baptism*, 79–80.
4. Harvey Cox, *Fire from Heaven*, 82–83.
5. Tillich, *History of Christian Thought*, 42–43.

time, it is not indicative of the entire Pentecostal experience, which will be discussed later.

PRE-TWENTIETH CENTURY PENTECOSTALISM

The close of the nineteenth century marked a significant era for Pentecostalism, with the ministry of Edward Irving. Many historians have written and discussed the spiritual awakening of the Church of England and its encounter with the Holy Spirit under the dynamic leadership of Irving. Gordon Strachan records that Irving was the minister of the National Scotch Church, Regent Square of London. He explains that Irving was tried for heresy for his teachings about the incarnation, which some viewed as dubious. After a series of trials and appeals, he was acquitted of the charges but not of the persecution.[6] Irving later became the center of attention for his so-called Pentecostal views, which developed through events and experiences that persuaded him that the Pentecostal experience was a valid contemporary experience for modern-day Christians.

Strachan claims that Irving reached his Pentecostal conclusions with the assistance of Miss Mary Campbell, who spoke in tongues and was also miraculously healed of consumption in March 1830. Also, in 1831, a Mrs. Cardale spoke in tongues and prophesied in her home in London. That same year, a Miss Hall spoke in tongues in the vestry of Regent Square Church. From that time, outbursts of tongues and prophecies began to fill the worship services.[7] Irving, who was the minister of the church, was asked to stop this unconstitutional behavior, "but Irving, believing them to the operation of the gifts of the Holy Spirit, refused."[8]

Because of this experience, Irving again found himself on trial for his religious beliefs. Finally, on May 2, 1832, after three days of hearing, the court decided against him, and he was ordered to be removed from his charge. Within days he found himself locked out of his church. After several appeals to the General Assembly of the Church of Scotland in 1832, he was deposed from the ministry of the Church of Scotland. Strachan writes that the majority of the members of Regent Square, who left with Irving, were formed into an ecclesial body that became known as the Catholic Apostolic Church. The first of its twelve apostles was

6. Strachan, *Pentecostal Theology of Edward Irving*, 25–28.
7. Strachan, *Pentecostal Theology of Edward Irving*, 25–28.
8. Anderson, *Vision of the Disinherited*, 36–37.

called in November 1832, and Irving, who now had no ministerial status, was ordained Angel or Pastor of the new congregation on April 5, 1833. However, soon after, his health began to fail, and he died of consumption in Glasgow on December 7, 1834, at the age of forty-two. Irving named twelve apostles after the pattern of the early church. Because of the attention given to the Pentecostal experience and its eschatological significance, the church never named any others, being assured by their experience of the imminent return of Christ.[9]

Strachan explains that many religious groups have claimed to have enjoyed the experience of Pentecost; however, only a few have actually spoken in tongues. He conjectures that after Montanism, only isolated cases were recorded. It was not until the late seventeenth century that it was claimed to be a sign of divine inspiration on a large scale. Extensive outbreaks of tongues occurred among the Huguenots of the Cevennes and the appellant (but still nominally Catholic) Jansenists. Strachan argues that there were no further instances until those associated with the ministry of Edward Irving. The Pentecostal experience in Irving's ministry was not attributed to emotionalism but faithful responses to the systematic study and preaching of the word of God. Theological understanding was central to all that happened and preceded all forms of experience of spiritual gifts. Strachan concludes that the centrality of the coherent theological system made the Pentecost of 1830–32 unique and distinct from all other previous Pentecostal revivals.[10]

Irving's Pentecostal position was almost identical to modern Pentecostalism. Strachan writes, "The center of his ministry was the systematic, doctrinal exposition of the Word of God and, from his intellectual and spiritual application to scripture, he developed the doctrine of the baptism with the Holy Spirit 'whose standing sign, if we err not, is the speaking with tongues.'"[11] Thus, any student of Pentecostalism can see the similarities between Irving and contemporary Pentecostals. Strachan contends that the doctrinal positions are so alike that it is thought the Apostolic Catholic Church passed down its beliefs to the modern Pentecostal movement of the early 1900s. However, there were no interactions between these two movements. The last of the Catholic Apostolic apostles died a few months after the modern Pentecostal movement started,

9. Anderson, *Vision of the Disinherited*, 38.

10. Strachan, *Pentecostal Theology of Edward Irving*, 29–30.

11. Anderson, *Vision of the Disinherited*, 37.

all the while with the two movements remaining completely ignorant of each other.[12]

TWENTIETH-CENTURY PENTECOSTALISM

The opening of the twentieth century was marked by new religious awakenings, such as the Jehovah's Witnesses and the Church of Christian Science. There was extreme racial hostility, lynchings, and laws to separate the races (Jim Crow), concepts that were reaffirmed by people and writings such as Charles Carroll and his book, *The Negro: A Beast or in the Image of God.* As noted in chapter 1, this book promoted social Darwinism, perpetuating the ideology that the superior race would rise to the top under any circumstance. This concept is sometimes referred to as "the survival of the fittest." Meanwhile, the Christian church was suffering from spiritual starvation while experiencing a large growth of members and wealth.

John Thomas Nichol contends that after the Civil War, the church suffered from spiritual stagnation, moral lethargy, and theological and practical problems that constantly haunted American Protestantism. Clifton Olmstead noted that the church was strong in membership but spiritually weak and unsound. Nichols observed that "Darwin's *Origin of Species* and *The Descent of Man* challenged the traditional orthodox theories of man's origin, producing sharp gaps between believers and dividing churches."[13] Trying to keep pace with the nation, the church became increasingly wealthy and institutionalized. The emotions of past religious experiences were considered undomestic, and robes and pews replaced religious experience. Thus, a deep-seated formalism became the mark and character of the church.

In this context, God sent the Pentecostal fire that spread throughout the world and remains the fastest-growing Christian experience in the world. According to Baer and Singer, the modern Pentecostal movement flowed from each of the following: The Latter Rain Revival in 1886 in Cleveland, Tennessee, the Western North Carolina Church of God, and the Fire Baptized Holiness Church.[14] While the Holiness movement and its branches are duly noted as the substratum of the modern Pentecostal

12. Anderson, *Vision of the Disinherited*, 39.

13. Nichols, *History of Christianity, 1650–1950*, 285.

14. Baer and Singer, *African-American Religion in the Twentieth Century*, 45–46.

movement, I believe that the observation and integration of African religious and Black church worship patterns played a role in forming what has become known as Pentecostalism.

Most white Pentecostals refer back to Charles Fox Parham's Bethel Bible School in Topeka, Kansas, for the origins of the movement. Parham and his students had a tongues-speaking experience in 1901. William J. Seymour, who is associated with the Azusa Street outpouring of 1906–09 in Los Angeles, is also considered a father of the movement.[15] The first official chartered Pentecostal church was started by a Black man, William J. Seymour. Parham and Seymour are commonly mentioned as founders of the modern Pentecostal movement. While modern Pentecostals trace their deep historical roots to Pentecost, they do not ignore the contributions of Parham and Seymour, who were vitally important in this modern-day phenomenon.

Strachan also notes that the twentieth-century Pentecostal revival began when Agnes Ozman spoke in tongues in December 1900 at Bethel Bible College in Topeka, Kansas, as a result of a spiritual quest based on a re-examination of Scripture, similar to that of Mary Campbell seventy years before. Many students at Bethel followed her, and during the next few years, the experience of tongues and other gifts of the Spirit were shared by thousands in various countries all over the world.[16] As the founder of Bethel Bible College, Charles Parham (a white man) has been given the place of preeminence in the Pentecostal movement by most white church historians. However, a closer look at the movement has made historians and scholars reconsider this estimate.

At the early age of fifteen, Parham held the office of lay preacher in the Congregational Church. Later on, he became associated with the Methodist Episcopal Church. Then he withdrew and joined the rapidly growing Holiness movement. He maintained that while many had experienced a move of sanctification, a great outpouring was yet to come to empower Christians. Parham opened Bethel Bible College in October 1900.[17] He was convinced that the narrative in Acts 2 meant a gift of languages (glossolalia) and instructed the students at his Bible college to seek the sign of the infilling of the spirit. Through this experience, one of his students, Agnes Ozman, was filled with the Holy Spirit and spoke in

15. Baer and Singer, *African-American Religion in the Twentieth Century*, 46–47.

16. Strachan, *Pentecostal Theology of Edward Irving*, 30–31.

17. Synan, *Holiness-Pentecostal Tradition*, 87–89.

tongues.[18] Indeed, "When glossolalia appeared among Parham and his students during a Bible school he was conducting, they believed this to be scriptural evidence of Pentecostal baptism."[19] C. Eric Nelson posits that Parham had a struggling ministry despite the initial enthusiasm at the beginning and some lively press coverage.[20] Because of health issues, Parham had to rest from his Kansas ministry in the winter of 1904–1905, leaving to spend time in recovery with his friends in Houston, Texas.

Once he regained his health, he began to preach again and opened a short-term Bible school in Houston, where he trained evangelists. There, he began to teach about the baptism in the Holy Spirit. It was here that William J. Seymour and Parham met. Seymour was intrigued by Parham's teaching on the baptism in the Holy Spirit, so he would come and listen to Parham teach. However, because of racism and social injustice, Seymour was not allowed to sit inside the class—he listened through a window. When it rained, he was allowed to sit in the hallway with the door cracked so he could hear. Seymour, a one-eyed Black preacher, studied under Parham for about a year.

Before receiving the baptism in the Holy Spirit, Seymour was called to Los Angeles to pastor a Holiness church. After going to the Holiness church, he began to preach about the baptism in the Holy Ghost, and because of this controversial teaching, he was dismissed as pastor and locked out of the church. From there, he began to teach a Bible study at the home of Richard Asbury at 312 Bonnie Brae Street in Los Angeles. On April 9, 1906, Seymour and seven others were filled with the Holy Spirit, thus beginning one the largest revivals the world has ever known, under the leadership of a Black man.[21]

The crowds that came to hear Seymour were so large that they would fill the streets. Therefore, Seymour and his followers moved to a larger facility. Seymour leased a ramshackle, barnlike former church building on Azusa Street in the old downtown Black ghetto. It had a dirt floor and had been used as a livery stable but cost only eight dollars per month. It could hold as many as 900 people. Services soon expanded to morning, afternoon, and night sessions, sometimes continuing without a break from morning to the next day.[22] Azusa drew racially mixed

18. Synan, *Holiness-Pentecostal Tradition*, 89–90.

19. Anderson, *Vision of the Disinherited*, 55.

20. Nelson, *Pentecostal Movement in the United States*, 12–13.

21. Synan, *Holiness-Pentecostal Tradition*, 99–101.

22. Robeck Jr., *Azusa Street Mission and Revival*, 56–59.

crowds, making it the first movement that allowed Blacks and whites to fraternize as equals. Paradoxically, at the height of Jim Crow and American segregation, Seymour and the Pentecostal movement were drawing people from all over the world. Indeed, among the seven historic Black denominations, Black Pentecostals have a unique historical origin. Unlike Black Methodists and Baptists, they trace their origin not to white denominations but to a movement initiated and led by a Black minister. Also, unlike Black Methodists and Baptists, Black Pentecostals began not as a separatist movement but as part of a distinctly interracial renewal movement from which whites subsequently withdrew.[23]

William J. Seymour had given birth to one of the most significant contributions by Blacks to the Christian church. This was, in my estimation, a prophetic moment in history. Modern Pentecostalism was led by a Black man, and the form of worship prevalent in the Holiness and Pentecostal churches of that time resembled that of African religious, slave worship styles present in the invisible institution of the slaves, and negro and Black church worship behavior. The Azusa revival lasted from 1906 to 1909.

Eyewitness reports state, "Some came to scoff and stayed to pray, and before long, blacks, whites, Mexicans, and Asians were praying together in a nation where Jim Crow was on the rise."[24] The modern Pentecostal movement, with its far-reaching effects, was begun by the son of a former slave and held in a rundown warehouse by a self-educated Black minister. Leonard Lovett writes that "the almost totally unplanned efforts of William J. Seymour, a descendent of African slaves shipped to America, were unprecedented."[25] Lovett records that the spiritual dynamism generated from that simple Black mission in Los Angeles caused Frank Bartleman to emphatically state "that the color line was washed away in the blood."[26] It is unfortunate that the blatant omission of Seymour by some classical Pentecostal historians is so obvious that it becomes a form of judgment on our ethnic and racial pride. Indeed, "Seymour, the one-eyed, unattractive apostle of Pentecost from Houston, defied the racist mentality of his time and opened the revival to everyone, a factor of supreme importance in explaining the success of the revival."[27]

23. Baer and Singer, *African-American Religion in the Twentieth Century*, 49–50.

24. Robeck Jr., *Azusa Street Mission and Revival*, 61.

25. Lovett, "Black Origins of Pentecostalism," 137.

26. Lovett, "Black Origins of Pentecostalism," 140–41.

27. Synan, *Holiness-Pentecostal Tradition*, 101.

A humble servant, Seymour would pray with his head in a shoe box to ensure he would get none of God's glory. Vinson Synan writes that no sooner had Seymour begun preaching in the Azusa location than a monumental revival began. Scores of people began to fall under the power and arise speaking in other tongues.[28] It was reported that there were no racial distinctions in these meetings—negroes, whites, Chinese, and even Jews attended side by side to hear the preaching of Seymour. This revival eventually became of interest to people all over the nation, regardless of race. Synan notes that the majority of the attendants were white, but there was always complete integration of the races in the services.

The Los Angeles Times covered the Azusa outpouring, denigrating things about the movement and Seymour, its leader.[29] The reporter said Seymour used his "stony optic" eye to hypnotize the people. The paper carried a prophecy given to a man in the revival meeting that warned the people of Los Angeles of awful destruction unless they adhered to the tenets of the new faith. Awful destruction did come the next day to San Francisco, as it suffered a great earthquake, and the tremors could be felt along the entire coast of California. The natural earthquake in San Francisco was followed by a tremendous spiritual earthquake.[30]

Record numbers began to flock to the Azusa meetings, being convinced that God was speaking in that movement. Daily, people traveled from across the continent to participate in this revival, and news accounts spread throughout the nation of the revival, both in the secular and religious press. People of all ages flocked to Los Angeles, some with skepticism and some with a desire to participate. The spiritual outpouring was characterized by speaking in tongues, dramatic worship services, and interracial mingling. Worship at 312 Azusa Street was frequent and spontaneous, with services going almost around the clock. Among those attracted to the revival were not only members of the Holiness movement but Baptists, Mennonites, Quakers, and Presbyterians.[31]

An observer at one of the services wrote: "No instruments of music are used. None are needed. No choir—the angels have been heard by some in the spirit. No collections are taken. No bills have been posted to advertise the meetings. No church organization is back of it. All who are in touch with God realize as soon as they enter the meetings that the

28. Synan, *Holiness-Pentecostal Tradition*, 101–2.

29. *Los Angeles Times*, "Weird Babel of Tongues," April 18, 1906.

30. Synan, *Holiness-Pentecostal Tradition*, 102–3.

31. Robeck Jr., *Azusa Street Mission and Revival*, 62–63.

Holy Ghost is the leader."[32] Singing was sporadic or a capella or occasionally in tongues. There were periods of extended silence. Among firsthand accounts were reports of blind people having their sight restored, diseases cured instantly, and immigrants who spoke German, Yiddish, and Spanish were spoken to in their native language by uneducated Black members, who translated the languages into English by "supernatural ability." Attendees were occasionally slain in the Spirit. Visitors gave their testimony, and members read aloud testimonies that were sent to the mission by mail. There was prayer for the gift of tongues. There was prayer in tongues for the sick and missionaries, and requests were given by attendees or mailed in. There was spontaneous preaching and altar calls for salvation, sanctification, and baptism of the Holy Spirit. Many people would continually shout throughout the meetings.

The members of the mission never took an offering, but there was a receptacle near the door for anyone who wanted to support the revival. The first edition of the *Apostolic Faith* publication reported a common reaction to the revival from visitors: "Proud, well-dressed preachers came to 'investigate.' Soon, their high looks were replaced with wonder, then conviction comes, and very often you will find them in a short time wallowing on the dirty floor, asking God to forgive them and make them as little children."[33]

The core membership of the Azusa Street Mission was never much more than fifty to sixty individuals, with hundreds and thousands of people visiting or staying temporarily over the years.[34] While Azusa was experiencing tremendous success under Seymour, Charles Parham was given a personal invitation from Seymour to participate in the revival. The movement had attracted spiritualists and mediums from numerous occult societies, who came in with their séances and other practices. Hence, Seymour sought assistance from Parham. However, upon his arrival to the Azusa mission, Parham was disturbed by what he saw: Blacks and whites worshiping together. Of greater concern was that white people were imitating the "unintelligent, crude negroisms of the Southland" and calling it the Holy Ghost.[35]

Parham had major problems with the behavior of the participants of the Azusa revival, for they reminded him of the "southern darkie camp

32. Bartleman and Robeck Jr., *How Pentecost Came to Los Angeles*, 58–59.

33. Bartleman and Robeck Jr., *How Pentecost Came to Los Angeles*, 58.

34. Robeck Jr., *Azusa Street Mission and Revival*, 71.

35. Martin, *Tongues of Fire*, 5.

meetings."[36] Parham, whom many have mildly called a racist, admired the Ku Klux Klan and objected to racial mixing or mingling during worship and at the altar. Thus, he had a difficult time embracing the Azusa experience. Parham initially preached at the revival, but when he objected to the mixing of the races, he was quickly uninvited.

Parham, Seymour's mentor, was sharp in his criticism: "Men and women, white and black, knelt together or fell across one another; a white woman, perhaps of wealth and culture, could be seen thrown back in the arms of a big 'buck nigger,' and held tightly thus, as she shivered and shook in freak imitation of Pentecost. Horrible, awful shame!"[37] Several other reasons can be given for Azusa Street's disassociation from Parham. Foremost, Parham had personality conflicts with Seymour and wanted to be the chief authority figure of the movement. However, the presiding leaders of the Apostolic Faith Mission were slow to make any changes to their methods or leadership. Parham spent the rest of his life disdaining Azusa and Seymour.

The participants in the Azusa Revival received criticism from secular media and Christian theologians for behaviors considered outrageous and unorthodox, especially at the time. The attendees of the meetings were often described as "holy rollers," "holy jumpers," "tangled tonguers," and "Holy Ghosters." Reports of the strange happenings in Los Angeles were published throughout the US and the world.[38] The *Los Angeles Times* scornfully reported:

> Meetings are held in a tumble-down shack on Azusa Street, and the devotees of the weird doctrine practice the most fanatical rites, preach the wildest theories, and work themselves into a state of mad excitement in their peculiar zeal. Colored people and a sprinkling of whites compose the congregation, and night is made hideous in the neighborhood by the howlings of the worshippers, who spend hours swaying forth and back in a nerve-racking attitude of prayer and supplication. They claim to have the "gift of tongues" and be able to understand the babel.[39]

A local newspaper reporter in September 1906 described the happenings as the

36. Synan, *Holiness-Pentecostal Tradition*, 104.
37. Anderson, *Vision of the Disinherited*, 80.
38. Robeck Jr., *Azusa Street Mission and Revival*, 65–66.
39. *Los Angeles Times*, "Weird Babel of Tongues."

> disgraceful intermingling of the races . . . They cry and make howling noises all day and night. They run, jump, shake all over, shout to the top of their voice, spin around in circles, and fall out on the sawdust-blanketed floor, jerking, kicking, and rolling all over it. Some of them pass out and do not move for hours as though they were dead. These people appear to be mad, mentally deranged, or under a spell. They claim to be filled with the Spirit. They have a one-eyed, illiterate negro as their preacher who stays on his knees much of the time with his head hidden between the wooden milk crates. He doesn't talk very much, but at times, he can be heard shouting, "Repent," and he's supposed to be running the thing . . . They repeatedly sing the same song, "The Comforter Has Come."[40]

Christians from many traditions were critical, saying the movement was hyper-emotional, misused Scripture, and lost focus on Christ by overemphasizing the Holy Spirit. Within a short time, ministers warned their congregations to stay away from the Azusa Street Mission. Some called the police and tried to get the building shut down.[41] Respected preachers and authors spoke harshly of the revival meetings. R. A. Torrey declared that this new Pentecostal movement was "emphatically not of God and founded by a Sodomite." G. Campbell Morgan called it "the last vomit of Satan." Harry Ironside said that it was "disgusting . . . delusions and insanities."[42] By the time the revival ended, it was thought by some that it was the result of spiritualism due to the fact that many occultists and spiritists attended the meetings. Yet, despite the controversy, today, historians consider the revival the primary catalyst for the spread of Pentecostalism in the twentieth century.

Nelson writes that "Seymour's life and leadership brought modern Pentecost a Christian perspective and dream forged in the fiery furnace of 300 long years under bitter slavery and brutal repression."[43] He says, "Seymour could grasp the meaning of Pentecost with a depth unattained and probably unattainable by any white leader of his time."[44] In sum, Seymour found an experience of new spirituality in Pentecostalism that extended beyond glossolalia and broke the color line. While

40. *Los Angeles Times*, "Weird Babel of Tongues."

41. Robeck Jr., *Azusa Street Mission and Revival*, 66–68.

42. Synan, Holiness-Pentecostal Tradition, 105.

43. Nelsen and Nelsen, *Black Church in the Sixties*, 92.

44. Cox, *Fire from Heaven*, 57.

glossolalia was important, it alone did not properly define Pentecostalism for Seymour, since he expected the baptism in the Holy Spirit to build Christian character. During his lifetime, Seymour established the aforementioned newspaper called *The Apostolic Faith*, which reached 50,000 subscribers.[45] This number is astonishing even to date. Unfortunately, because of the effects of racism, Seymour was soon forgotten. Organized religion had packaged the movement, and he died a poor, lonely man.[46]

PENTECOSTALISM GOES INTERNATIONAL

The Apostolic Faith was published occasionally until May of 1908, mostly through the work of Seymour and a white woman named Clara Lum, a member of the Apostolic Faith Mission. *The Apostolic Faith* was distributed without charge, and thousands of laypersons and ministers received copies worldwide. Seymour purchased a printing press, and 5,000 copies of the first edition were printed; by 1907, his press run reached over 40,000 people. This was quite a notable accomplishment, particularly for a Black man in a segregated society. The publication reported the happenings at the Azusa Street Mission to the world. As it and many secular publications publicized the events of the Azusa Street Revival internationally, thousands of individuals visited the mission to witness it firsthand.[47]

"Missionary Bernt Bernsten traveled all the way from North China to investigate the happenings after hearing that the biblical prophecy of Acts 2:4 was being fulfilled. Other visitors left the revival to become missionaries in remote areas all over the world."[48] Reverend K. E. M. Spooner visited the revival on Azusa Street in 1909 and became one of the Pentecostal Holiness Church's most effective missionaries in Africa, working among the Tswana people of Botswana. In 1904, the Welsh Revival took place, and approximately 100,000 people in Wales joined the movement. Joseph Smale, pastor of the First Baptist Church in Los Angeles, went to Wales personally to witness the revival.[49]

Internationally, many evangelical Christians took this event as a sign of fulfilling the prophecy in Joel 2:23–29. The Apostolic Church was

45. Synan, *Holiness-Pentecostal Tradition*, 101.

46. Synan, *Holiness-Pentecostal Tradition*, 107.

47. Robeck Jr., *Azusa Street Mission and Revival*, 85–87.

48. Wikipedia, "Azusa Street Revival."

49. Synan, *Holiness-Pentecostal Tradition*, 97–98.

the first Pentecostal church to be formed in the United Kingdom. This was followed by the Elim Foursquare Gospel Alliance, later known as the Elim Pentecostal Church, founded in 1914 by George Jeffreys. In Sweden, the first Pentecostal church was the Philadelphia Church in Stockholm. Pastored by Lewi Pethrus, this congregation, originally Baptist, was expelled from the Baptist Union of Sweden in 1913 for doctrinal differences. Today, this congregation has about 5,400 members and is one of the largest Pentecostal congregations in northern Europe.[50] As of 2024, the Swedish Pentecostal Movement has approximately 89,000 members in nearly 480 congregations.[51] These congregations are all independent but cooperate on a large scale. Swedish Pentecostals have been very missionary-minded and established churches in many countries. In Brazil, for example, churches founded by the Swedish Pentecostal mission claim several million members.[52]

Thousands of people were leaving Azusa Street with the intention of evangelizing abroad. Many missionaries went out from Azusa (thirty-eight in October 1906 alone), such that within two years, the movement had spread to over fifty nations, including Britain, Scandinavia, Germany, Holland, Egypt, Syria, Palestine, South Africa, Hong Kong, China, Ceylon, and India. A. G. Garr and his wife were sent from Azusa Street as missionaries to Calcutta, India, where they managed to start a small revival. (Speaking in tongues in India did not enable them to speak the native language, Bengali.) Garr significantly contributed to early Pentecostalism through his later work in redefining the "biblical evidence" doctrine and changing the doctrine from a belief that speaking in tongues was explicitly for evangelism to a belief that speaking in tongues was a gift for "spiritual empowerment."[53] Such "empowerment" is an important factor in the contemporary church.

Other small-scale revivals were taking place in Minnesota, North Carolina, and Texas. By 1905, reports of speaking in tongues, supernatural healings, "physical demonstrations of emotion," and significant lifestyle changes accompanied these revivals. As news spread, evangelicals across the United States began praying for similar revivals in their congregations. By the end of 1906, most leaders from Azusa Street had spun

50. Bundy, "Swedish (Pentecostal Movement)," 1123–24.

51. Bundy, "Swedish (Pentecostal Movement)," 1123–24.

52. Bundy, "Swedish (Pentecostal Movement)," 1123–24.

53. Synan, *Holiness-Pentecostal Tradition*, 106–8; Robeck Jr., *Azusa Street Mission and Revival*, 125–27.

off to form other congregations, such as the 51st Street Apostolic Faith Mission, the Spanish Apostolic Faith Mission, and the Italian Pentecostal Mission. These missions were largely composed of immigrant or ethnic groups.[54]

The southeast US was a particularly prolific area of growth for the movement since Seymour's approach appealed to the charismatic spiritual climate growing in those areas. Other new missions were based on preachers who had charisma and energy. Nearly all of these new churches were founded among immigrants and the poor.[55]

CONTEMPORARY PENTECOSTALISM

Contemporary Pentecostalism also owes its beginnings to another important Black man, C. H. Mason, one of the founders of the Church of God in Christ. C. H. Mason and C. P. Jones founded the Church of God in Christ as a part of the Holiness movement. This church had its beginnings in Mississippi, Tennessee, and Arkansas in 1897. Both Mason and Jones were former Baptist preachers who adopted the Wesleyan view of sanctification. After Mason heard of the Azusa outpouring, he felt drawn to Los Angeles to investigate. Jones, who was not keen on speaking in tongues, did not attend. Mason traveled to the Azusa Street Mission in 1907 with two fellow ministers, J. A. Jeter and D. J. Young. After staying at Azusa for five weeks, all three men were baptized in the Holy Spirit and spoke in tongues. They then traveled back to Memphis as persuaded Pentecostals.[56]

After Mason returned with the message and experience of Pentecost, Mason and Jones had a major dispute, which caused them to split up. The Pentecostal experience had been a point of dissension and division from Irving to Seymour and now Mason. In a general assembly of the church in Jackson, Mississippi, in August 1907, the Pentecostal controversy dominated the agenda. This conflict led to those who were convinced about the Pentecostal experience following Mason and those who were not so persuaded following Jones. Mason continued to use the name, while Jones changed his group's name to The Church of Christ (Holiness) USA. However, the Church of God in Christ became the most

54. Robeck Jr., *Azusa Street Mission and Revival*, 136–38.

55. Anderson, *Vision of the Disinherited*, 95–96.

56. Synan, *Holiness-Pentecostal Tradition*, 109–10.

important Pentecostal church of the day while remaining under the leadership of Mason, a Black man who had great respect for African religious practices.[57]

The Pentecostal movement was mainly an interracial movement from 1906 to 1924, when there was a separation based on race. However, until this time, the Church of God in Christ served a unique role in Pentecostalism, especially from 1907 to 1914. During this time, it was the only church allowed to issue ordinations, for it was the only Pentecostal church licensed as a denomination. Thus, ministers in the Pentecostal movement, seeking to be ordained, which enabled them to perform weddings and obtain minister's discounts (especially on railroad fares), had to come through Mason and the Church of God in Christ. The Church of God in Christ was and is one of the largest Pentecostal churches in the world. While many Holiness churches that experienced the baptism in the Holy Spirit remained holiness in teaching, it was the Church of God in Christ that taught Pentecostal theology, that is, the doctrine that one needed to be filled with the Spirit and demonstrate it by speaking in tongues to be fully sanctified.[58]

The Church of God in Christ enjoyed being the only Pentecostal church licensed to ordain Pentecostal ministers for eight years. However, because of the interracial following of Mason, he was placed under official FBI national surveillance, which worked closely with the War Department, Justice Department, and local police. Mason had the challenge of conducting urban ministry during a time of Black lynchings and Blacks being burned alive. The Church of God in Christ served as a force to be reckoned with in a racist society because of its growth, revenue, and interracial connections.[59]

The year 1914 marked another important date for Pentecostalism, for that was when white Pentecostals formed their own groups to detach from the "Black" Pentecostal church. This gave birth to the first white Pentecostal denomination, the Assemblies of God. William W. Menzies points out that, by 1914, being Pentecostal carried a social disgrace for whites because of the perceived behavior of Pentecostalism's followers. Thus, white Pentecostals were rejected by the Holiness church, fundamentalists, and the larger church world. Menzies writes, "Emotionalism

57. Menzies, *Anointed to Serve*, 337–38.

58. Synan, *Holiness-Pentecostal Tradition*, 109–10.

59. Clemmons, *Bishop C. H. Mason*, 75–77.

was a common complaint from the quarter of conservative Christianity."[60] Hence, to be Pentecostal was to be despised, and one cannot help but wonder if this was simply because the interpretation was, "To be Pentecostal is to be Black, and to be Black is to be Pentecostal."[61]

The 1914 Hot Springs Pentecostal convention aimed to form an all-white Pentecostal denomination that excluded Blacks—the Assemblies of God. White Pentecostal and Holiness churches were invited to participate in this new Pentecostal church organization. No Black churches were invited. Note that until the Hot Springs Convention, all Pentecostal ministers were ordained through the Black Pentecostal church. Yet, within ten years, the Assemblies of God became the largest Pentecostal church in the world that also ordained Pentecostal preachers. Thus, what started with a Black man in Azusa as an interracial movement was now, in less than a decade, tossed once again in the garbage heap of racism that fights God by any means necessary. By 1943, Pentecostals were accepted as a part of the National Association of Evangelicals. In 1948, eight of the largest Pentecostal churches formed the Pentecostal Fellowship of America.[62]

Pentecostal education marked another important era in Pentecostalism. It was not until the time of the Vietnam War that Pentecostal seminaries were established. The Church of God in Christ founded the first Pentecostal seminary in Atlanta in 1970, the Charles H. Mason Theological Seminary.[63] This Black Pentecostal seminary was the only one with full accreditation. Other, checkered Pentecostal graduate schools included California Theological Seminary (Fresno), CBN University, Jimmy Swaggart Theological Seminary, Melody Land School of Theology, and Oral Roberts University. Menzies states that the fresh young leadership that becomes a part of the Pentecostal church promises to make contributions in the following four areas:

- Ecclesiastical leadership that will provide frontline leadership;
- Scholarship that has so long been missing;
- Attention to strong church growth, especially in areas outside the United States, such as Latin America;

60. Menzies, *Anointed to Serve*, 56.

61. Lovett, *Black Origins of Pentecostalism*, 141–42.

62. Menzies, *Anointed to Serve*, 309–11.

63. Synan, *Holiness-Pentecostal Tradition*, 188; Clemmons, *Bishop C. H. Mason*, 145–46.

- Bridging the gap with those who claim to have experienced the spiritual gifts outside the Pentecostal church.[64]

BLACKS AND PENTECOSTALISM

As we discuss the origin of the Black church and its Pentecostal roots, it is important not simply to examine the Black Pentecostal church but the Black church in general, because the foundation of Pentecostalism was lying somewhat dormant in the Black church movement. From the preferred worship styles and practices of Blacks dating back to the bush church, we see these styles traveled through the Methodist, Holiness, independent, and Baptist churches. When we consider the turbulent past of Pentecostalism and the racial and doctrinal issues that plagued this very powerful movement, we still cannot help but recognize the potential power of the Pentecostal church to impact change in the world and especially the Black community.

This is why I confidently say that the birth of the Black Pentecostal church was in the DNA of the Black church, waiting for the season of full manifestation, which was realized under the Black leadership of Seymour and the stimulus of Mason and the Holiness/Methodist movement. Needless to say, Blacks gravitated to Pentecostalism; it was an organic expression of their passion for God. Blacks were drawn to Pentecostalism because of the following reasons:

(1) The Pentecostal worship was reminiscent of the old revival meetings the Methodists and Baptists launched. It was also akin to African religious expression.

(2) The lack of formality in the worship experience was beginning to shape American Protestant worship practices.

(3) Pentecostalism is a religion of the socially disinherited and the economically underprivileged. For the most part, Pentecostals come from the lower socioeconomic class, though not exclusively.

(4) Also, it attracted those who felt a call to preach because its ministers had no educational requirements.

64. Menzies, *Anointed to Serve*, 337–38.

(5) The movement marked perhaps a decrease in racial tensions since it began as an interracial movement. Pentecostalism demonstrated the true meaning of perfect love for God and humans. [65]

WOMEN AND PENTECOSTALISM

Like African Americans, women were actively involved in the early Pentecostal movement and served as pastors, missionaries, evangelists, and in other governance roles. Women were the catalysts of the early Pentecostal movement. Since they believed in the presence and interaction of the Holy Spirit in their assemblies, and since these gifts came to men and women, the use of spiritual gifts such as speaking in tongues, interpreting tongues, laying on of hands, and healing were all encouraged. The unconventionally intense and emotional environment created other forms of participation, such as personal testimony and spontaneous prayer and singing. Women did not shy away from engaging in this setting, and in the early movement, the majority of converts and churchgoers were female. Agnes Ozman herself evangelized throughout the Midwest after leaving Kansas. When Parham moved his ministry to Houston, eight of the fifteen workers were women. Since the movement relied on the efforts and participation of lay members, both in the church and outside, women gained great cultural influence and helped shape Pentecostalism. Women wrote religious songs, edited Pentecostal papers, and taught and ran Bible schools.[66]

The availability of these opportunities to women from the start of the movement may help explain the preponderance of female adherents. In addition, evidence from three of the oldest Pentecostal groups—Assemblies of God, the Church of God (Cleveland, Tennessee), and the International Church of the Foursquare Gospel—shows the numbers of women in clergy and missionary positions. Shortly after the Assemblies of God formed in 1914, clergy rolls showed that one-third of its ministers were women. Though by 1925, the number of female ministers had dropped significantly, still two-thirds of its overseas missionaries were women. When the Church of God was formed in 1906, one-third of its founders were women. Moreover, when Aimee Semple McPherson started the International Church of the Foursquare Gospel in 1927, single

65. Anderson, *Vision of the Disinherited*, 96–100.

66. Blumhofer, *Restoring the Faith*, 128–30.

women served in one-third of the church branches as pastors and married couples served as co-pastors to another sixteen congregations.[67]

Other aspects of Pentecostalism also promoted the participation of women. Pointing to Peter's proclamation of the biblical prophecy of Joel 2:28 on the day of Pentecost, Pentecostals focused on the end days during which Christ would return. Given that the baptism of the Holy Spirit led to speaking in tongues, whoever was blessed with this gift would be responsible for using it to prepare for Christ's second coming. Due to this responsibility, any restrictions that culture or other denominations placed on women were often disregarded in the early part of the movement. Joel 2:28 also specifically included females, saying that both sons and daughters and male and female servants would receive the Holy Spirit and prophesy in the end days. Thus, the focus on spiritual gifts, the nature of the worship environment, and dispensationalist thinking encouraged women to participate in all areas of worship.[68]

While William J. Seymour is typically regarded as the leader of the Azusa Outpouring, a number of women also contributed significantly to the revival, and depending on which firsthand accounts are considered, women's leadership in the revival is either neglected or emphasized. More historical accounts have been available from men, and these authors tend to pose William J. Seymour as the principal leader, with other men like Charles Fox Parham and Edward Lee in important supporting roles. However, women like Julia Hutchins, Lucy Farrow, and Neely Terry were de-emphasized. Regardless of who had the greatest share in leading the revival, it seems generally safe to conclude that the overall leadership at Azusa Street Revival was shared between women and men.

Women, of course, also came out of the Azusa Street Revival. Florence Crawford was a prominent convert on Azusa Street. While at the Azusa Mission, she was active in *The Apostolic Faith* newspaper and became one of the first from Azusa to evangelize primarily through the Midwestern United States. Later, she moved to Portland, Oregon, where she established the Apostolic Faith Mission and ministered. Clara Lum was also a significant figure of Azusa Street. She co-edited *The Apostolic Faith* with Seymour. Ophelia Wiley also worked for the newspaper, writing articles. She preached at Azusa and then evangelized throughout the northwestern United States. Jennie Moore was an active leader of the

67. Blumhofer, *Pentecost in My Soul*, 95–97.

68. Synan, *Holiness-Pentecostal Tradition*, 159–61.

Azusa Street Revival, who married Seymour and helped lead the congregation. Abundio and Rosa Lopez were active at Azusa and later led worship in the streets of the Hispanic sections of Los Angeles. Other evangelists and missionaries from Azusa Street include Ivey Campbell, who preached throughout Ohio and Pennsylvania; Louisa Condit, who went to Oakland, California, and then Jerusalem; and Lucy Leatherman, who evangelized in Israel, Egypt, Palestine, Chile, and Argentina. Julia Hutchins and G. W. and Daisy Batman were missionaries in Liberia. Overall, about half of the traveling evangelists and overseas missionaries were women.[69]

Over time, the roles of women changed. Despite the leadership of women in the early movement, many were uncertain about the roles women held at this time and wavered in their struggle to gauge the proper role and position of women within their Pentecostal churches. While restorationism emphasized the role of the Holy Spirit and Joel's egalitarian prophecy, Paul's writings in the Newer Testament also had to be considered. In doing this, restorationism also highlighted the seemingly contradictory nature of the theology regarding women's roles. On the one hand, Paul's instructions on the propriety of worship in 1 Corinthians 11 seemed to concede the existence of women prophesying and praying in the church. However, in other passages, namely 1 Timothy 2:12, he warned that "I do not permit a woman to teach or to have authority over a man; she must be silent" (NIV). Thus, while the immediacy and the fervor of the initial revival atmosphere were subsiding, questions of authority and the organization of churches arose.

Institutionalism took root again, as repeated throughout church history, and brought new concerns to the forefront. While it was clear that both men and women spoke in tongues, many started to see this gift as a nonintellectual one and asserted that more intellectual acts, such as preaching, should be undertaken by women only in conditions controlled by male leaders. In addition, culture also contributed to the restriction of women's roles in Pentecostal churches. The social vision of women as the moral keepers of society faded as flappers in the 1920s came onto the scene, provoking suspicions about women's morality. Since Pentecostals wanted to distance themselves as much as possible from modernity, the "new woman" was a fearful image. Pentecostals instead clung to more traditional views of women in the home and society. A

69. Robeck Jr., *Azusa Street Mission and Revival*, 139–45.

more socially conservative approach to women settled in, and as a result, female participation was channeled into more supportive and traditionally accepted roles.[70]

Institutionalism brought gender segregation, and the Assemblies of God, along with other Pentecostal groups, created auxiliary women's organizations. At this time, women became much more likely to be evangelists and missionaries than pastors, and when they were pastors, they often co-pastored with their husbands. It also became the norm for men to hold all official positions, such as those of board members, college presidents, and national administrators. While the early movement eschewed denominationalism because of the dead spirituality they saw in Protestant denominations, later Pentecostal churches began to mirror the more traditional evangelical community. Thus, the more democratic way of addressing others, whether male or female, lay person or leader, as either "brother" or "sister," gave way to more institutionalized titles like "reverend."[71]

PENTECOSTAL THEOLOGY

Pentecostal theology basically fits within one of three modes of interpretation. The following lists the three possible positions of Pentecostals, according to Donald W. Dayton:

(1) Those teaching a doctrine of sanctification in the Wesleyan Holiness tradition (the "three works of grace"—Pentecostals who maintain that the Christian experience normally finds expression in a pattern of conversion, "entire sanctification" as a distinct subsequent experience, and a further baptism in the Holy Spirit empowering the believer for witness and service, evidenced by speaking in tongues);

(2) Those reducing this pattern to "two works of grace" by collapsing the first two into one "finished work" supplemented by a process of gradual sanctification (thus advocating a pattern focusing on conversion and a subsequent baptism in the Holy Spirit as just defined);

70. Blumhofer, *Restoring the Faith*, 133–36.

71. Anderson, *Vision of the Disinherited*, 228–30.

(3) And those holding a "Oneness" or "Jesus Only" view of the Godhead (thus proclaiming an "Evangelical Unitarianism" of the second Person of the Trinity).[72]

Ray Hughes has written on the unique characteristics of Pentecostal preaching. He observes that Pentecostal preaching:

(1) convicts of sin and produces revival;

(2) moves men and women to be baptized in the Holy Spirit;

(3) produces faith;

(4) confronts demonic powers;

(5) produces godly fear and respect for the church;

(6) and is confirmed by the operation of spiritual gifts.[73]

The Spirit-filled life produces spiritual men and women who proclaim the gospel of Jesus Christ to a dying world by the power and the gifts of the Spirit through the charisma that is upon their lives.

THE CHARISMATIC MOVEMENT

On the surface, the Charismatic movement seems identical to Pentecostalism, and in some cases it is. But the Charismatic movement does not share the same history as Pentecostalism. Therefore, most Charismatic churches refer back to the first-century church as their model for ministry. At the same time, many Charismatic churches lean heavily upon the Azusa Outpouring for its contemporary validation. The Charismatic movement is not of great necessity for this study, so only a few major highlights of the movement will be mentioned.

Donald Gee described the Charismatic movement as the New Pentecostals.[74] Its theology is very similar to Pentecostal theology, except for Charismatics a heavy emphasis is placed on the operation of spiritual gifts according to 1 Corinthians 12. Key figures in this group include The Full Gospel Business Men's Fellowship International, Oral Roberts, and Dennis Bennett, whom some consider to be the father of the movement. The Charismatic movement took place among denominational churches.

72. Dayton, *Theological Roots of Pentecostalism*, 17.

73. Hughes, *Pentecostal Preaching*, 15–18.

74. Gee, *Pentecostal Movement*, 112.

Hence people spoke in tongues without having to join the classic Pentecostal church.

This movement was seen as a renewal, and it spread throughout the major Protestant denominations in America and extended into the Roman Catholic Church. Magazines by both Protestant and Catholic churches were produced to further introduce this movement to its members and constituency. David Edwin Harrell Jr. writes that for a time in the 1960s and 1970s, the charismatic revival overflowed traditional religious barriers.[75] The joyous embracing of the Holy Spirit ignited extraordinary ecumenical experiences, gatherings small and large that pushed into the background old theological and denominational distinctions. Catholics and Protestants, rich and poor, Black and white mingled freely, sharing the gifts of the Holy Spirit. However, as the heat of revival cooled in the 1980s, Charismatics and Pentecostals began to look again at the vast theological, liturgical, and cultural differences beneath their charismatic experiences. The Holy Spirit united, but history and culture divided. In the 1980s, many who spoke in tongues did not speak to one another.

The Charismatic movement is sometimes referred to as the subculture of the Pentecostal church, which has a heritage of demonic and angelic visitations, of supernatural prophets and gifted seers, of healing lines and prosperity messages. Harrell further notes that the Charismatic movement and the Catholic Renewal movement have turned the attention of serious scholars and churchmen to the Holy Spirit; they have spent two decades grounding the Pentecostal experience in biblical scholarship and historical theology.[76] Shocked by Pentecostal faith teachers such as Kenneth Hagin and Kenneth Copeland, who were regarded as unsavory extremists, and embarrassed by the grandiose personal experience of Oral Roberts, these moderate charismatics have searched for guidelines to try the Spirit without quenching the Spirit. As a result, the Pentecostal/Charismatic movement of the 1980s is so theologically and culturally diverse (even in the crucial area of understanding the workings of the Holy Spirit) that it remains a movement only in terms of historical connections and common roots.

Harrell contends that many Protestant denominational churches initially reacted negatively to the Charismatic movement, especially in its birthing. Nevertheless, by the mid-1970s, most had come to welcome or

75. Harrell Jr., *All Things Are Possible*, 171–73.

76. Harrell Jr., *All Things Are Possible*, 178–80.

at least tolerate the movement.[77] This negative reaction was partly due to denominational fears of membership losses to these thriving Pentecostal/Charismatic churches. The Charismatic movement was largely influenced by the personal ministries of healing evangelists such as Oral Roberts and T. L. Osborne and by the Full Gospel Business Men Fellowship International. Publications such as *The Voice of Healing and Abundant Life* were also formed. In the 1970s and 1980s, the movement was influenced by the international Charismatic publication *Charisma* magazine and the television ministries of Jimmy Swaggart, Oral Roberts, Jim Bakker, Pat Robertson, and scores of others.[78] During the 1980s, Oral Roberts and Pat Robertson began to reach many through their educational institutions and television.

The essential elements of the Charismatic Renewal are:

(1) focus on the Lordship of Jesus

(2) exuberant praise and worship

(3) love of the Bible

(4) the prophetic, *rhema*, "right-now" Word of God; God still speaks today

(5) evangelism

(6) awareness of evil

(7) spiritual gifts

(8) eschatological expectation

(9) spiritual power

(10) a respect for the fivefold ministry of Ephesians 4:11

(11) the concept of cell groups[79]

The Charismatic movement has had internal and external controversy over its position on faith healing and Christian prosperity. Charismatics have been nicknamed by some of their detractors as "health and wealth" or "name it and claim it" people; it has also been referred to as the "Word of Faith" movement. James R. Goff Jr. says that the movement is known

77. Harrell Jr., *All Things Are Possible*, 176–78.

78. Synan, *Holiness-Pentecostal Tradition*, 214–17.

79. Synan, *Century of the Holy Spirit*, 389–90.

for its emphasis on healing the sick, getting rid of the devil, turning one-dollar bills into twenties, and positive confession.[80]

Harold B. Smith records that while the Charismatic movement brings a sense of celebration to the worship experience in contemporary churches, it seems to be borderline humanism and has a kind of materialistic orientation. He records the words of Raymond E. Carlson: "We need that balance of the Word and the Spirit—we need to anchor solidly in the Word of God."[81] The Charismatic movement was not only experienced by denominational churches; it also gave way to an independent church movement with various and diverse theological and ecclesiologies.[82]

Blacks were almost nonexistent in the early Charismatic movement of the 1960s. Two Black leaders came to be recognized in the movement: Bishop Vernon Bird and John Bryant, both of the AME Church. Leaders in the Church of God, Anderson, Indiana, were Benjamin Reed and Milton Granuin. Bishop John Meares, a white pastor with roots in the Church of God, Cleveland, Indiana, who pastored a large Black congregation, published *Bridge Builders*. Synan notes that, according to Meares, there has never been true reconciliation between Blacks and whites since the Civil War. His purpose was to bring about that reconciliation through the Pentecostal/Charismatic movement.[83] By the end of the 1980s, there were signs of major charismatic and ecumenical breakthroughs into the Black Christian community. Black preachers such as Ben Kinchloe, Carlton Pearson, and Frederick Price became televangelists of national influence, commanding the allegiance of millions of whites as well as Blacks.[84]

On the other hand, the Pentecostal church was a crucial factor in the life of the Black church and the American religious experience. Hollenger describes the Pentecostal movement as including "the miracle of the Spirit, where 'the color line' was washed away in the blood, [but] was not only forgotten but sometimes even shamefully hidden away."[85] The Pentecostal revival was a contribution from the Black community to the white one. White Pentecostals have never denied this—it has just been forgotten. The reason for this "forgetting" was the fact that between 1908 and 1914, the Pentecostal revival was—in opposition to what was declared

80. Goff Jr., *Fields White Unto Harvest*, 199–200.

81. Carlson, quoted in Smith, ed., *Pentecostals from the Inside Out*, 138.

82. Smith, ed., *Pentecostals from the Inside Out*, 138.

83. Synan, *Holiness-Pentecostal Tradition*, 167.

84. Smith, ed., *Pentecostals from the Inside Out*, 48.

85. Hollenweger, *Pentecostals*, 54.

the beginning of the revival—divided into two parts, one Black and one white. However, most Black denominations included white members, and a few Black members remained in some white denominations.

The main reason for this segregation was the very heavy criticism of the traditional white denominations against the Pentecostals, who disqualified Pentecostalism by pointing to its humble Black beginnings. It would, therefore, be unfair to put the blame for this development wholly on the white Pentecostals. They just adapted themselves to what was considered decent American Protestantism.[86]

According to a study done by David Barrett, a cross-section of worldwide Pentecostalism reveals a composite "international Pentecostal" that is more urban than rural, more female than male, more third world (66 percent) than the Western world (32 percent), more impoverished (87 percent) than affluent (13 percent), more family-oriented than individualistic, and younger than age eighteen.[87] The Pentecostal church, which received its missionary thrust on Azusa Street in 1906 under the leadership of William J. Seymour, now lays claims up to 600 million affiliated church members worldwide, 13 million new members a year, 35,000 new members a day, $34 billion annually donated to Christian causes, activity in 80 percent of the world's 3,300 large metropolises, with 80 percent of the membership in the developing world.[88]

These statistics demonstrate the effectiveness of the Pentecostal message and movement, which has grown dramatically since its humble beginnings on 312 Azusa Street in 1906.

PENTECOSTALISM AS A DENOMINATION

Most Pentecostals consider themselves part of broader Christian groups. For example, Pentecostals often identify as evangelicals. Furthermore, many embrace the term "Protestant," while others the term "Restorationist." Pentecostalism is also theologically and historically close to the Charismatic movement, as mentioned; the latter was influenced by the Pentecostal movement. (Some Pentecostals use the two terms interchangeably.) It should be noted that the Pentecostal denomination is,

86. Hollenweger, *Pentecostals*, 33–35.
87. Barrett, Kurian, and Johnson, *World Christian Encyclopedia*, 284–89.
88. Synan, *Century of the Holy Spirit*, 406–8.

worldwide, currently second in size only to the Roman Catholic Church and is the fastest-growing form of Christianity today.

- The Pentecostal church, which received its missionary thrust on Azusa Street in 1906, now lays claim to more than 279 million adherents, sometimes referred to as the "third force of Christianity." When Charismatics are included, the number increases to more than a quarter of the world's two billion Christians; there are more than 580 million Pentecostal and Charismatic believers across the globe.[89]
- Jeffrey K. Hadden of the University of Virginia collected statistics from the various large Pentecostal organizations and the work by David Stoll, demonstrating that the Pentecostals are experiencing rapid growth. The movement enjoys its greatest growth in the Global South (where many nations are classified as developing countries), which includes Africa, Latin America, and most of Asia. At the same time, North America retains significant leadership within the movement. Hadden notes that the Pew Research Center has noted that about 80 percent of Pentecostals reside in developing regions, particularly in sub-Saharan Africa (44 percent) and Latin America (37 percent). Asia and the Pacific regions also have significant Pentecostal populations. These areas are generally considered part of the Global South.[90]

Gordon-Conwell Theological Seminary's Center for the Study of Global Christianity corroborates this, highlighting the significant growth of Pentecostalism in developing regions.[91] The movement has seen explosive growth in these areas due to its appeal to the "poorest of the poor," as a 1999 UN report indicated. Academic studies and reports on global Christianity also emphasize that while Pentecostal leadership often remains centered in North America, the demographic majority of adherents now come from developing countries in Africa, Latin America, and Asia.

The largest Pentecostal denomination in the world, the Assemblies of God, claims over 13,000 churches in the US, 442,000 churches and outstations in many countries, and approximately 85 million adherents

89. Pew Research Center, *Global Christianity*, 68–70.

90. Hadden, "Pentecostalism."

91. Johnson and Zurlo, *Introducing Spirit-Empowered Christianity*, 15–16.

worldwide.[92] The largest single Pentecostal church in the world is the Yoido Full Gospel Church in South Korea.[93] Founded and led by David Yonggi Cho in 1958, it had nearly 830,000 members at its peak.[94] According to a spring 1998 article in *Christian History*, about 11,000 different Pentecostal or Charismatic denominations exist worldwide.[95]

With 6.5 million members, the Church of God in Christ is the largest Pentecostal denomination in the US. Other organizations in the US are the Assemblies of God, 3.3 million; the Pentecostal Assemblies of the World, 1.5 million; and the Church of God (Cleveland, Tennessee), 1 million. The size of Pentecostalism in the US is estimated to be more than 10 million, counting all unaffiliated congregations. However, the numbers are uncertain because some tenets of Pentecostalism are held by members of non-Pentecostal denominations in the Charismatic movement.[96]

Pentecostal churches are becoming increasingly market savvy, with significant dollars expected to be spent on public relations and newspaper, TV, and radio advertising. Australia's largest church, Hillsong, has weekly attendance figures ranging from approximately 130,000 to 150,000 across more than twenty countries. Its songs are sung in churches around the world. Hillsong is a member of Australian Christian Churches, the Australian branch of the Assemblies of God.[97] These statistics demonstrate the effectiveness of the Pentecostal message and movement, which has grown dramatically since its humble beginnings on 312 Azusa Street in 1906.[98]

92. Assemblies of God, "Our Statistics."
93. Anderson, *Introduction to Pentecostalism*, 102–3.
94. Synan, *Century of the Holy Spirit*, 404.
95. Synan, *Century of the Holy Spirit*, 6–7.
96. Pew Research Center, *Global Christianity*, 68–70.
97. Atherstone, *Hillsong Church*, 2–4.
98. Robeck Jr., *Azusa Street Mission and Revival*, 1.

3

The Black Church, Pentecostalism, and Community and Economic Empowerment

THE BLACK CHURCH AND THE INFLUENCE OF PENTECOSTALISM

THE HISTORY OF THE Black church and Pentecostalism laid a strong foundation under Black leadership. We understand that African religious worship patterns through the physical expression of dancing, singing, rhythmic and metric complexity and syncopation of music, and vocal expression in worship have been a part of the religious practices of Black people beginning with the import of slaves in the transatlantic slave trade. These styles and traditions characterized the Baptist, Methodist, and Holiness churches, the incubators of the Black Pentecostal church movement. Often, when people speak of the Black church, they cite emotionalism and culturalism, as though the Black church is substandard and subordinate to the white church. Hopefully, the historical outline of how the Black church developed has enlightened you and caused you to increase your respect and honor for her as equal to any other church. The Black church was born out of the racist rejection of the white church. But what history has also shown us is that the Black church is the sole reason for the survival and perpetuation of Black people, not least in the US.

The history of the Black church helps us to understand that those who were Pentecostal used to be affiliated with another church movement that stopped being spiritually fulfilling. The people were on a quest for more. When we look at the Great Awakening movements, we see that one of the traits that made them appealing was the physical engagement, shouting, falling down, dancing, and just all kinds of spiritual expressions that were abnormal in other church movements. I think that it is crucial to see the stages of development of the Black church from the invisible institution in the bush, to the negro church, to the Black church, and ultimately to the Pentecostal church. I am intentional about not saying "Black" Pentecostal church here because the twentieth-century Pentecostal movement was an inclusive, multiracial movement. It was multicultural until the pressure of the culture of racism broke it apart.

After whites racially cleansed the Pentecostal movement and began their own isolated brand of white Pentecostalism under the Assemblies of God, which excluded Black churches, it gave birth to the Black Pentecostal church, not by preference but by abandonment. Thank God for men like Seymour and Mason and the strong women who stood by them to formally introduce us to official Pentecostal churches that were filled with the Holy Spirit. For the founders of the twentieth-century Pentecostal experience, race wasn't an issue—it was an issue of grace.

Remember, it was the Black church that clandestinely carried the worship style and experiences that we now claim as authentically Pentecostal. However, these practices were seen throughout the evolution of the Black church and revival movements of this country. Thus, just as the Holiness movement evolved into Pentecostal churches, many Black churches, some Baptist and Methodist, are clandestinely Pentecostal by worship style (minus speaking in tongues). The Black Baptist church carried the DNA of Pentecost in its organizational loins and was waiting for the right season to give birth to her.

All Black people know that the most popular church in the Black community is the Black Baptist church. Still, only some Black people know that the only differences between the Black Baptist church and the Pentecostal church is the latter's quest for holiness, speaking in tongues, and deliverance ministry. However, outside of these practices, the worship patterns, songs, and expressions are very similar. It is not difficult for a Pentecostal to sit in a spirited Black Baptist church and for a Baptist to sit in a Bible-centered Pentecostal church.

I believe that we do the Black Pentecostal church a disservice by disconnecting Pentecostalism from the historic Black church, which was the feeder that helped establish the Pentecostal church. I have been in ministry for forty years and have met ministers throughout the country in almost every denomination. I am Pentecostal, but I refer to myself as "neo-Pentecostal" because I did not come out of the COGIC Church, Pentecostal Assemblies of the World (PAW), Church of God, or independent holiness Pentecostal churches. I came out of the missionary Baptist church, where people shouted, screamed, fell out in the pew and at the altar, prophesied, and sometimes spoke in tongues, though they were looked at strangely. Many leaders I have met used to be Baptist, but so was Bishop C. H. Mason.

We can validate my hypothesis that the Black Baptist church carried the DNA of Pentecostalism in worship by observing one of the most remarkable organic movements the Black church had ever seen: the Full Gospel Baptist Church Fellowship (FCBCFI). The FGBCFI began primarily through the leadership and vision of Bishop Paul S. Morton Sr. The movement started in the early 1990s, with the formal founding year often cited as 1994. The movement combined the elements of traditional Baptist theology with Pentecostal/Charismatic practices, such as speaking in tongues, prophecy, healing, and other gifts of the Holy Spirit. Many of its early members and leaders came from the National Baptist Convention, USA, Inc., and other historic African American Baptist denominations.

Bishop Paul S. Morton Sr., originally a pastor within the National Baptist Convention with a background in Pentecostalism, became increasingly drawn to Charismatic and Pentecostal practices, something we witness throughout our examination of the Black church history. Morton envisioned a movement that maintained Baptist doctrines but embraced the fullness of the Spirit-filled experience, hence the term "Full Gospel." As he shared his vision, other Baptist leaders and congregations with similar experiences began aligning with his vision.

The FGBCFI started informally through the sharing of ideas and beliefs. However, as noted, the FGBCFI was officially established as a formal fellowship in 1994. The FGBCFI grew rapidly, attracting numerous churches and followers who sought a blend of Baptist teaching and Pentecostal/Charismatic worship. Key components of the movement included annual conferences, leadership training, and a strong emphasis on unity and doctrinal integrity.

The FGBCFI emphasizes maintaining a balance of sound biblical teaching (core to traditional Baptist beliefs) and the empowerment of spiritual gifts (core to Pentecostalism). The FGBCFI also strongly emphasizes leadership development and provides resources and training for pastors and church leaders to minister effectively within their communities. The movement, which is true to the spirit of Pentecost, is based upon inclusivity and diversity. It has become known for its inclusive approach, appealing not only to African Americans but also to a broader demographic searching for a more expressive worship experience. Bishop Morton became the International Presiding Bishop and played a vital role in shaping the Fellowship's direction and policies.[1]

The FGBCFI is now under the leadership of Presiding Bishop Joseph Walker III. I would refer to such Baptist leaders as "Bapti-costal," because there is in them a merger of the two traditions. Their Pentecostalism was under the surface, waiting to emerge. The FGBCFI represents a significant movement within contemporary Christianity, bridging traditional Baptist principles with the dynamic expressions of the Black Pentecostal and Charismatic movement.

The Black Church as a Source of Empowerment

It is my contention that any ground that has been gained in America since the Emancipation Proclamation, and one of the main drivers and independent sources of change for Blacks in every arena, has been the Black church. Concerning political changes, community programs, and broader societal efforts aimed at promoting equity and inclusion, the traditional Black church engaged in activism to bring these changes to pass. However, another important aspect of Black empowerment that must be considered is the empowerment that comes from within (internal change). This is where I believe the Black Pentecostal church comes into play, due to her history of Black resilience and empowerment.

One of the differences between the traditional non-Pentecostal churches and the Black Pentecostal churches was that the traditional Black church primarily worked on external factors to bring about change. In contrast, the Black Pentecostal churches worked on internal factors. Due to their otherworldliness theology, many if not most Pentecostals shunned trying to impact the external world and spent more time separating from the external world. They focused more attention on deliverance ministry, which involved casting out demons that were believed to be root causes of mental illness and destructive practices such as irresponsible sexual behavior, addictions, and other fleshly sins.

In Pentecostalism, the healing ministry is an area of focus that reflects the ministry of Jesus. But closely related to the healing ministry was deliverance ministry. Donald G. Bloesch, in his *The Holy Spirit: Works*

1. Yong and Alexander, eds., *Afro-Pentecostalism*, 249–52.

and Gifts, states that the deliverance ministry was based upon the supposition that the ultimate adversary of humanity is Satan or demonic powers. Bloesch says that here sickness is not only attributed to sin but also demonic incursion. He shares that what is needed is not simply prayer for healing but the exorcism of the demons that pull us down into the depths of misery and depravity and render us helpless to help ourselves.[2]

The concept of deliverance ministry was based upon expelling the demonic presence that seeks to inhabit the human body and control the human mind (see, e.g., Mark 5). Deliverance ministry requires the commanding of demons out of individuals in the name of Jesus (Mark 16:17). As a part of deliverance ministry, many churches would have all-night prayer meetings for a breakthrough, and moaning bench sessions were held to purge those who were struggling to get delivered by the laying on of hands. This approach to deliverance and empowerment is a mentality with much more to offer the Black community than meets the eye.

When we consider the devastation of the Black community and the establishment of the inner-city ghetto colonies, it provides a very challenging context and environment for success and opportunity. One of the facts of history is that whenever Blacks were given an opportunity to compete on equal or unequal grounds, they emerged successful, as in science, math, technology, politics, sports, or entertainment. Blacks are some of the leading inventors in the world when given an opportunity. However, years and years of Black programming have smitten the hearts and confidence of Africans of the diaspora, particularly African Americans. A significant number of Blacks have resigned from hope and opportunity.

The Black church, the seedbed for the twentieth-century Pentecostal church, has always been both a silent and a vocal partner for Black empowerment. Black strength and Black excellence emerged out of the Black church in almost every field, both secular and sacred. Due to the emotional damage to the Black community from centuries of slavery and oppression, change requires more than external efforts for empowerment. Negative programming of Black people and white people about Black people hinders African Americans internally and externally. It is a known fact that change must begin on the inside before it can manifest on the outside. Thus, the Black church and Black religious empowerment groups have attempted to assist Black communities in the quest for liberation.

2. Bloesch, *Holy Spirit*, 107–9.

Black Liberation Theology

Black liberation theology is a theological perspective that emerged in the 1960s and 1970s, primarily in the United States. It aims to address the contextual realities and experiences of Black Americans by integrating the Christian gospel with the struggle for liberation from racial and socio-economic oppression. Black liberation theologians have for years attempted to provide a paradigm and platform to argue for Black liberation from a theological perspective in order to help Black people understand their value and significance, even though America continues to disparage us and devalue our worth and contributions to this nation. Black liberation theologians set their eyes like a flint toward Black liberation through the Bible and social platforms.[3]

This liberation theology prioritizes the liberating aspects of Christian doctrine, emphasizing the concept that God is deeply concerned with the plight of the oppressed and actively involved in their struggle for justice and equality. The core belief of liberation theology is that God is the God of the oppressed. Black liberation theology posits that God's primary concern is for the marginalized and oppressed in society, not least Blacks. God sides with the oppressed against their oppressors, seeking justice and liberation for those who suffer under systems of racism and economic exploitation. Jesus Christ is seen as a liberator who challenged the unjust structures of his time and whose life and ministry offer a model for contemporary struggles for justice. The cross and resurrection are understood as symbols of ultimate resistance and victory over oppressive powers. The theology advocates for a holistic view of salvation that encompasses spiritual emancipation and social, economic, and political liberation. It holds that the kingdom of God involves the establishment of just relationships and the transformation of society. It also emphasizes the importance of context in theological reflection. It asserts that theology must speak to the lived realities of Black people and address their historical and social contexts.

James Cone is often regarded as the father of Black liberation theology. His key work was *A Black Theology of Liberation*. Cone's work was pivotal in framing the theological discourse around the Black experience of oppression and the struggle for liberation. Cone articulated that God's revelation in Jesus Christ is deeply intertwined with the liberation of the poor and oppressed. He emphasized the need for a theology that

3. Bradley, *Liberating Black Theology*, 19–25.

resonates with the Black church and community, highlighting the liberating themes in the Bible and stressing that any theology that ignores the plight of the oppressed is inauthentic.[4]

Another supporter of liberation theology is Gustavo Gutiérrez. Though technically a proponent of Latin American liberation theology, Gutiérrez's work has significantly influenced Black liberation theology due to the overlapping concerns with social and economic oppression. His main work was *A Theology of Liberation*.[5] He introduced the concept of God's "preferential option for the poor," highlighting a need for the church to be an agent of social change and an ally in the struggle against systemic injustice.

Another liberation theologian is Cornel West, a contemporary thinker who bridges academia and public life. West has advanced and expanded upon Black liberation theology, making it relevant for modern discussions on race, politics, and justice. His key work is *Prophesy Deliverance! An Afro-American Revolutionary Christianity*. West integrates various elements such as Marxism, existentialism, and pragmatism, within his theological discourse, emphasizing the role of Christian faith in social activism and the moral imperative to confront systemic injustice.[6] Other liberation theologians include:

- Kelly Brown Douglas, an Episcopal priest and scholar, who has been a significant voice in contemporary Black liberation theology, particularly in exploring issues related to gender and sexuality. Her key work is *The Black Christ*. Douglas has expanded the discussion to include feminist perspectives, addressing how Black liberation theology can incorporate issues of gender and advocate for the broader inclusion of oppressed voices within the theological narrative.[7]
- J. Deotis Roberts, a notable theologian who has contributed significantly to bridging the gap between Black theology and broader ecumenical dialogues. His key work is *Liberation and Reconciliation: A Black Theology*. Roberts emphasized the need for reconciliation between oppressed and oppressors, thus adding a crucial dimension of dialogue and unity to liberation theology.[8]

4. Cone, *Black Theology of Liberation*.
5. Gutiérrez, *Theology of Liberation*.
6. West, *Prophesy Deliverance!*
7. Douglas, *Black Christ*, 112–15.
8. Roberts, *Liberation and Reconciliation*, 21–23.

Black liberation theology has had a profound impact on both academic theology and grassroots Christian activism. It has contributed to a greater awareness of the ways racism and economic exploitation intersect with religious life, inspiring a range of social movements and forming the theological backbone of much contemporary Black church activism. The theology remains a vital, evolving discourse that continues to address new challenges and contexts in the ongoing struggle for justice and equality. There have been multiple attempts by the traditional Black church and its split cells to try to address the economic, health, and community issues of the Black community, which has made an impact, but not enough. Many great thinkers and activists, such as Martin Luther King Jr., and an array of others in politics, have sought to change, modify, and transform the Black condition and the Black community, but we remain a penny short and a day too late.

The Nation of Islam

Elijah Muhammad, Malcolm X, and the Nation of Islam have for many decades attempted to improve the Black condition separate from the white man's version of God in Christianity and present what they consider a more palatable approach to a non-white God through the Nation of Islam. The Nation of Islam (NOI) is a religious and sociopolitical organization founded in the United States in 1930. It primarily seeks to improve the spiritual, mental, social, and economic condition of African Americans. It was founded in Detroit during the Great Depression, a period marked by severe economic hardship and social discrimination for African Americans. It was a time when many Black individuals were seeking new means of spiritual and social empowerment amidst the pervasive racism and segregation in the United States.

The founder of the Nation of Islam was Wallace D. Fard Muhammad (also known simply as W. D. Fard). His teachings centered on empowering Black Americans through self-sufficiency, economic independence, and spiritual enlightenment. He advocated for a separate Black identity and community that was distinct from the dominant white society. He taught that African Americans were the true descendants of an original, powerful race and promoted the idea of Black self-reliance and the rejection of Western Christianity, which he saw as a tool of oppression.[9]

9. Lincoln, *Black Muslims in America*, 46–52.

The movement really grew legs under the leadership of Elijah Muhammad (born Elijah Poole; 1897–1975). Elijah Muhammad assumed the leadership of the Nation of Islam after W. D. Fard mysteriously disappeared in 1934. Under Elijah Muhammad's guidance, the NOI grew significantly. He emphasized the teachings that Fard introduced and institutionalized the organization, spreading its influence through speeches, writings, and establishing temples and schools. Elijah Muhammad authored several influential books, such as *Message to the Blackman in America*[10] and *The Fall of America*.[11] He mentored influential members, including Malcolm X and Louis Farrakhan, who would later become prominent figures within the organization.[12]

The Nation of Islam holds that Fard Muhammad was an incarnation of Allah (God), and Elijah Muhammad was his messenger. Under the leadership of Elijah Muhammad, it emphasizes economic independence, community self-sufficiency, and the importance of Black-owned businesses. It encourages strict moral behavior, including dietary restrictions (e.g., a pork-free diet) and principles of discipline, cleanliness, and abstinence from drugs and alcohol. It advocates for racial separation as opposed to integration, believing that true freedom and justice for African Americans can only be achieved by forming their own independent nation or community.[13]

Over the years, the Nation of Islam has undergone various transformations, especially after Elijah Muhammad's death in 1975. His son, Warith Deen Mohammed, briefly led the NOI towards mainstream Sunni Islam, forming what is now known as the American Society of Muslims. Meanwhile, Louis Farrakhan revived the original teachings of Elijah Muhammad, retaining the Nation of Islam's identity and its emphasis on Black empowerment. The Nation of Islam continues to be a significant religious and sociopolitical entity, advocating for the uplift and empowerment of African Americans while remaining controversial due to its racial and political stances.[14]

If history teaches us one thing about the Black church and Pentecostalism, it is that religious presence and practice have been one of the main drivers for Black liberation. The Black Baptists realized that the

10. Muhammad, *Message to the Blackman in America*.

11. Muhammad, *Fall of America*.

12. Turner, *Islam in the African-American Experience*, 108–15.

13. Turner, *Islam in the African-American Experience*, 100–105.

14. Turner, *Islam in the African-American Experience*, 100–105.

Black church was uniquely positioned to drive Black empowerment, and the Black Methodists realized the same thing. Black Pentecostalism also realizes that the Black church will be instrumental in Black empowerment. Acknowledging that fact, the Nation of Islam, led by the Honorable Louis Farrakhan, launched a historic march on Washington, coalescing the Black church—Baptists, AMEs, Methodists, Holiness, Charismatics, and Pentecostals alike. Farrakhan knew that the key to empowering the Black community was to lift the Black man first.

The Million Man March (MMM) was held on October 16, 1995, in Washington, DC, and aimed to promote unity, atonement, and empowerment among African American men.[15] The goal of the MMM was to bring together African American men from various walks of life to demonstrate unity and collective strength. The march was intended to show the world that Black men could come together in peace and cooperation, cross-denominationally and ecumenically, for the purpose of empowering the Black man, the Black family, and the Black community. It sought to encourage participants to engage in self-reflection and seek forgiveness for any wrongdoings they had committed in their lives, both personally and within their communities. The event served as a call for spiritual and moral renewal, urging Black men to be better fathers, husbands, and role models.[16]

The MMM also sought to motivate men to become more involved in community service, to combat social issues such as violence and poverty, and to strive for economic independence and self-sufficiency. The march set out to increase awareness and participation in political engagement, voter registration, and civic participation among Black people. It aimed to raise political awareness and activism, motivating attendees to influence public policies that affected their communities. It demonstrated to the world that a large number of disciplined Black men could gather in Washington for a peaceful gathering, seeking positive change in their family, community, and economic condition.

History repeatedly reveals that Black empowerment is possible and heavily contingent upon internal and external factors of spiritual renewal and political justice that lead to economic freedom. Some of the most powerful movements, like those just discussed, involved Black Pentecostal leaders; and even if the entire church was not involved, the movement

15. Bynoe, *Stand and Deliver*, 129–32.

16. Bynoe, *Stand and Deliver*, 85–89.

still had the DNA of Pentecostals embedded in its efforts. Space will not permit me to discuss the NAACP, the Southern Christian Leadership Conference, the Black Panthers, the Urban League, and, most recently, Black Lives Matter. But regardless of the movement, the motivation is the same—Black empowerment. Some movements turned to politics and policies, and some to religion and relationships (integration). However, the secret sauce to making a difference in Black empowerment is Pentecostals and power. Holy Spirit empowerment can help combat and transform social issues such as violence and poverty and spearhead initiatives for economic independence and self-sufficiency based upon the internal work of God.

Liberation Through Pentecostalism

The Holy Spirit is a liberator. I contend that the future of Black Americans is not in the hands of the political leadership of our country but in the hands of Black Pentecostal churches. They have played significant roles in the Black liberation and civil rights movements in the United States. Black Pentecostalism's involvement in social justice issues is not generally known due to their hard stance on holiness and coming out of the world and being separated. The theology of Pentecostalism, which teaches believers to be in the world but not of the world, has traditionally led to a very clandestine approach to Black liberation. Interestingly, this position has been held by both Black and white Pentecostals; however, white Pentecostals still encouraged members to vote and be involved in politics.

It is often stated that Dr. King's March on Washington demonstrated his strong allies were Roman Catholicism and Judaism, though he was a Baptist pastor. However, Black Pentecostal churches provided a spiritual and communal foundation for resistance against racial oppression. Their worship services, which emphasized emotional expression and communal support, offered a refuge and an empowering space for the Black community and Black people. Pentecostal leaders such as Bishop Charles H. Mason actively advocated for racial justice. Mason and other leaders used their influence to organize and support civil rights activities. The COGIC church played a pivotal role during the Memphis Sanitation Strike in 1968. Dr. King gave his famous "I've Been to the Mountaintop" speech at the Mason Temple, the headquarters of COGIC, the night before he was assassinated.[17] This event highlights the significant support from COGIC in the civil rights movement. And Pentecostal worship music, characterized by gospel music, provided anthems of the civil rights movement. Artists like Mahalia Jackson, who was associated with Pentecostalism, used their music to inspire and mobilize people.

Many Black Pentecostal churches provided economic support for the movement. They organized fundraisers, donated money, and supported boycotts and strikes, helping sustain the movement financially. Pentecostal churches often served as meeting spaces and organizing hubs for civil rights activities. They provided training for activists and were involved in voter registration drives and educational initiatives to combat racial discrimination. Pentecostal bishops and pastors frequently spoke out against racial injustice from their pulpits, educating their congregations about civil rights issues and encouraging active participation in the movement. Members of Black Pentecostal churches participated in marches, sit-ins, and protests. Their collective action and presence were crucial in demonstrating the widespread demand for civil rights and equality. The Black Pentecostal churches offered leadership and empowerment to the Black community through economic support and active participation, significantly contributing to the fight for black liberation and the success of the civil rights movement.

BLACK EMPOWERMENT THROUGH ECONOMIC AND COMMUNITY DEVELOPMENT

What we have consistently seen throughout the history of the Black church is the power of the Holy Spirit to do what humans have been unable to do. As we look at the state of Black America and the devastation she continues to suffer from the fruit and residual effects of slavery, social injustice, the lack of access to quality education, the lack of healthcare and economic freedom, we must ask the question—is there any hope for the Black community? The state of Black America encompasses various statistics related to health, economics, housing, education, and other aspects of life. These indicators provide insights into the disparities and progress experienced by black Americans. Here are some key statistics:

17. Alexander, *Black Fire*, 322–23.

Economic Statistics of Black America	
Income—The median household income for Black families was approximately $45,870 in 2020, compared to $71,564 for white families.[18]	• Poverty Rate—The poverty rate for Black Americans is approximately 19.5 percent, compared to 10.1 percent for white Americans.[19] • Unemployment Rate—Historically, the unemployment rate for Black Americans is higher. As of August 2021, the Black unemployment rate was around 8.8 percent, compared to 4.5 percent for white Americans.[20] • Wealth Gap—The median wealth of Black households is significantly lower than that of white households. In 2016, the median net worth of Black households was $17,150 compared to $171,000 for white households.[21]
Housing	• Homeownership—As of the first quarter of 2021, the homeownership rate for Black Americans was around 45.1 percent compared to 73.8 percent for white Americans.[22] • Housing Affordability—Black Americans spend a higher share of their income on rent. They are more likely to experience a housing cost burden, with approximately 53 percent of Black renters spending more than 30 percent of their income on housing.[23] • Subprime Mortgages—Black borrowers are more likely to receive subprime mortgage loans with higher interest rates and less favorable terms, contributing to financial instability.[24]
Education	• High School Graduation—The high school graduation rate for Black students was about 79 percent for the 2018–2019 school year, compared to 89 percent for white students.[25] • College Enrollment and Completion—Black Americans constitute about 14 percent of all college students. However, they have lower college completion rates, with approximately 42 percent of black students graduating within six years compared to 64 percent of white students.[26] • Student Debt—Black college graduates owe, on average, $25,000 more in student loan debt than white graduates four years after graduation.[27]

18. Shrider et al., "Income and Poverty in the United States."

19. Shrider et al., "Income and Poverty in the United States."

20. U.S. Department of Labor, "Employment Situation—August 2021."

21. Board of Governors of the Federal Reserve System, "2016 Survey of Consumer Finances."

22. U.S. Census Bureau, "Quarterly Residential Vacancies and Homeownership, First Quarter 2021."

23. Joint Center for Housing Studies of Harvard University, *State of the Nation's Housing 2021*.

24. Choi, "Breaking Down the Black-White Homeownership Gap."

25. Irwin et al., *Report on the Condition of Education 2021*.

26. De Brey, Zhang, and Duffy, *Digest of Education Statistics, 2020*.

27. Scott-Clayton and Li, "Black-White Disparity in Student Loan Debt More Than

Criminal Justice	• Incarceration Rate—Black Americans are incarcerated at disproportionately higher rates. Black men are about six times more likely to be incarcerated than white men.[28] • Policing—Black people are more likely to be stopped, searched, and arrested by police.[29]
Health	• Life Expectancy—Black Americans have a shorter life expectancy compared to white Americans. As of 2020, the life expectancy for Black Americans was approximately 72 years, compared to 78 years for white Americans.[30] • Infant Mortality—Black infants have a higher mortality rate, with approximately 10.8 deaths per 1,000 live births compared to 4.6 for white infants.[31] • Chronic Diseases—Black Americans have higher rates of chronic conditions such as diabetes, hypertension, and heart disease. Approximately 41 percent of Black adults have hypertension compared to 28 percent of white adults.[32] • Obesity—Around 49.6 percent of Black adults are considered obese, compared to 42.2 percent of white adults.[33] • Mental Health—Black Americans are less likely to receive mental health services, with about 30.6 percent of Black adults receiving mental health treatment compared to 48 percent of white adults.[34] • Health Insurance Coverage—The uninsured rate for Black Americans is higher than for white Americans. Approximately 9.7 percent of Black Americans were uninsured in 2020 compared to 5.4 percent of white Americans.[35]

These statistics highlight significant disparities and challenges faced by African Americans in various sectors. Efforts to address these issues involve policy changes, community programs, and broader societal shifts aimed at promoting equity and inclusion. The statistics can vary slightly depending on the source and year of the data, but they generally illustrate

Triples After Graduation."

28. Bureau of Justice Statistics, *Prisoners in 2019*.

29. NAACP, *Criminal Justice Fact Sheet*.

30. National Center for Health Statistics, "Health, United States, 2020–2021: Annual Perspective."

31. Ely and Driscoll, "Infant Mortality in the United States, 2019."

32. U.S. Department of Health and Human Services, "Chronic Disease Indicators."

33. Centers for Disease Control and Prevention, *National Health and Nutrition Examination Survey*.

34. Substance Abuse and Mental Health Services Administration, "National Survey on Drug Use and Health (NSDUH)."

35. Artiga, Hill, and Damico, "Health Coverage by Race and Ethnicity, 2010–2022."

ongoing disparities. Comparing the condition of Black Americans to other ethnic groups, including Asians and Latinos, Blacks are lagging in their overall economic and community health status.

The Black economic condition in America includes a lack of wealth generation, access to capital for entrepreneurial endeavors, lack of access to quality healthcare, poor quality of educational resources that have led to a school-to-prison pipeline, the discrimination of the criminal justice system, lack of access to adequate housing, and high subprime interest rates charged to Blacks by banks. While I can add and add to the list the challenges faced by the Black community, it all boils down to one thing—how can the Black community engage in lifting themselves above and beyond these cyclical problems that began in the early 1600s? Before we get into what I argue is the prophetic hope of the Black community—which is the authentic message and experience of the kingdom of God that we have seen traces of throughout the historical worship styles and practices of the invisible institution, the negro church, the Great Awakenings, the Black church, and the Black Pentecostal church—we must examine and consider the economic and community development challenges of Black people.

Earning graduate degrees such as a Duke Global Executive MBA and a University of Houston masters in economic development and entrepreneurship gives me a different perspective and interest in Black empowerment through economic and community development than most pastors. When considering economic and community development in the Black community and Pentecostalism, we are talking about a two-pronged approach: internal through the power of the Holy Spirit and external through principles and practices of sound economic and community development acumen. History has demonstrated that one or the other is once again a penny too short and a day too late. So, let's explore "Black empowerment" and Black Pentecostalism in real terms.

Black liberation or Black empowerment refers to the movements and efforts aimed at achieving freedom, equality, and justice for Black people, particularly those of African descent. It encompasses the struggle against systemic racism, oppression, and exploitation directed at societal institutions and within the global context. The roots that led to Black liberation movement can be traced back to the transatlantic slave trade, colonialism, and the racist systems that arose from these eras. As mentioned previously, movements such as abolitionism, civil rights, and Black power have all played significant roles in the pursuit of Black liberation.

The goal of Black empowerment and liberation is to dismantle institutional and structural racism that causes discrimination in areas like employment, education, criminal justice, and housing. It involves the fight for civil and human rights, legal reform, and equal treatment under the law. Black empowerment aims to rebuild the damaged self-esteem that has been cast upon the Black community and emphasizes pride in Black culture, history, and identity by encouraging knowledge about Black history and Black contributions to society. Black empowerment challenges negative stereotypes and promotes a positive representation of Blacks, not least in the biblical arena of theology. Black empowerment also focuses on achieving economic self-sufficiency and addressing economic disparities, such as wealth gaps and unemployment. It encourages entrepreneurship, community ownership, and equitable access to resources.

Black empowerment refers to the process through which Black individuals and communities gain the power, control, and confidence to make decisions that affect their lives and allow them to assert their rights. It focuses on improving the socio-economic and political status of Black people and ensuring access to quality education and opportunities for academic and personal growth. Black empowerment focuses on economic independence by promoting financial literacy, entrepreneurship, and the creation of Black-owned businesses, while advocating for fair wages and improved economic conditions in Black communities.

Black empowerment understands that the significance of policies and politics is the long-term sustainability of justice, and so encourages voter registration, political activism, and representation in government. It understands the necessity of working to elect officials who will advocate for policies that benefit Black communities. Black empowerment aims to build a stronger sense of community by strengthening community bonds through mutual support, cultural events, and local organizations. Building a strong Black community requires that we foster a sense of unity and collective action against common challenges. Black empowerment also targets the inefficient and inadequate health services rendered to the Black community. It also addresses healthcare access and outcomes disparities, promoting mental health awareness and offering support systems. Lastly, Black empowerment strives to attack the negative media representation of Black people that portrays Black culture in a demeaning way; it demands a more diverse representation of Black life and culture, not just "thug life."

It's most unfortunate that the counterpart to the Black church, the white church, doesn't want to discuss these issues and sees social issues that do not involve them as non-spiritual issues. For example, George Floyd was connected to the Black community, which connected him and his family members to the Black church. Yet, while he was caught begging and pleading for his life on video, some church leaders saw it and deemed it beyond the concerns of the church—the white church, that is. Still, the murder of George Floyd garnered attention from around the world. The Sunday after his death, there was probably not a Black church in the country that did not have to provide some commentary to their congregation concerning this issue and what we were going to do to stop the police from killing Black males.

I must state this: while I know that Black-on-Black crime is one of the leading killers of Black boys in the country, this doesn't justify law enforcement becoming judge, jury, and executioner in the streets. Everyone has a right to due process, not to be "tried" and given a death sentence on the spot. After Floyd's murder, however, the church was divided along race lines. White Pentecostals and Black Pentecostals, white and Black denominations, took opposing sides because, for whites, it was an issue of law and Black stereotyping. For Blacks, it was an issue of social and spiritual justice.

Black liberation and Black empowerment are interconnected in their aim to overcome systemic barriers and improve the lives of Black individuals and communities. While Black liberation seeks to address and reform broader societal structures, Black empowerment focuses on personal and community development within these contexts. Together, these efforts contribute to the broader pursuit of equality, justice, and human dignity for Black people around the world.

Yet, for Black liberation or empowerment to have a profound effect, I believe it must be approached from a spiritual perspective that involves the whole person. This is the foundation for change in the Black community, starting with each individual that makes up that community. Thus, Black empowerment is a call for the individual and personal change of those who must elevate above the oppressive ideologies and stereotypes that have contributed to their inability to prosper and be in good health (3 John 2).

Black empowerment includes economic and community development. But what exactly are we talking about? Community and economic development simply means improving the economic well-being of citizens, which leads to a higher quality of life. Unfortunately, while this is the goal of economic and community development, people of color continuously get left out.

The ideal of economic development assumes that improving a citizen's economic well-being results from wealth creation in the community through increased individual incomes. Wealth creation, a primary goal of economic development, is based on three basic activities: starting businesses, growing and retaining existing businesses, and attracting new businesses. In addition, dynamic economic development rests on a foundation of communities with a high quality of life. The fruits of economic growth and development are used to further improve the lives of people in the community. Black empowerment through economic development involves wealth generation that requires financial literacy. This necessary requirement automatically disqualifies Blacks and Browns due to their lack of exposure to financial knowledge.

One of my former professors, who taught economic development, provided me with the following training tool.

As the model shows, economic growth and development have as their foundation high quality-of-life communities. Simply put, high quality-of-life communities are communities where people want to live. The Heartland Center for Leadership Development states that these types of communities often have many of the following characteristics:

- Evidence of Community Pride: Successful communities are often showplaces of care, attention, history, and heritage.
- Emphasis on Quality in Business and Community Life: People believe something worth doing is worth doing right.
- Willingness to Invest in the Future: In addition to the brick-and-mortar investments, all decisions are made with an outlook on the future.
- Participatory Approach to Community Decision-Making: Even the most powerful of opinion leaders seem to work toward building consensus.
- Cooperative Community Spirit: The stress is on working together toward a common goal, focusing on positive results.
- Realistic Appraisal of Future Opportunities: Successful communities have learned to build on strengths and minimize weaknesses.

- Awareness of Competitive Positioning: Local loyalty is emphasized, but thriving communities know who their competitors are and position themselves accordingly.
- Knowledge of the Physical Environment: Relative location and available natural resources underscore decision-making.
- Active Economic Development Program: An organized, public/private approach to economic development exists.
- Deliberate Transition of Power to a Younger Generation of Leaders: People under age forty regularly hold key positions in civic and business affairs.
- Celebration of Diversity in Leadership: Women, minorities, youth, and newcomers are welcomed into leadership circles where their ideas are treated as opportunities.
- Strong Belief in and Support for Education: Good schools are the norm and centers of community activity.
- Problem-Solving Approach to Providing Healthcare: Healthcare is considered essential, and smart strategies are in place for diverse methods of delivery.
- Strong Multigenerational Family Orientation: The definition of family is broad, and activities include younger and older generations.
- Strong Presence of Traditional Institutions that are Integral to Community Life: Churches, schools, and service clubs are strong influences on community development and social activities.
- Sound and Well-Maintained Infrastructure: Leaders work hard to maintain and improve streets, sidewalks, water systems, and sewage facilities.
- Careful Use of Fiscal Resources: Frugality is a way of life, and expenditures are considered investments in the future.
- Sophisticated Use of Technology Resources: Leaders access information that is beyond the knowledge base available in the community.
- Willingness to Seek Help from the Outside: People seek outside help for community needs, and many compete for government grants and contracts for economic and social programs.
- Conviction that, in the Long Run, You Have to Do It Yourself: Thriving communities believe their destiny is in their own hands. Making

> their communities good places is a proactive assignment, and they willingly accept it.[36]

High quality-of-life communities are fertile grounds for economic development that encourages entrepreneurship, business growth, and the attraction of firms to the community. Consequently, when we consider this description of a high quality-of-life community in which wealth generation and creation are built, we understand that the Black urban or rural community does not qualify as a high quality-of-life community. In order for the Black community to become such a community, it must begin with community-building strategies that are executed by high-esteemed and Holy Ghost-filled individuals. Only God can do exceedingly above all that we ask or think according to the power that is at work in us (Ephesians 3:20). This was written by Paul, the Pentecostal, as he was led by the prompting and power of the Holy Spirit.

Our challenge in empowering the Black community is that no one wants to live there, including Blacks. Thus, when they can afford to leave, a great percentage elect to do so. The next challenge is that other ethnic groups do not prefer to live with a high population of Black people. Thus, successful Blacks can tend to feel displaced unless they have an exorbitant number of resources. When they have such resources, they escape the title of being Black; they are just wealthy.

The final goal of economic development activities is economic growth and development, which, in turn, feeds additional improvement in the community's quality of life. Economic growth is expanding economic opportunities and the economic well-being of all citizens in the community. Economic development is focused on sustainable and stable economic growth that fits the vision and values of the community. In other words, development is planned economic growth that will provide a stable, high quality of life for the community.

What is wealth? This great question must be answered before discussing the wealth creation process. Edward Wolff, an economics professor at New York University, defines wealth as "the stuff that people own."[37] Webster's dictionary defines wealth as "all property that has a money or an exchange value."[38] Both definitions portray wealth as the collection of

36. Heartland Center for Leadership Development, "Building Strong Leaders Through Programs for Community Vitality."

37. *Multinational Monitor*, "Wealth Divide."

38. *Merriam-Webster*, s.v. "wealth."

things we own that have value. In his best-selling book *Rich Dad, Poor Dad*, Robert Kiyosaki takes a different approach. Kiyosaki states that the rich don't work for money. The rich work for and accumulate assets (wealth) that produce an income.[39]

Consequently, true wealth is accumulating assets that create an income. For example, the family home is not considered to be wealth, in Kiyosaki's definition, because it doesn't create income but rather consumes income to maintain it. Corporate stocks, a business, and savings are examples of assets that create income and are classified as wealth.

I tend to side with Kiyosaki in concentrating more on assets that create additional wealth than just any asset with monetary value. Therefore, I see starting and building a business (entrepreneurship) as the ultimate form of wealth creation. The results of entrepreneurial activity are often measured in terms of new employment, increased income, and additional tax base. These are some primary goals of economic development. Therefore, wealth creation, the goal of economic development, results from creating new businesses, growing and retaining existing businesses, and recruiting new businesses.

Wealth is the accumulation of assets over time and results from investment decisions. Therefore, the quality of the investment decision influences the value of accumulated wealth. Often, economic developers do not have control over investment decisions. Consequently, economic developers often use increasing income as a primary measure of economic progress. Sources of income include more and better quality jobs (the most common measure of economic progress), increased business profits for business owners, capital investment in the community, increased income from individual asset accumulation (i.e., stocks, bonds, real estate, retirement accounts, etc.), and the level of transfer payments from government and nongovernment sources. Investment in assets from various sources that produce income leads to wealth accumulation.

Why create wealth? In the final analysis, wealth is the primary tool to enhance the overall quality of life for all citizens. Economically prosperous communities, regions, states, and nations can provide citizens with amenities such as high-paying and stable jobs, quality education, access to healthcare, safe and clean environments, a variety of arts, etc., that improve the overall quality of life.

39. Kiyosaki, *Rich Dad, Poor Dad*, 51–53.

In order for Blacks to advance as a people, there has to be an internal change that lifts our self-esteem and engenders courage to be innovative and creative problem-solvers and solution-finders, at a profit. One of the models for my argument of how Pentecostalism can transform the Black community if the Spirit is given opportunity is the model of George Washington Carver. A prominent African American scientist and inventor, Carver is widely known for his agricultural innovations, particularly those involving peanuts. His connection to Pentecostalism, however, is an interesting aspect of his life less frequently discussed. George Washington Carver and the peanut are a prototype for what can happen when Spirit-filled believers solve problems and find solutions.

Carver was closely connected with the Methodist denomination. He was mainly involved with the African Methodist Episcopal Church (AME), one of the first independent Black denominations in the United States. The AME Church emerged in the early nineteenth century and emphasized education, social justice, and the betterment of African American communities. Carver was a devout Christian, and his faith played an essential role in his life and work. He often spoke about his belief that his scientific discoveries were guided by divine inspiration. He was known to rise early to pray and meditate, regularly seeking guidance from God on his scientific endeavors. And it has been said that when Carver wanted new ideas on how to use the peanut, he prayed in tongues, for he was Pentecostal.[40]

While the specific denominations Carver was associated with are not very clear, it is believed that his spiritual practices and outlook were influenced by the Pentecostal movement, known for its emphasis on direct personal experience with God through baptism with the Holy Spirit. Carver's faith intersected with his scientific work. He believed in the harmony of science and religion and often stated that his scientific inquiries were a form of worship. He attributed many of his creative insights and advancements in agricultural science to divine revelation rather than solely to his own intellect or effort.

Carver is famously associated with developing numerous products derived from peanuts, including food items, dyes, plastics, and gasoline substitutes. His work drastically improved the agricultural economy of the southern United States by promoting crop rotation and soil enrichment, which included alternative crops like peanuts to restore soil fertility. Carver was a pioneer in promoting sustainable agricultural practices.

40. McMurry, *George Washington Carver*, 235–40, 283–88.

His ideas helped transform agricultural practices and provided new economic opportunities for farmers, especially in the African American community.

The Black Pentecostal church was an unspoken catalyst for change and transformation in the Black community even before it was known as Pentecostal. The disciplined lifestyle, the high trust in God, and the physical and vocal expression of joy, even in pain, have been a bulwark for change among Black people. The Holy Spirit has been at work through the Pentecostal church in known and unknown ways. The same Spirit that was upon Jesus in Luke 4 in baptism, that led him into the wilderness and empowered him after the wilderness, and rested upon him and anointed him for deliverance ministry, has never ceased to move on earth. This same Spirit raised Christ from the dead, gave Seymour Pentecostal power, gave Mason Pentecostal power, and gave George Washington Carver Pentecostal power to make a change in the culture!

4

The Kingdom of God and the Ministry of the Holy Spirit

THUS FAR, WE HAVE discovered how pertinent Pentecostalism has been historically to both the white church and the Black church. The pre-formation of Pentecostalism can be seen in the fibers of the invisible institution of the church in the bush, and its continued DNA appears in both the negro and Black church movements. The Pentecostal church movement was latent in the fabric of the Great Awakening revivals of both the eighteenth and nineteenth centuries and began to informally materialize in both the Methodist and Holiness movements. These movements prepared the way for formal Pentecostalism and the Azusa Outpouring at the turn of the twentieth century, led by William J. Seymour, culminating with Bishop C. H. Mason. The Pentecostal movement ushered in a solid theological foundation on the ministry of the Holy Spirit. Before Edward Irving and the Holy Apostolic Catholic Church movement of England in the late nineteenth century, the church had not seen manifestations of the gifts of the Spirit since the Montantist movement.

Pentecostalism, with its focus on the ministry of the Holy Spirit and his gifts, combined with strict discipline for living, has proven to be a significant chemistry for change. The presence and power of the Holy Spirit served as the substratum for the ministry works of Jesus. Through the power and presence of the Holy Spirit, Jesus performed the mighty acts of God in his life and ministry. Most evangelicals (an interdenominational term for Christians who primarily emphasize evangelism) embrace the teaching of the virgin birth of Jesus. We embrace the incarnation statements recorded in the Gospel of John, "In the beginning was the Word and the Word was with God and the Word was God" (John 1:1). John goes on to say, in verse 14, that "the Word became (*ginomai*) flesh and dwelt among us." The Greek term *ginomai* denotes the beginning of something that was not, suggesting that the Word, God, took upon itself a new reality—flesh. Thus, in the incarnation, God didn't stop being God; he just *became* man.

Orthodox Christianity espouses the doctrinal belief that Christ was a product of the virgin birth. He was not the seed of Joseph but was born of the Holy Spirit (Gal 4:4). The Gospel of John states that he was not born of the will of man but was the Father's only begotten (1:13, 14, 18). Paul speaks of the incarnation in what is referred to as the kenosis chapter of Philippians 2—that Christ veiled himself from his divinity and took upon himself the form of a servant, not making a reputation of being God (Phil 2:5–11). In essence, Paul teaches us that the works of Christ were not based upon his divinity but his empowerment.

Christ's ministry to the world was not powered by him being God, but his empowerment was based upon the indwelling presence of the Holy Spirit and the baptism of the Spirit. Jesus transformed the world not as God but as a man, driven by the Holy Spirit in the virgin birth and the baptism of the Holy Spirit in his baptism. Jesus is the model of what believers can do when sold out to God and led by the Holy Spirit. Jesus stated, "These works that I do, greater works shall you do because I go to the Father" (John 14:12). Jesus emphasized that the soon-to-be born-again and filled with the Holy Spirit believers would be able to do what he did, post-Pentecost.

I firmly believe that due to times and seasons, racism, and denominationalism, the doctrine of the Holy Spirit has not been given the balance or fair treatment that the subject and experience require. We see the power and work of the Holy Spirit in both the Older Testament and Newer Testament. However, the work of the Spirit is always hindered by the acts and behaviors of humans who impede the flow of the Holy Spirit. The Holy Spirit is such a dominant player in the affairs of believers that even Jesus stated that you can attack Jesus and be forgiven, but he that blasphemes the Holy Spirit cannot be forgiven (Matt 12:32). So, I want to discuss the ministry of the Holy Spirit and then how the Spirit and the kingdom of God work in tandem with the will of God as demonstrated in the ministry of Jesus.

THE HOLY SPIRIT AND PNEUMATOLOGY

We are living in critical times as Christians. If Jesus does not cut the times short, even the very elect could be deceived (Matt 24:22–24)! We live in a period when people evaluate Christian orthodoxy not based on Scripture but on popularity, publicity, and church size. For instance, if you have a sizable congregation, that is supposedly a sign that God is with you. Others evaluate Christianity based on economics and the Protestant work ethic: "If God's on your side, you're prospering. If you are poor, you must not be in right relationship with God."[1] However, a study of kingdom theology would be incomplete without more insight into God the Holy Spirit. I want us to understand the Holy Spirit and his relationship to the power of the kingdom of God.

My religious background included attending a Black Baptist church and then becoming an associate pastor at a Black Baptist church. Later, I became charismatic and evolved from neo-Pentecostalism to recently kingdom-minded neo-Pentecostalism. My progression to how I identified my faith, in terms of doctrine, has been a spiritual evolution that has always been built upon the firm foundation of the reality, the Person, and the power of the Holy Spirit. The ministry of the Holy Spirit is paramount to any Spirit-filled movement. You cannot experience the existential reality of the kingdom of God without the power and ministry of the Holy Spirit.

It was the power of the Holy Spirit that lifted this high school dropout out of the muck and mire of inner-city conditioning and African American low self-esteem. Indeed, it was the baptism of the Holy Spirit that revolutionized my life. This is one of the reasons that I strongly believe in the power of the Holy Spirit manifesting through a renewal of kingdom theology that expands its borders beyond eschatology and embraces the existential value of kingdom theology. The Holy Spirit is the key to the power of the kingdom that can transform worldwide communities, particularly the Black community. Jesus provides the foundation for our pneumatology through his teachings and modeling.

The Holy Spirit was the basis for the power ministry of Jesus in the first century. The Scriptures teach us that the focus of the ministry of Jesus was the existential message of the kingdom. John the baptizer announced both Jesus and the coming of the kingdom, saying, "Repent

1. For discussion, see Weber, *Protestant Ethic and the Spirit of Capitalism*, 171–72; and Bowler, *Blessed*, 7–9.

for the kingdom of God is ready—are you?" (if you don't mind me paraphrasing).[2] Thus, John ushered in the coming of the Messiah, the Lamb of God, reflecting his twofold kingdom ministry as Lord and Savior. Christ came to establish the kingdom of God among humanity and provide access to the kingdom through his redemptive works of the cross.

It is understood in orthodox Christology through the Scriptures and the church creeds that Christ was both fully God and fully man. Jesus was God incarnate in the flesh, born of a virgin through the power of the Holy Spirit. Thus, as a man, the ministry of Jesus reveals the ministry of the Holy Spirit in his life. He was born by the Holy Spirit. He grew in the spirit by the presence of the Holy Spirit. He was baptized in the Holy Spirit. He was filled with the Holy Spirit. He was led by the Holy Spirit, he did ministry in the power of the Holy Spirit (Luke 4:14), and he was anointed by the Holy Spirit. The Scriptures even state that Jesus rejoiced in the Spirit. Jesus was a Spirit-filled and led man.[3]

Jesus did not perform miracles through his divine nature as the Son of God but through his human nature as the Son of Man. Yet, we must never forget that Jesus had a pure and unblemished soul and spirit that was not connected to the first Adam and the fall of man. He was obedient and had access to an unlimited measure of the power and presence of the Holy Spirit. Jesus did not come to demonstrate what God could do; the universe is proof of that. He came to demonstrate what humans with a new nature could do by the power of the Holy Spirit. Based on the interpretation of Scripture and proper Pentecostal exegesis, my strong position is that Jesus' kingdom ministry and works were the results of the power of the Holy Spirit.

Jesus' ministry focused upon the arrival of the kingdom or the gospel of the kingdom, not simply as an eschatological reality but as an existential reality that ushered the power of the future age of the kingdom of God into the present age. The Scriptures teach that when Jesus began his Galilean ministry, he entered the Jewish synagogues preaching and teaching the gospel of the kingdom. Jesus engaged in the threefold kingdom ministry of proclamation, explanation, and demonstration. He preached the inauguration of the kingdom in his Personhood as the *shaluach* or the sent representative of God. The Scriptures then state that after he preached and taught kingdom principles and values, he demonstrated

2. See Matt 3:2, 4;17; Mark 1:15.

3. Luke 1:35, 80; 3:21–22; 4:1, 14, 18; 10:21.

the power of the kingdom over sickness and disease and healed the sick.[4] Jesus' kingdom ministry impacted the condition of the oppressed people of Israel who were under Roman rule and government.

Jesus himself was from a ghetto of Galilee called Nazareth. Jesus was born in what we would consider a low-income community. It was somewhat offensive to the Pharisees and others to think that the Messiah would have originated in Nazareth. Nazareth, during the time of Jesus, was a small, relatively obscure village in the region of Galilee. Archaeological and historical evidence suggests it was not a large or wealthy settlement. It was considered a humble and modest village, likely with a largely agrarian economy, where people engaged in farming, herding, and small-scale trades.

The perception of Nazareth as a humble place is echoed in the Newer Testament, in the Gospel of John, where Nathanael asked, "Can anything good come out of Nazareth?"[5] This reflects the view that it was not a place of prestige or wealth. While home to several larger and more prosperous towns like Sepphoris and Tiberias, Galilee as a whole was generally more rural and poorer compared to the urban centers of Judea, like Jerusalem.

However, Jesus never forgot where he came from and was intentional about not just preaching to the middle and upper class but also to the poor, neglected, and rejected. When Jesus approached the Jewish population as the people of God, as a whole, they were similar to inner-city dwellers, ridden with many woes as a nation. The Scriptures state that when Jesus looked at the condition of the people, not just spiritually but socially, mentally, financially, and otherwise, he was moved with compassion. In fact, he stated that they were like sheep without a shepherd.[6]

Jesus knew his ministry was holistic and non-exclusive, accessible to anyone regardless of race, class, or gender. He stated that he was anointed to preach the gospel to the poor; he was sent to heal the broken-hearted and proclaim liberty to the captives, recovery of sight to the blind, and to set free those who were oppressed, by proclaiming the year of acceptance or the Year of Jubilee.[7] Jesus' ministry touched all classes and genders. While I'm not a liberation theologian, I do espouse that Jesus had a heart for the poor, which is not a part of the watershed theology of today.

4. Matt 4:23–25; 9:35.
5. John 1:46.
6. Matt 9:36.
7. Luke 4:18–19.

When Jesus wanted to authenticate his ministry qualifications to John and his disciples, he stated, "Go and tell John the things which you hear and see: The blind see and the lame walk; the lepers are cleansed and the deaf hear; the dead are being raised, and the poor have the gospel preached to them. And blessed is he who is not offended because of Me."[8] At the same time, Jesus touched every class and condition of people, including Samaritans and gentiles, such as the Roman centurion. But to emphasize: Jesus' invitation to the kingdom was not just for the wealthy and the healthy; his kingdom message was for everyone regardless of their status and condition. Jesus' invitation to the kingdom was, "Come to Me, all you who labor and are heavy laden, and I will give you rest. Take My yoke upon you and learn from Me, for I am gentle and lowly in heart, and you will find rest for your souls. For My yoke is easy and My burden is light."[9] Jesus used the power of the Holy Spirit to address an oppressed nation under Roman rule, a people who had a history of slavery and colonization. Thus, the message of the kingdom of God allowed Jesus to liberate all of those who would give themselves over to the kingdom.

Jesus' discussion with the Pharisee named Nicodemus, a prominent and middle-class man, focused on the importance of connecting with the Spirit of God before entering the kingdom of God. Jesus' kingdom message was tied to his pneumatology. He told Nicodemus in John 3:1–8 that in order to enter the kingdom of God, he must be born *anothen* (ἄνωθεν) or "from the above world" or "from God" (John 3:31; 19:11, 23).[10] Being born again is an adaptation of the Jewish hope of a new creation.[11] Words with the suffix -θεν answer the question "whence?" or "from where?"[12] The word can also mean "again" or "anew" (Acts 26:5). The translation "reborn from above" includes both meanings of the word.[13] However, this phrase stands in contrast to the belief that being of the seed of Abraham was sufficient.[14] For Jesus, the rights or privileges of seeing and entering the kingdom of God was a work of the Holy Spirit. Thus, Jesus instructed Nicodemus that he must be born of the Holy Spirit and that when one is born of the Holy Spirit, he is under the leadership and control of the

8. Matt 11:4–6.

9. Matt 11:28–30.

10. Carson, "Nicodemus and Jesus."

11. Beasley-Murray, *John*, 47–48.

12. Morris, *Gospel According to John*, 219.

13. Morris, *Gospel According to John*, 219–20.

14. Brown, *Gospel According to John I–XII*, 130–32.

Spirit. For Jesus, entering the kingdom of God involved a spiritual transformation and experience.

Let's discuss the Person of the Holy Spirit so that we can be on the same page about who he is and what he does. In systematic theology, the property of the Father is generation. He is unbegotten, but he begot the Son, and from him the Holy Spirit proceeds. The Father's gifts—eternal life, faith, grace, and the Holy Spirit—are supernaturally distinct and unique because they create the means by which we have a relationship with him. His gifts are preeminent; without them, we have no relationship with God. Thus, the Holy Spirit is a gift of the Father, and only those who desire God holistically receive his gifts.

Many misconceptions exist regarding the identity of the Holy Spirit. For example, while some regard the Spirit as an impersonal, mystical force, others refuse to believe in the Spirit's existence at all. They attribute alleged manifestations of his presence to fanatical hysteria. However, the Bible declares that the Holy Spirit is a divine Person of the triune Godhead, a being with a mind, emotions, and a will, sent by God as a gift to man. Of all the gifts given to humanity by God, the gift of the Holy Spirit, because he is God, is the primary conductor or vehicle by which most spiritual things come to pass for the modern-day believer. Yet, few would likely refer to him as a gift from God. However, Luke, the writer of the book of Acts, quoted Peter as referring to the Holy Spirit in this manner: "Then Peter said to them, 'Repent and let every one of you be baptized in the name of Jesus Christ for the remission of sins, and you shall receive the gift of the Holy Spirit.'"[15]

The Holy Spirit is the catalyst for all godly and spiritual things; Jesus told the disciples that the Holy Spirit "convicts the world of sin, and of righteousness, and of judgment."[16] Thus, the Holy Spirit's presence in the life of the believer follows the act of repentance unto salvation. This presence activates its outcome—the conversion of the spirit of the human, but it also precedes it with conviction. Jesus stated, "And I will pray for the Father, and He will give you another Helper, that He may abide with you forever—the Spirit of truth, whom the world cannot receive because it neither sees Him nor knows Him; but you know Him, for He dwells with you and will be in you."[17]

15. Acts 2:38.

16. John 16:8.

17. John 14:16–17.

The Greek word for "helper" is *paraklétos* (παράκλητος, par-ak'-lay-tos), which is defined as "one summoned or called alongside to render aid; an advocate." Thus, the Holy Spirit was sent by God to assist and render aid to humans. "Comforter," "Counselor," and "Advocate" (Isa 11:2; John 14:16; 15:26; 16:7) are all translations of the Greek word *paraklétos*, from which we get *paraclete*, another name for the Holy Spirit.[18] When Jesus went away, his disciples were greatly distressed because they were about to lose his comforting presence. But he promised that the Father would send another comforter, the Spirit, to comfort, console, and guide those who belong to him.

Before the death, burial, and resurrection of Christ, the Spirit could not and did not constantly abide with the people of Israel. Even though the children of Israel were God's covenant people and participated in animal sacrifice for the remission of sin, there was still a gulf between God and humanity. The Holy Spirit would abide or come upon God's people at will and then return; he was not an ever-abiding presence. However, when Jesus reconciled the world to God, the Holy Spirit became the indweller of believers.[19] Now, the Holy Spirit resides in the hearts of God's people, and that indwelling is the distinguishing characteristic of the regenerated person. From within, the Spirit directs, guides, comforts, and influences us, producing the fruit of the Spirit in us.[20] He provides the intimate connection between God and his children. All true believers in Christ have the Spirit residing in their hearts. I am convinced that this premise has the potential to transform the internal state of the Black community, reshape our thinking, and help to empower us by boosting our self-esteem and confidence.

The apostle Paul wrote in 2 Corinthians 1:22; 5:5 and Ephesians 1:13–14 that the Holy Spirit is a "guarantee" in the hearts of believers, which Christ had promised and secured for us at the cross. The Bible uses three words in this respect—"deposit," "seal," "earnest"—to reflect God's claim on us as his own. Because the Spirit has sealed us, we are assured of our salvation. No one can break the seal of God. The presence of the Holy Spirit can lift the worth of the individual and help them see their value, not through racial eyes, but through the lens of God. The Holy

18. Bauer, Danker, Arndt, and Gingrich, *Greek-English Lexicon of the New Testament and Other Early Christian Literature.*

19. Rom 8:9–11; Eph 2:21–22; 1 Cor 6:19.

20. Gal 5:22–23.

Spirit's presence can revolutionize the mind, heart, and thoughts of the individual. The Holy Spirit also bears witness in three ways:

(1) He bears witness to our human spirit that we are children of God.[21]

(2) He bears witness to the fact that we are saved every time the Word convicts us, when we are baptized in the Holy Spirit, and when we flow in spiritual gifts.[22]

(3) He bears witness to the world that Jesus and the disciples who performed miracles were sent by God,[23] that the books of the Bible are divinely inspired,[24] and that kingdom citizens belong to God when we operate with signs and wonders.[25]

But to whom does the Spirit bear witness? The answer is clear in the context of Romans 8:15, which indicates that our spirits cry, "Abba, Father." So, our witness is to God the Father.[26] This is in keeping with the Older Testament principle that all matters must be established by at least two or three witnesses.

The Holy Spirit is the *Hagios Pneuma* (ἅγιος πνεῦμα [hag-ee-os pnyoo'-mah] in Greek).[27] The adjective "Holy" is used for the Spirit of God because there are a lot of invisibles and intangibles in the spirit realm. But the "Holy" Spirit is separate, and he is sacred. Any other spirit is a defiled spirit. Demons are spirits, but they are unholy. The Bible even tells us that God is a Spirit, and they that worship him must worship him in spirit and truth.[28] +

21. Rom 8:16.

22. Heb 10:15–18.

23. Heb 2:4.

24. 2 Tim 3:16.

25. 2 Cor 4:7.

26. Rom, 8:15.

27. Bauer, Danker, Arndt, and Gingrich, *Greek-English Lexicon of the New Testament and Other Early Christian Literature*, s.v. "πνεῦμα."

28. John 4:24.

But no matter how much you learn the letter of the word, you must have the Spirit of God. He is vital in your walk and relationship with God. We discover in the Scriptures that the power of the Holy Spirit is responsible for placing us in the body of Christ via regeneration, which produces the fruit of the Spirit and positions us to be filled with the Spirit so that the Spirit can lead us.

Geiko Muller-Fahrenholz states that an encounter with the Holy Spirit is a powerful yet gentile experience. He emphasizes how these experiences bring transformation, guidance, and comfort. He further writes that the essential role of the Holy Spirit in the life of the church includes worship, community, and mission. He addresses how the Spirit empowers believers for service and fosters unity among diverse members of the body.[29] Based on this analysis, he concludes that the Spirit can empower people, and for the sake of our context, I include Black empowerment through Pentecostalism. In his work, Muller-Fahrenholz speaks to the contemporary relevance of the Holy Spirit, which lends itself to my thesis that the power of Pentecost can transform communities and, in particular, the Black community. He argues that the relevance and power of the Holy Spirit addresses current issues in society and how the church can engage social injustice, peace, and reconciliation.[30]

This is an important issue when addressing the power of the Holy Spirit in facilitating racial reconciliation, for the Spirit is a catalyst for world change. If the Holy Spirit can facilitate world transformation by people yielding to the Spirit, undoubtedly people empowered by the Spirit can impact the Black community. I'm not talking about idealism; I'm talking about the potential of a twenty-first-century revival that can shake the world and beginning, this time, in one of the most neglected communities in America, the Black community. Muller-Fahrenholz speaks of the mystery of the Spirit and how his presence is both immanent and transcendent, working in ways that are beyond the human intellect or understanding. In his *God's Spirit: Transforming a World in Crisis,* he attempts to deepen readers' understanding and experience of the Holy Spirit. He seeks to challenge and inspire believers to be more attuned to the Spirit's movements and to live in response to the Spirit's divine promptings.[31]

29. Müller-Fahrenholz, *God's Spirit*, 109–10, 135, 144–47.

30. Müller-Fahrenholz, *God's Spirit*, 109–10, 135, 144–47.

31. Müller-Fahrenholz, *God's Spirit*, 87–92, 140–44.

When you take a purely analytical approach to try to have a relationship with God and misunderstand the Holy Spirit, you will miss God. One of the reasons it is so difficult to understand the Holy Spirit is that we see the Father as transcendent and far off in heaven. Additionally, we see the Son as far removed by 2,000 years of history. But, when it comes to the Holy Spirit, unlike the Father and Jesus, he is an invisible Person who is always among us today. Yet, most people have a difficult time qualifying their time with God when it comes to relating to God the Holy Spirit because it is a relationship that requires sensitivity and spiritual discernment. The Holy Spirit challenges people who tend to be too intellectual, rational, or analytical in their relationship with God. It is easier to ritually quote Scripture than to qualify a statement like, "The Spirit of God is moving in me."

There are innumerable things about God that your head will never learn. God is infinite, and we are finite. If God shows us too much of himself, we will have a nervous breakdown trying to understand him! You cannot fully understand God, no matter how sharp and deep you think you are, even though you are made in his image. Thus, people try to avoid things they cannot control intellectually. While it is clear that Jesus moved and performed his ministry by the power of the Holy Spirit, the twenty-first-century church has a difficult time understanding the ministry of the Holy Spirit, even through the lens of Acts, which is about the acts of the Holy Spirit through the apostles and the church.

One of the difficulties in understanding the Holy Spirit, as it relates to the Father and the Son, is that there is more written directly about the Father and the Son than there is about the Holy Spirit. A second difficulty is the lack of concrete imagery about the Holy Spirit. We have analogous human relationships that help us conceptualize the Father and the Son. We know what a father and a son are, but where is our model of a Holy Spirit?

There is so much profundity in the working and moving of the Spirit of God. Acts 8:26–40 describes how Philip baptized the Ethiopian eunuch. When Philip emerged from baptizing the eunuch, the Spirit of the Lord "caught Philip away" (v. 39) and transported him to the Gaza Strip somewhere. This is like a *Star Trek* episode! Mind you, this was not the Older Testament; this was a Newer Testament phenomenon! The Spirit of God had the ability to take a man's natural body and make it appear whole in another place. What is the science behind God transporting

Philip within time but outside of time from one geographical location to another? No one knows.

Philip traveled from Jerusalem to Ashdod, which would have equated to thirty miles from the Gaza Strip to Ashdod or Azotus, and in a millisecond.[32] The Holy Spirit confounded technology with a supernatural form of transportation. This should tell us that we have never scratched the surface of what the Holy Ghost can do! I don't believe that we have seen or experienced the potential power of the Holy Spirit to transform the world in the twenty-first century. So, I ask, why can't the Holy Spirit transform individuals in the Black community and empower them to progress in economic and community development through the power of his Spirit? The Holy Spirit assisted Philip and those after him in taking the gospel from Jerusalem, Judea, Samaria, to the uttermost parts of the world for the sake of evangelism. Revival is about preaching the gospel of the kingdom around the world (Matthew 24:14).

The Bible declares that the Holy Spirit is a Person who has a personality. He's not just a force; he is a Person, and the Bible uses masculine pronouns to identify him! For example, Jesus said, "However, when He, the Spirit of truth, has come, He will guide you into all truth; for He will not speak on His own authority, but whatever He hears He will speak; and He will tell you things to come. He will glorify Me, for He will take of what is Mine and declare it to you. All things that the Father has are Mine. Therefore, I said that He will take of Mine and declare it to you."[33]

- The Holy Spirit is intelligent:
  - » *For it seemed good to the Holy Spirit, and to us, to lay upon you no greater burden than these necessary things. . .*[34]
  - » The Holy Spirit has a will:
  - » *Now, when they had gone through Phrygia and the region of Galatia, they were forbidden by the Holy Spirit to preach the word in Asia.*[35]
- The Holy Spirit has feelings:
  - » *But they rebelled and grieved His Holy Spirit, so He turned Himself against them as an enemy, and He fought against them.*[36]

32. Bruce, *Book of Acts*, 188–89.
33. John 16:13–15.
34. Acts 15:28.
35. Acts 16:6.
36. Isa 63:10.

   - » *And do not grieve the Holy Spirit of God, by whom you were sealed for the day of redemption.*[37]
   - » *You can vex or grieve the Holy Spirit! You can get on the Holy Ghost's nerves. (When the Scripture says that we should not grieve the Holy Spirit,*[38] *it uses language to indicate how God feels about a given behavior. It's not like God is surprised. This same thing applies when the Scripture says God repented that he made humanity (Gen 6:6). God is immutable! He is omniscient! He knows what man will do, but he put that language in place to help us understand how he feels emotionally about our behavior. Thus, when you grieve the Holy Ghost, it's not like he was expecting something else from you. He knew when he chose you that you would grieve him!)*[39]

- The Holy Spirit glorifies the Son:
   - » *However, when He, the Spirit of truth, has come, He will guide you into all truth, for He will not speak on His own authority, but whatever He hears, He will speak, and He will tell you things to come. He will glorify Me, for He will take of what is Mine and declare it to you. All things that the Father has are Mine. Therefore I said that He will take of Mine and declare it to you.*[40]
   - » *John 14:26 refers to the Holy Spirit as a "Comforter."*[41] *In Greek, "Comforter" means paraklétos (παράκλητος),*[42] *or "helper; one called alongside to help, one who appears on another's behalf, advocate, defender, helper, counselor, or intercessor." The Bible says He will teach us "all things."*[43] *Still, you cannot simply open and understand a text without exegesis. But the Holy Spirit can teach you and give you discernment on how Scripture should be applied to your life with the proper understanding.*

- The Holy Spirit speaks:

37. Eph 4:30.

38. Eph 4:30.

39. Eph 4:30.

40. John 16:13–15.

41. John 14:26.

42. Bauer, Danker, Arndt, and Gingrich, *Greek-English Lexicon of the New Testament and Other Early Christian Literature*, s.v. "παράκλητος."

43. John 14:26.

- *"He who has an ear, let him hear what the Spirit says to the churches. To him who overcomes I will give to eat from the tree of life, which is in the midst of the Paradise of God."*[44]
- *Some people have never been taught that the Holy Spirit can speak. Others try to hear the Holy Ghost without living a spiritual life. This is because they don't have the word in their lives yet are trying to hear "a voice."*[45] *People have breakdowns because of this! When you start talking about living a spiritual life and listening to the Spirit, you're talking about a serious matter that cannot be played with. An untrained ear can listen to the wrong spirit.*
- *A popular adage says it's okay if you start hearing voices, but you only have a problem when you start talking back to them! "He who has an ear to hear, let him hear" is stated in Matthew 11:15, and the almost identical wording is in Mark 4:9 and Revelation 2:7. It means that he who has spiritual sensitivity should hear what the Spirit is saying. The Holy Spirit is trying to lead and speak to you, but if you are inundated with carnality, overwhelmed with concerns of your flesh and natural provisions, you cannot hear the Spirit. All you can hear is the intellect.*
- *The Bible says that "There is a way that seems right unto man, but the end thereof is destruction."*[46] *You must learn how to hear the Spirit of God. A kingdom citizen should not desire to go anywhere that the Holy Spirit does not lead them. The Bible says, "For as many as are led by the Spirit of God, these are sons of God."*[47] *That speaks of a submissive attitude towards the voice of God. A believer should say to themselves, "If God is leading me, He is not going to take me any place that He's not been first." This is the whole concept of shepherding. A shepherd goes before the sheep. So, any place the Spirit leads you, you can be assured that it will lead you to heaven. That's why we can say, like David said, "Yea, though I walk through the valley of the shadow of death, I will fear no evil, for You are with me"* [48]

44. Rev 2:7.
45. Ervin, *Spirit Baptism*, 73–76.
46. Prov 14:12 .
47. Rom 8:14.
48. Ps 23:4.

- The Holy Spirit teaches us:
  - » *But the Helper, the Holy Spirit, whom the Father will send in My name, He will teach you all things, and bring to your remembrance all things that I said to you.*[49]
  - » *The Holy Spirit can teach us "all" things; therefore, Jesus told his hearers that all things are possible to those who believe.*[50]
  - » *For what man knows the things of a man, except the spirit of the man which is in him. Even so, no one knows the things of God except the Spirit of God.*[51]
- The Holy Spirit guides us:
  - » *However, when He, the Spirit of truth, has come, He will guide you into all truth, for He will not speak on His own authority, but whatever He hears, He will speak, and He will tell you things to come.*[52]
  - » *The Holy Spirit is well-cultured and understands every person's situation and context. The Holy Spirit can help us figure it out or instruct and guide us in the ways of deliverance and emancipation of the oppressed if we adhere to his voice.*

THE WORK OF THE HOLY SPIRIT

In the Older Testament, the work of the Holy Spirit is seen in creation in Genesis 1:2 when it says, "the Spirit hovered." When there was a prophetic word, the Holy Spirit would give prophecy, as seen in Ezekiel 2:2; 8:3; 11:1, 24 and 1 Samuel 10:6, 10. The Holy Spirit gifted people for various tasks (Exod 31:3–5, Zech 4:6) like the gifts for administration (Gen 41:38, Num 11:25, Deut 34:9). In the era of the judges, it was the moving of the Spirit that gave them power for service. They were not judges in the judicial sense; instead, they were charismatic figures upon whom the Holy Spirit would come, and they would do mighty exploits in the name of the Lord, and then the Spirit would leave (Judg 3:10; 6:34). The Holy Spirit would endow the kings for service (1 Sam 10:10; 16:13; Neh 9:20;

49. John 14:26.
50. Mark 9:23.
51. 1 Cor 2:11.
52. John 16:13.

Ps 143:10; 51:11; Isa 63:10). It was the work of the Holy Spirit that convicted and changed the lives of the people as they prophesied (Isa 11:2–5; 32:15–20; Ezek 36:26–28). In the days to come, a more prominent role of the Spirit was prophesied—"I will pour out My Spirit upon all flesh" (Joel 2:28–29).

Three very important aspects of the Spirit's work are Pentecost (Acts 2), the fruit of the Spirit (Gal 5:22–23), and the gifts of the Spirit (1 Cor 12). The Holy Spirit changed the Jewish nation forever because, on Pentecost, he came upon Jewish believers from all over the world. Paul, speaking of the power of the Holy Spirit in a supernatural way, stated that the "Spirit helps us in our infirmities."[53] It was a Jewish expectation that when the Messiah came, he would have healing in the hem of his garments and that he would overpower the Roman government through the power of the age to come or the kingdom age. Through his disciples, John the Baptist asked if Jesus was the Christ (Messiah) or if they should look for another. Jesus answered and said to them, "Go and tell John the things which you hear and see: The blind see and the lame walk; the lepers are cleansed and the deaf hear; the dead are being raised, and the poor have the gospel preached to them. And blessed is he who is not offended because of Me."[54]

We do not have a dictatorial and non-compassionate King. He can sympathize with our infirmities and knows what it means to suffer. Christ was incarnated, not voted into his position. He has walked in our shoes and knows what it means to be tempted and tried as we are. He related not simply to the middle and upper class, but was concerned about the lower class or the poor. Therefore, when you ask him, "Have mercy on me,"[55] he can be merciful. The power and authority of the King sets people free from their infirmities—spiritually, physically, and socially.

Paul also wrote, "My grace is sufficient for you,"[56] which points to the simple ability to forgive weaknesses and the power to help us through every situation by the power of the Holy Spirit. As a principle, Paul wrote, "My strength is made perfect in weakness. Therefore, most gladly, I will rather boast in my infirmities that the power of Christ may rest upon me. Therefore, I take pleasure in infirmities, reproaches, needs, persecutions, distresses, for Christ's sake. For when I am weak, then I am strong" (2

53. Rom 8:26.

54. Matt 1:2–6.

55. Matt 9:27, Mark 10:47, Luke 18:38.

56. 2 Cor 12:9.

Cor 12:9–10). I believe we have not allowed the power of the Holy Spirit to be at work in challenging situations outside of the work of salvation, sanctification, and anticipated glorification.

We must not lock the Holy Spirit into a box based upon examples found only in the Scriptures, because the Holy Spirit is relevant today. Just because we don't see works of the Holy Spirit in the Bible that we can clearly identify doesn't limit the Holy Spirit in the twenty-first century. William J. Seymour witnessed many miracles, such as people playing musical instruments without any lessons. These accounts are part of the larger narrative of the Azusa revival, emphasizing the extraordinary and supernatural experiences reported by participants. The miracles we see in the Scriptures were the miracles needed then. But everything that the Holy Spirit is capable of was not noted in Scripture, and we must not limit the power and ability of the Holy Spirit. Therefore, I believe that the Holy Spirit can provide supernatural acts and works that are needed today that were not needed during biblical days.

The Holy Spirit can work in many different ways to manifest healing in the lives of people! Notice that the Bible mentions "gifts of healings."[57] We use the plural of this because the gifts of healings are what the Holy Spirit has in diversity. He has different kinds of healings: the gift of healing might manifest over cancer in one moment, AIDS in another moment, asthma in the next moment. At those moments, people will be cured of that particular illness. Because these gifts belong to the Spirit, they manifest, they work, and then they go away.

THE EARLY CHURCH'S PERSPECTIVE OF THE HOLY SPIRIT

The book of Acts informs us that, in the early church, the apostles and the laypeople held the Holy Spirit in divine esteem. The book of Acts serves as a history book of the Newer Testament church. It marks our beginning, our Pentecost, and our spread to Jerusalem, Judea, Samaria, and the ends of the earth. When we look at the book of Acts, we see that the Holy Spirit played a tremendous role in the spread of the gospel. It can be argued that the book should not be called the "Acts of the Apostles." It should be called the "Acts of the Holy Spirit working through the Apostles"!

57. 2 Cor 12:28.

It has been said that the book of Acts can be summed up in three words: ascension, descension, and extension. Christ ascended, the Holy Ghost descended, and the church extended to Jerusalem, Judea, Samaria, and the ends of the earth.[58] This verse of Scripture can serve as a table of contents for the book of Acts:

- Chapters 1–7 Jerusalem and Judea
- Chapter 8 Samaria
- Chapters 8–10 and beyond (uttermost parts, beginning with Philip and the Ethiopian Eunuch and extending to Peter in Rome in the house of Cornelius)[59]

Is this a coincidence? Absolutely not! The Holy Spirit is still working throughout the uttermost parts of the world. We are a part of the book of Acts. Its fulfillment has never stopped—it is still being written. It is picking up lives, eras, and dispensations, and we are continuously a part of that tremendous work with God.

Beginning with the patristics (the so-called church fathers and mothers), there have always been Christians who believed in the work and power of the Holy Spirit. During the patristic era, which is divided into three periods and starts at the time of the apostles and extends to the mid-eighth century, creeds gave each of the three persons of the Godhead equal status. In the Nicene Creed, the deity of Christ was established.[60] In the Constantinople Creed, the deity of the Holy Spirit was established.[61] Then, Athanasius gave us a Trinitarian creed. Finally, the Chalcedon and Ephesus Creeds addressed Christ's two natures and union to help us further clarify who he is.[62] These creeds also make clearer the belief that the Holy Spirit is God. God the Holy Spirit is still working among believers on earth for the glory of God; there has never been a total silencing of the work, gifts, and power of the Holy Spirit.

As Christians, we tend to honor God the Father and glorify God the Son but totally neglect God the Holy Spirit! Many churches are stagnant to this day because every week, they go to the cross to celebrate what Jesus did—and that's where they stop! The problem is that the salvation story

58. Acts 1:8.

59. Acts 1:8.

60. Kelly, *Early Christian Doctrines*, 233.

61. Kelly, *Early Christian Doctrines*, 251.

62. Kelly, *Early Christian Doctrines*, 310–15, 339–42.

doesn't stop with the cross! It doesn't stop at "Jesus got up, and he's got all power!" What ends up happening is that we celebrate the resurrection but don't participate in the Great Commission; but both are the result of the working of the Spirit. Therefore, the church tends to celebrate Jesus for dying for our sins, but we don't realize the role that the Holy Spirit plays in our regeneration. Why? I believe it is because we celebrate Christ as Savior but do not submit to him as Lord. We preach the cross and ignore the crown. We do not embrace Christ as Lord; we simply celebrate him as Savior.

It's only after you know Jesus as Lord that you genuinely understand the role of the Holy Spirit in your life. This makes kingdom theology of the utmost importance, for it examines the importance of honoring the rule and reign of God as King and not simply as Savior. Because many Black church services today focus on lifting the people, we thank Jesus for being Savior, but we ignore his Lordship. Knowing God as Savior causes us to praise but not be obedient to his Lordship, which tells us to spread the gospel of the kingdom around the world as a witness. The challenge of the contemporary church today is to stop simply celebrating the historical power of the Holy Spirit but also to embrace the existential power of the Holy Spirit!

We have come to celebrate the resurrection while ignoring the fact that Jesus was raised by the power of the Holy Spirit.[63] We have learned to celebrate the resurrection of Jesus apart from the kingdom mission and power of the source of the resurrection, who was the Holy Spirit. The Great Commission is an option in the contemporary church, where we simply celebrate the reality of the resurrection but not the purpose of the resurrection. I believe this reality is due to what I call "watershed theology."[64] In short, we have learned to interpret the Scriptures through the lens of Westernized thought, not through the lens of Second Temple Judaism and the kingdom message of Jesus. According to the Scriptures, the mission of Jesus was to preach, teach, and demonstrate the kingdom.[65] The Great Commission is an extension of the ministry of Jesus—he died for our sins, and we live for his kingdom mission!

63. Rom 8:11.

64. Carson, *Five Watersheds.*

65. Matt 4:23; 9:35.

5

The Kingdom as a Global Experience and Empowerment

THE FIRST TIME I traveled to Johannesburg, South Africa, I was mesmerized by the strong Pentecostal presence I encountered, especially the "Seymourites," followers of William J. Seymour. I was totally impressed with the work that Seymour had done there. At that time, several thousand Seymourites claimed their spiritual origin in the founder of the Azusa Street Revival in 1906. It felt like a page out of history as they told me stories about what they experienced and were told. It helped me understand the global significance of the Azusa experience, even as I knew that many had come from different parts of the world to experience the outpouring of the Holy Spirit. I learned that Azusa was not simply an experience but a global movement that had not just touched the world but changed it.

I was in South Africa working with several leaders and hosting a kingdom leadership conference. We talked about how the kingdom was a global experience, and empowerment was the original intent of God. God has always been concerned not just about Israel but the entire world. Abraham, the father of the faith in Judaism, Christianity, and Islam, was given a global vision. In Genesis 12, God told him that "all the nations" of the world would be blessed through him.[1] Though God began the process of globalization with Abraham, Isaac, and Jacob, he always had the gentile world in mind as well.

1. Gen 12:1–3.

Paul stated that the gospel was for the Jew first and then the gentile (Romans 1:16–17). The gospel was intended to offer salvation to the entire world, as many as would receive him. The gospel of Christ is synonymous with the gospel of the kingdom, and the good news of God's reign is meant for the whole world. From a Pentecostal perspective, the kingdom of God and the concept of globalization are intricately connected, reflecting both theological priorities and practical engagements by Pentecostal communities worldwide. This chapter will explore how Pentecostal churches can interpret the kingdom of God in the context of globalization and how they can engage constructively within this global framework.

THE KINGDOM IS A GLOBAL MESSAGE

When we examine the Scriptures, we understand that the plan of salvation began with the Semitic people of the Bible and, as mentioned, the patriarch Abraham. God began his plan of salvation by selecting Semitic people and forming a covenant with them, calling them a kingdom of priests (Exod 19:6).[2] While we know that salvation is unto the Jew first, it is also to the gentile. Though Jesus stated that he came to his own, all that believed upon his name would be saved (John 1:11–12).[3] Salvation was always a global plan of God that had to begin somewhere. Thus, God chose a people to cut covenant with in order to save the world.

God told Abraham that in him, all the nations of the world would be blessed (Genesis 12:3). One could become a Jew by way of circumcision, observation of the Torah, and participation in the feasts. Non-Jews were proselytized and converted to Judaism by adhering to the covenantal laws of God as prescribed in the Torah. Torah was considered the yoke of the kingdom. Later, Jesus told the disciples to make disciples everywhere they went. Indeed, the disciples, apostles, and the universal church's commission is to take the gospel of the kingdom around the world as a witness to the nations (Matt 28:19–20; 24:14; Mark 16:19–20; Luke 24:49; John 21:15–19; Acts 1:8).

The gospel of the kingdom was not to be hindered by culture, ethnicity, race, language, class, or gender. Thus, on Pentecost, the power of the Holy Spirit penetrated global barriers. The Scriptures state:

2. Exod 19:6.
3. John 1:11–12.

> And there were dwelling in Jerusalem Jews, devout men, from every nation under heaven. And when this sound occurred, the multitude came together and were confused, because everyone heard them speak in his own language. Then they were all amazed and marveled, saying to one another, "Look, are not all these who speak Galileans? And how is it that we hear, each in our own language, in which we were born? Parthians and Medes and Elamites, those dwelling in Mesopotamia, Judea and Cappadocia, Pontus and Asia, Phrygia and Pamphylia, Egypt and the parts of Libya adjoining Cyrene, visitors from Rome, both Jews and proselytes, Cretans and Arabs—we hear them speaking in our own tongues the wonderful works of God." So they were all amazed and perplexed, saying to one another, "Whatever could this mean?" (Acts 2:5–11)

When the Holy Spirit was released on Pentecost, he fell on everyone who believed. Those who were baptized began breaking barriers of language and gender and doing the supernatural. Somewhat illiterate people became linguists on the spot in order to effectively communicate God's message in different foreign languages that were represented from the Jewish diaspora. We must understand that God desires to reach every person where they are before we begin limiting the power of the Holy Spirit. No one, including the disciples, was expecting glossolalic speech in the form of tongues of angels or people. But the Holy Spirit broke global barriers of speech on day one, in my estimation, to express to the church its global mission and the call to communicate to every person in a way they can relate to the message, even if it requires supernatural power. The power of the kingdom message and mission gives me great confidence that the kingdom of God has the power to transform communities that will yield themselves to him. I am convinced that Pentecostalism and its kingdom power emphasis can impact and empower Black and Brown communities globally.

As previously noted, Acts 1–8 can serve as a table of contents for the entire book of Acts because it demonstrates how the gospel spread from Jerusalem, Judea, and Samaria, and, in chapter 8, to the ends of the earth, beginning with the Ethiopian eunuch.[4] It's fascinating that God began the spread of the gospel in the kingdom with the African gentiles. Church tradition suggests Philip evangelized the Ethiopian eunuch named

4. See Bruce, *Book of Acts*, 36–37.

"Judich" from the kingdom of Meroe. He is believed to be the founder of the Coptic Church, which is the oldest Christian church in the world.[5]

Africa has always served as a special place in the heart and geography of God. Africa is mentioned in the garden of Eden, among the sons of Noah, and during the exodus and promised land narrative (proselytized Egyptians, Jethro, Zipporah, etc.).[6] God mentioned Egypt as his people in Isaiah 19:25: "whom the Lord of hosts shall bless, saying, 'Blessed is Egypt, My people, and Assyria the work of My hands, and Israel My inheritance.'" Africa and Africans have always seemed to play an important role in the covenant of God. In the Newer Testament, Mary and Joseph hid the baby Jesus in Egypt. And Simon the Cyrene from Africa was chosen to bear the cross of Christ on the road to Golgotha. During the patristic period, Africans played a crucial role in the foundation of Christian thought and doctrine before the Muslim crusades. These North African leaders in the church, some of whom attended the school of Alexandria in Egypt, included the black dwarf, Athanasius, Augustine, Cyprian, and others.[7] If it were not for African participation in the fight against heresy, we could not even imagine where Christianity would be.

In the book *Pentecostal Spirituality: A Passion for the Kingdom*, Steven Land argues that Pentecostalism places significant emphasis on the kingdom of God, interpreting it as both a present reality and a future hope. Central to Pentecostal belief is the transformative power of the Holy Spirit, who empowers believers to live in accordance with kingdom values—such as justice, peace, and love—and to spread the gospel message globally. Land indicates that Pentecostals view the kingdom as already manifesting through the work of the Holy Spirit in individuals and communities but also anticipate its full realization upon Christ's return.[8] The Pentecostal expression produces a vibrant spirituality that suggests a personal and communal experience with God's presence, a taste of the kingdom on earth that fosters a sense of immediacy and expectancy in believers' lives. From a Pentecostal perspective, the kingdom of God offers social impact by coupling spiritual empowerment and social action, positioning itself as an agent of change and justice aligned with kingdom principles. The Pentecostal church and the power of the Holy Spirit can offer change in a global context.

5. Carson, *One True King*, 91.
6. Oden, *How Africa Shaped the Christian Mind*, 31–36.
7. Oden, *How Africa Shaped the Christian Mind*, 43–58.
8. Land, *Pentecostal Spirituality*, 118–27.

Globalization, characterized by increased interconnectedness and cultural exchange, presents both opportunities and challenges for churches. For Pentecostalism, which is inherently global due to its rapid growth and spread, globalization offers a unique potential for mission and influence. Global interconnectedness accelerates the dissemination of Pentecostal beliefs and practices, using technology and media to reach diverse populations.

Peter White observes that immigrant communities often become focal points for Pentecostal mission work, enhancing cross-cultural exchanges. He postulates that Pentecostal churches engage with a multiplicity of cultural expressions, facilitating a diverse worship experience that embraces various languages, music styles, and communal forms. Not only do Pentecostal churches engage in cultural exchange, but they are also involved in global social engagement.[9]

In facing global challenges such as poverty and injustice, Pentecostal communities often partner with international NGOs, advocating for transformative social justice initiatives aligned with kingdom values. Pentecostal churches constantly face the global landscape's pluralistic nature, which poses questions about maintaining doctrinal orthodoxy while dialoguing with other faith traditions and secular cultures. However, when we examine the global call to ministry to take the gospel worldwide, the early church faced the same challenge, if not more so. The Spirit of God will help the church to overcome these barriers and transform deviant beliefs. Pentecostal churches must actively engage globalization through varied mission strategies that reflect their dynamic and adaptive characteristics.

Adeneken-Koevoets suggests that the following strategies can impact the global communities from a Pentecostal perspective:

(1) Church Planting and Development Initiatives—Planting churches in diverse regions remains a primary mode of expansion. These efforts often emphasize local leadership and contextualized expressions of worship and organizational structure.

(2) Media and Technology—Pentecostals utilize television, radio, and the internet to spread the gospel, offering online services and media broadcasts that transcend physical boundaries.

9. White, "Pentecostalism and Migration."

(3) Education and Training—Bible schools and training centers equip believers with theological and practical skills necessary for effective ministry, fostering leadership development in global contexts.

(4) Diaspora Networks—Addressing the diasporic nature of many modern communities, Pentecostal churches often function as hubs for migrants, providing both spiritual community and material support.[10]

I have had firsthand experience and can validate that Pentecostal churches are engaging in these strategies or similar ones. My ministry has supported and helped to establish orphanages in the Philippines, and I founded a school in Nairobi, Kenya, providing Bible training for pastors and leaders. We are now trying to establish capacity-building institutions in Liberia and theological and leadership institutions in South Africa. Our experience and initiatives are not unique. The future of Pentecostalism in the globalized world is wide open. Pentecostalism's global expansion continues to reshape the religious landscape, driven by its adaptable approach to the kingdom of God in a dynamic world.

As Pentecostalism in a global world has the opportunity to impact countries worldwide, its potential to shape global culture, politics, and society increases, advocating for policies and practices in line with a holistic understanding of God's kingdom. Carrying the gospel of the kingdom around the world, Pentecostals will have the opportunity to have interfaith dialogue. It will allow the Pentecostal church to engage respectfully with other faith traditions and contribute constructively to broader peace-building initiatives, offering Spirit-led reconciliation and understanding. Lastly, the vibrancy and energy of Pentecostalism can profoundly affect youth. Pentecostalism, as a movement, appeals mainly to younger populations. Pentecostal churches continue to attract youth through vibrant worship and meaningful engagement with global issues, shaping future generations.

From a Pentecostal perspective, the kingdom of God unfolds dynamically amid globalization—inviting believers to participate actively in world transformation while maintaining faithfulness to spiritual truths. Through intentional engagement, Pentecostalism aligns its profound spiritual experiences with initiatives that meet the pressing needs of the

10. Adenekan-Koevoets, "Nigerian Pentecostal Diasporic Missions and Missionary Churches in Europe."

global community, guided by a vision of God's kingdom that transcends borders and languages.

AFRICANS AND AFRICAN AMERICANS NETWORKING AND SUPPORT

The disconnection of people of African descent in the diaspora from their homeland due to the transatlantic slave trade has led to numerous significant consequences. Yet, Black empowerment does not have to be domestically focused. The majority of Black people are not aware of how broad the African diaspora was and how intentional it was that Blacks stayed separated from one another. The Black Pentecostal church can empower the continent of Africa in light of the diaspora. While globalization includes all six inhabitable continents, it is well known that the continent of Africa is having church growth explosions, growing by leaps and bounds in comparison to the churches in North America.

The Black diaspora is critical when discussing the Black Pentecostal church, the kingdom of God, and empowerment. Black Pentecostalism is poised and structured for a tremendous global movement due to the strategic placement of Blacks in Africa and the entire Western hemisphere (North, Central, and South America). During the African diaspora, enslaved Africans were sold and transported to various regions across the Americas, including North America, Latin America, the Caribbean, South America, and Europe. Slaves were sold in the following places:

The Caribbean Islands

- Barbados, one of the earliest British colonies to develop a plantation economy reliant on slave labor, primarily for sugar production. Jamaica, another major site of sugar plantations under British rule, had a large enslaved African population.[11]
- Saint-Dominique (now Haiti), a French colony that, at its peak, was one of the wealthiest due to its sugar, coffee, and indigo plantations worked by enslaved Africans.[12]

11. Klein and Vinson III, *African Slavery in Latin America and the Caribbean*, 77–85.

12. Klein and Vinson III, *African Slavery*, 112–18.

- Cuba, which was known for its sugar plantations, became a significant destination for enslaved Africans, especially in the nineteenth century.[13]
- Puerto Rico, which was under Spanish rule, also participated in the slave trade, though on a smaller scale.[14]
- Trinidad and Tobago, initially under Spanish and then British control, engaged in plantation agriculture depending on enslaved labor.[15]

Central and South America

- Brazil, the largest single destination for Africans during the transatlantic slave trade, was primarily used for sugar and coffee plantations, as well as gold mining.[16]
- Colombia and Venezuela had African slaves who worked in agriculture and mining.[17]
- Guyana and Suriname, which are known for plantations producing crops like sugar and coffee, were heavily reliant on African slave labor.[18]

North America

- The British Colonies (later the United States) and eastern and southern colonies had extensive plantations, especially in Virginia, South Carolina, and Georgia, focusing on tobacco, rice, and indigo.[19]
- French Louisiana, which focused on sugar and indigo plantations, later became a part of the United States.[20]

13. Klein and Vinson III, *African Slavery*, 155–63.
14. Klein and Vinson III, *African Slavery*, 163–67.
15. Klein and Vinson III, *African Slavery*, 167–70.
16. Klein and Vinson III, *African Slavery*, 51–72, 130–45.
17. Klein and Vinson III, *African Slavery*, 145–54.
18. Klein and Vinson III, *African Slavery* , 170–77.
19. Berlin, *Many Thousands Gone*, 69–105.
20. Hall, *Africans in Colonial Louisiana*, 45–68.

Europe

- Though Europe did not have slave plantations, arrivals of enslaved Africans were evident in domestic labor or through servitude arrangements. Various ports in countries like Portugal, Spain, and England participated in the trade economy. Liverpool, Bristol, Lisbon, and Seville were key cities involved.[21]

The process of slave trading was quite involved, and there were routes and markets that supported the diaspora. Specific ports on the West African coasts specialized in handling slave products, such as Elmina, Whydah, Gorée, and Bonny. These ports were major starting points for slave ships.[22] They were transported to enslavement centers, which were marketplaces where slaves were sold, either in these ports or the hinterlands, ensuring that captive Africans could be "processed" and sent on to their destinations overseas.[23]

These various regions reflect the widespread reach of the transatlantic slave trade and the integral role that enslaved Africans played in the development of economies across the Americas and beyond. The legacy of this diaspora is still evident today in the diverse cultural and demographic compositions of these regions. The greatness of the cultures of which they boast is due to the free labor that cost millions of lives and the perceived sublevel status of Black people.

When we consider the impact of Black people who were dispersed around the world and treated like animals or some subpar species, I contend that not just the Black Pentecostal church should be involved in a specific movement to empower Blacks, but the entire church should be involved. When we consider the significant role that people of color played in church history and how the institutions in North Africa preserved the doctrine of the Christian faith, the church owes a profound debt and deep compassion. More attention is needed toward a culture that has helped many other cultures, yet no one has helped them as a whole.

The Jewish Holocaust was a tragedy among tragedies, yet the Jews were able to recover as a people because they were able to return to their homeland. They regained a sense of identity, pride, and dignity rooted

21. Eltis and Richardson, *Atlas of the Transatlantic Slave Trade*, 12–20.

22. Eltis and Richardson, *Atlas of the Transatlantic Slave Trade*, 22–35.

23. Thomas, *Slave Trade*, 165–72.

in their history and hope. We are encouraged by the Scriptures to pray for the peace of Jerusalem, and thus, we are compelled to do so. But the Scripture also instructs us to preach the gospel to the poor and to set the captives free.

It is my strong conviction and prophetic understanding that Egypt (Africa) is in a unique position with God, as mentioned in Isaiah 19:18–25. I have noted a portion of this passage earlier, but here let me quote it in full:

> In that day, five cities in the land of Egypt will speak the language of Canaan and swear by the Lord of hosts; one will be called the City of Destruction. In that day, there will be an altar to the Lord in the midst of the land of Egypt and a pillar to the Lord at its border. And it will be for a sign and for a witness to the Lord of hosts in the land of Egypt; for they will cry to the Lord because of the oppressors, and He will send them a Savior and a Mighty One, and He will deliver them. Then the Lord will be known to Egypt, and the Egyptians will know the Lord in that day and will make sacrifice and offering; yes, they will make a vow to the Lord and perform it. And the Lord will strike Egypt, He will strike and heal it; they will return to the Lord, and He will be entreated by them and heal them. In that day, there will be a highway from Egypt to Assyria, and the Assyrian will come into Egypt and the Egyptian into Assyria, and the Egyptians will serve with the Assyrians. In that day, Israel will be one of three with Egypt and Assyria—a blessing in the midst of the land, whom the Lord of hosts shall bless, saying, "Blessed is Egypt My people, and Assyria the work of My hands, and Israel My inheritance."

The Bible mentions Africa and Ethiopia in various contexts, including prophecy, historical narratives, and poetic passages. One prominent mention of Ethiopia in a prophetic and poetic context is in Psalm 68:31. This verse is often quoted as "Ethiopia shall stretch out her hands unto God." It is a declaration that signifies a future where Ethiopia turns to worship God. This is symbolic of African or gentile nations recognizing and praising God. Another notable mention is found in the book of Isaiah, where Ethiopia is referenced in multiple passages. Isaiah 18 describes a prophecy concerning Ethiopia, often depicted as a land "beyond the rivers of Cush" (Cush typically refers to areas south of Egypt, including parts of Africa like modern-day Sudan and Ethiopia).

Isaiah 20:4 also refers to Assyria leading Cushite (Ethiopian) and Egyptian captives as a sign, further tying Ethiopia into biblical prophecy. While Africa is not Israel and does not share the same destiny as Israel, she seems to have a prophetic moment when she will return to the Lord and be blessed, but in the end, she may fall because of her blessings.[24] However, God declared that Africa and African people, while being slanderously accused of having the curse of Ham upon them, will have God's hand upon them. As mentioned in earlier chapters, Africans have served a tremendous purpose in the plan of God.[25]

The diaspora came with a consequence of disconnectedness. Black people, in a global and national sense, have suffered from a loss of cultural identity. Many African diasporic communities have experienced a loss or dilution of specific cultural practices, languages, and connections to ancestral histories. This significant loss in a world that boasts racial superiority both directly and indirectly impacts Black self-esteem. The diaspora has also brought with its historical trauma the forced separation and subsequent conditions of slavery and colonialism, which have contributed to enduring psychological and societal traumas.[26]

The diaspora has caused global poverty for Black people and the descendants of the African diaspora. Today, Black people face glaring economic disparities. The displacement and systemic discrimination have often resulted in economic disenfranchisement and reduced opportunities for wealth accumulation within Black communities. The social disconnection of Black people has created social fragmentation.[27] This suggests that cultural disconnection can lead to challenges in forming a shared identity or common cause among people of African descent globally. Blacks in different regions that have the same historical background and victims of the diaspora and slave trade no longer see themselves as related to one another.

I believe that the lack of awareness of Black history impairs the Black intellect and education by creating educational gaps. Limited awareness or education about African history and contributions can perpetuate narratives of inadequacy and dependency and cause one to wonder about how they got into their situation and status in life. I believe that God has a

24. Ezra 30:4–6.

25. Carson, *Kingdom, Globalization and You*, 87–95.

26. Manning, *African Diaspora*, 196–202.

27. Manning, *African Diaspora*, 200–204; Darity Jr. and Mullen, *From Here to Equality*, 35–48.

special purpose for those whom he allowed to experience the most brutal form of slavery that the world has ever known.

The Black Pentecostal church and African and African American networks can produce Black empowerment on a global level that involves collaboration for mutual benefits, particularly in business. The following are some empowering strategies and ways in which African Americans and Africans can collaborate for mutual benefits, particularly in business through reconnection.

(1) Cultural Exchange and Education: Initiatives promoting learning and sharing cultural history can strengthen identity and solidarity. This can be achieved through exchange programs, heritage tours, and cultural festivals celebrating African traditions.[28] My Pentecostal church employs this strategy to foster educational empowerment, which leads to economic empowerment.

(2) Genealogical Research: Tools and services that help individuals trace their ancestry and understand their ethnic roots can foster a sense of belonging and personal empowerment.[29]

(3) Diaspora Engagement Policies: Governments and organizations can create policies that foster stronger ties with diasporic communities, such as offering dual citizenship or investment incentives for those wishing to repatriate or invest in their homeland.[30] This is a strategy that Ghana has employed, offering many African Americans dual citizenship. We can't forget that Ghana is where the great Harvard scholar W. E. B. Dubois retired to and was granted citizenship.

(4) Economic Partnerships: Facilitating business collaborations between African and diasporic entrepreneurs, offering diaspora investment platforms, and removing barriers for diasporans to invest in Africa can enhance economic empowerment.[31]

When we consider the concept of empowerment, there is no empowerment without the opportunity to build wealth. The world is a global market, and the church must act like an international player. The Black Pentecostal church is no different. Where there is no vision, the

28. Manning, *African Diaspora*, 209–12.

29. Manning, *African Diaspora*, 209–12.

30. Akurang-Parry, "Ghana's Year of Return."

31. Manning, *African Diaspora*, 205–10.

people perish,[32] and where there are no provisions, the vision perishes. Economic synergy and energy are necessary for Black Pentecostal empowerment and the kingdom of God.

Many don't realize how business and economically savvy Jesus was because we don't investigate the cultural background of his parables. Jesus discussed real estate, entrepreneurship, investments, leadership and business management, and human resources. I didn't even become keenly aware of Jesus' business and economic mind until I received my MBA. If we are going to be globally minded, we must understand business globally and enter the foreign exchange market. One of the hindrances of African and African Americans collaborating and engaging in joint ventures is the lack of knowledge of the marketplace nationally and globally.

The Black Pentecostal church is no longer just the tongue-talking Pentecostal church. It is the Pentecostal church that is being empowered by the Holy Spirit, executing the Great Commission throughout the world, and empowering the poor. When we look at the similarities in struggles of Africans and African Americans, it is mind-blowing why we have not chosen to collaborate and work together in business opportunities.

Africans and African Americans must work together for a better future, and the most powerful and holistic way for this to happen is through the empowerment of the Holy Spirit. While erasure and assimilation in many parts of the world are implemented through policies aimed at erasing African cultural identities and enforcing assimilation into Western cultures, further contributing to the disconnection from their African origins, we must be intentional about connecting. Here are a few ways in which we can engage in business opportunities between African Americans and Africans:

- Investment in African Markets

  African economies are proliferating, with technological, agricultural, and renewable energy opportunities. African Americans can leverage these markets by investing in or partnering with African firms.[33]

32. Prov 29:18.
33. Bright and Hruby, *Next Africa*, 145–75.

- Export-Import Relations

  Strengthening trade links to export American products to Africa and importing African goods can diversify markets and boost economies on both sides.[34]

- Technology and Innovation Partnerships

  Collaborative ventures in tech, such as setting up fintech startups or engaging in knowledge exchanges, can significantly benefit both communities under the ACFTA (African Continental Free Trade Area).[35]

- Tourism Development

  Promote Africa as a prime tourism destination, emphasizing cultural and heritage sites that appeal to the African diaspora, which can lead to significant economic benefits.[36]

- Art and Culture Industry

  Investing in African art, cinema, music, and literature can enrich global culture and provide financial return and empowerment to the communities involved.[37]

By addressing the legacies of disconnection and fostering avenues for reconnection, Black communities worldwide can create synergies that lead to cultural revival and economic empowerment.

There are many opportunities for the Black Pentecostal church to assist in the collaboration of Africans and African Americans who don't have a lot of investment monies. And there are numerous small business opportunities that Africans and African Americans can explore to foster economic collaboration, cultural exchange, and entrepreneurship, even with limited starting capital. Here are some possible ways in which

34. United States International Trade Commission, *U.S. Trade and Investment with Sub-Saharan Africa*, 1–15; Bright and Hruby, *Next Africa*, 120–35.

35. Bright and Hruby, *Next Africa*, 145–60.

36. Adu-Ampong and Mensah, "African Diaspora Tourism."

37. United Nations Conference on Trade and Development, *Creative Economy Outlook*, 2–3.

the Black Pentecostal church can engage in kingdom-building through economic empowerment:[38]

Cultural Goods and Crafts	• Handmade crafts and art: Selling traditional African crafts and art in American markets or African American art in African markets. • Fashion and accessories: Designing and selling clothing, jewelry, and accessories that incorporate traditional African textiles and designs.[39]
Food and Cuisine	• Catering services: Specializing in African or African American cuisine for events. • Food trucks or pop-up restaurants: Offering a fusion of African and African American meals. • Packaged food products: Creating spice blends, sauces, or mixes that represent African culinary traditions.[40]
Educational and Cultural Exchange Programs	• Online courses and workshops: Teaching languages, arts, crafts, or African and African American history and culture. • Study and travel programs: Organizing tours or cultural exchange trips that foster deeper connections between communities.[41]
Digital and Information Services	• Blogging/vlogging: Creating content focused on shared cultural heritage, travel, food, or business experiences. • Online marketplaces: Developing platforms that connect African and African American product sellers to a global audience.[42]
Agricultural Ventures	• Organic or specialty farming: Collaborating on farming projects, particularly those emphasizing traditional crops or sustainable practices. • Cooperative models: Forming cooperatives for exporting goods like coffee, chocolate, or unique agricultural products endemic to Africa.[43]

38. Lincoln and Mamiya, *Black Church in the African American Experience*, 205–35.
39. African Development Bank, *Investing in the Creative Industries*, 15–28.
40. Harris, *High on the Hog*, 200–215.
41. Falola and Afolabi, eds., *African Diaspora*, 320–35.
42. Falola and Afolabi, eds., *African Diaspora*, 300–315.
43. African Development Bank, *Feeding Africa*, 55–64.

Health and Wellness	• Herbal and natural products: Producing and selling traditional African remedies, skincare, or wellness products. • Fitness and nutrition coaching: Leveraging African and African American health practices and diet models.[44]
Arts and Entertainment	• Music production and promotion: Collaborating on projects blending African and African American influences. • Film and digital media projects: Producing documentaries or films that portray the shared histories and stories of African and African American peoples.[45]
Social Enterprise and Nonprofits	• Community building: Initiating projects aimed at solving social issues that impact African and African American communities. • Collaborative workspaces and events: Establishing spaces or events that nurture entrepreneurial collaboration and innovation.[46]

These business ideas enable both cultural preservation and innovation. Small investments, creativity, and leveraging existing networks and technologies can make these ventures feasible and impactful.

When we consider globalization, the kingdom of God, and Black empowerment, we must not lose the place of economic stability. In Pentecostalism, we often approach money with an evil eye, but the Scripture does not admonish us to do so. The Bible doesn't say money is evil; it simply states that the *love* of money is the root of all evil (1 Tim 6:10). Jesus only had one official officer on his team. It was an accountant or treasurer—someone in charge of the money, Judas. The point is not that Judas was the treasurer, but that Jesus was conscious of the money. When God provided Moses with the Ten Commandments in one hand, he also provided him with the blueprints for the tabernacle, the place of sacrifice, in the other. The Black Pentecostal church cannot engage in globalization and transforming communities without transforming education, economics, and exposure.

44. World Health Organization, *WHO Global Report on Traditional and Complementary Medicine 2019*, 45–62.

45. Bright and Hruby, *Next Africa*, 175–90.

46. Bright and Hruby, *Next Africa*, 150–70.

6

The Man and the Woman of God and the Anointing to Do Good in the Black Community

THERE IS A VERY sensitive area in the body of Christ and the Black community that needs discussion, and that is gender-based roles. When looking at the Black heritage of the diaspora versus a Eurocentric heritage, the foundation of the African-derived family is more matriarchal. Also, universally, the African familial structure is the extended family model, and the Eurocentric model is nuclear. Thus, there must be a high regard for the matriarchal structure if we intend to transform and empower the Black community. While history records that countless numbers of Black men have done good in and for the Black community, to be respected in the Black community, one must hold Black women in high regard.

While discussing Black Pentecostalism, the kingdom of God, and empowerment, I thought it necessary that I broach the subject of the man and the woman of God. Some of the challenges of the twenty-first century rest upon three of the top historical issues that even Jesus and Paul had to address during Second Temple Judaism: racism, classism, and sexism. Even though Jesus had close female companions, such as Mary and Martha, sexism continues to diminish the role and value of women in ministry. The prophetic declaration of Joel 2:28 announced that both "your sons and daughters shall prophesy." Peter affirmed it on Pentecost (Acts 2:17). In modern times, some European denominations, such as the Southern Baptists, argue that women should not allowed be to preach; some other denominations, regardless of race, join in on their stance.

Even though it took some time and intentional effort, the Pentecostal churches allowed women to share with such titles as missionaries, supervisors, and mothers. Several circles in Pentecostalism today affirm and others tolerate women bishops, pastors, and preachers. I'm not writing to defend a particular theology as it relates to God using women, because I think that it is a no-brainer that God uses women. The Pentecostal church has to loosen its grip a little more on leadership roles while not developing a feminist or womanist theology. Let's first define feminist and womanist theology and the difference between the two.

Feminist and womanist theology are two distinct yet related theological frameworks that address issues of gender, race, and social justice. They emerge from different contexts and emphasize different aspects of women's experiences and perspectives. Feminist theology is a movement that reevaluates and reinterprets religious texts, traditions, and practices from a feminist perspective, aiming to challenge patriarchy and promote gender equality within religious contexts. It critically examines how religious traditions have historically perpetuated patriarchal structures, often questioning interpretations of Scripture that undermine women's roles and contributions. It seeks to discover and highlight women's voices and experiences within sacred texts, often advocating for interpretations emphasizing equality and justice. Feminist theology addresses a variety of issues, such as sexism, the roles of women in religious institutions, and the often exclusive use of male imagery and language for the divine. Feminist theology emerged in the latter half of the twentieth century, especially within Western contexts and academia, as part of the broader feminist movement.[1]

Womanist theology, on the other hand, is a theological approach that centers on the experiences and perspectives of Black women, integrating concerns about race, class, and gender in its critique of religious and social practices. While sharing concerns about gender oppression with feminist theology, womanist theology mainly addresses the intersections of racial and gender oppression experienced by Black women. It draws heavily from the cultural, social, and religious experiences of African American women, incorporating elements like storytelling, communal wisdom, and traditions from the Black church. Womanist theology often emphasizes liberation and justice for marginalized groups, advocating

1. Ruether, *Sexism and God-Talk*, 11–30.

for broader social change. Womanist theology arose in response to the perceived limitations of both feminist and Black liberation theologies, pointing out that neither adequately addressed the unique experiences of Black women.[2]

While both feminist and womanist theology advocates for the equality of women, there are some differences between the two. Feminist theology generally arose within predominantly white contexts and focused on gender inequality broadly, while womanist theology specifically centered on the lived experiences of Black women.[3] Womanist theology inherently deals with the intersections of race, gender, and class, reflecting the complex identities of Black women.[4] Although feminist theology can also address intersectionality, it often starts with a primary focus on gender.

The term "womanist" was popularized by author Alice Walker, differentiating it from "feminist" by emphasizing a unique worldview that includes but transcends gender issues. Both frameworks have contributed significantly to expanding and diversifying theological scholarship by bringing various marginalized perspectives and experiences to light. Thus, when we discuss the empowerment of the Black community, we must take into consideration the Black female as the head of household, single parenting, matriarchs of the family, the missing male influence, the disappointed Black male child, and the Black family, while also taking into account the socioeconomic issues and social injustice.

My first dissertation, written for a Boston University degree, was entitled "How Independent Churches in Select Areas Were Reaching Young Adult African American Males Between the Ages of 14–35."[5] I wrote it in 1995, and at that time the acting Surgeon General stated that if Black men were animals, they would be on the endangered species list. This statement was made because Black men led the charts in several distressing socioeconomic health indicators. Black males had the highest mortality rate and one of the lowest life expectancy rates among all other ethnic groups. Nearly 40 percent of Black men were in prison, or on parole or

2. Williams, *Sisters in the Wilderness*, 1–20.

3. Williams, *Sisters in the Wilderness*, 1–15.

4. Cannon, *Black Womanist Ethics*, 25–35.

5. Carson, "How Independent Churches in Select Areas Are Reaching Young Adult African American Males."

probation, in the age group I studied.[6] The Black community is plagued with the reality of missing fatherhood and positive role models.

I once talked to a young Black male about his future, and he said he wasn't expecting to live to be twenty-five years old. So when we talk about empowering the Black community, we must empower the family, which means we must restore Black manhood and identity while raising the consciousness of the value of Black women. The empowerment of the Black community means that our theology must be a theology that doesn't discriminate against women while affirming manhood and promoting family unity.

COMMUNITY EMPOWERMENT: THE BLACK MALE

The community is people; thus, when we discuss empowerment, we are talking about people. A biblical approach to building the family must begin with building the man. Adam came first, and he was responsible for caring for his family. And this is the challenge of the Black community—the absenteeism of Black manhood. As a result, Black women suffer. Approximately 31 percent of African American families are headed by single women, making them the racial group with the highest proportion of female-headed households.[7] While overall poverty numbers have decreased for people of color, in 2021, Black women continued to experience the highest poverty rates of any group as measured by both the OPM (official poverty measure) and the SPM (supplemental poverty measure).[8] The inner cities are filled with men who are struggling with all kinds of issues—some they are responsible for and others due to systems of neglect and racism that have relegated them to mediocrity.

The challenges faced by Black males in inner-city contexts are both educational and economic, as well as in areas such as the criminal justice system and healthcare, all of which are complex and intertwined. Here are some statistics and insights into these issues.

(1) Black males historically have had lower high school graduation rates compared to their peers. According to data from the National

6. Carson, "How Independent Churches in Select Areas Are Reaching Young Adult African American Males," 11.

7. Pew Research Center, "Facts about the U.S. Black Population."

8. Center for American Progress, *The Latest Poverty, Income, and Food Insecurity Data Reveal Continuing Racial Disparities.*

Center for Education Statistics, the graduation rate for Black males has been consistently below that of white males and the national average in recent years.[9]

(2) Test score disparities persist, with Black students often scoring lower on standardized tests like the National Assessment of Educational Progress, as compared to white students.[10]

(3) Black males are disproportionately disciplined in schools, facing higher suspension and expulsion rates, which correlates with worse educational outcomes.[11]

(4) Unemployment rates for Black males are typically higher than the national average. Structural factors contribute to this disparity, including discrimination and fewer job opportunities in some urban areas.[12]

(5) Black men often earn less than their white counterparts, and the racial wage gap persists across various sectors and levels of education.[13]

(6) Black males are significantly overrepresented in the US prison population. While they make up about 13 percent of the US male population, Black males account for a substantial percentage of those incarcerated.[14]

(7) Research indicates that Black defendants often receive harsher penalties than white defendants for similar offenses, contributing to higher incarceration rates.[15]

(8) Disproportionate school discipline and policing policies contribute to what is termed the "school-to-prison pipeline," disproportionately impacting Black males.[16]

9. Heckman and Lafontaine, "American High School Graduation Rate."

10. National Center for Education Statistics, "National Student Group Scores and Score Gaps."

11. Learning Policy Institute, *Pushed Out.*

12. Wilson and Darity Jr., "Understanding Black-White Disparities."

13. Wilson and Darity Jr., "Understanding Black-White Disparities."

14. Bureau of Justice Statistics, *Prisoners in 2021.*

15. United States Sentencing Commission, *Demographic Differences in Federal Sentencing.*

16. American University SOE Online, "Who is Most Affected by the School-to-Prison Pipeline."

(9) Black males often face disparities in healthcare access and outcomes, including lower life expectancy compared to other racial groups.[17]

(10) There are higher incidence rates of chronic conditions, such as hypertension and diabetes, among Black men, partially attributed to socioeconomic factors and poor access to healthcare.[18]

(11) Black males experience mental health issues at similar rates to other groups. Still, they are less likely to receive treatment due to stigma, access issues, and a lack of culturally competent care.[19]

(12) Many inner-city areas where Black males live face issues like poverty, underfunded schools, and limited economic opportunities, exacerbating these outcomes.[20]

(13) Historical and systemic racial inequalities contribute to these disparities, necessitating comprehensive policies and community efforts to address the root causes.

The efforts to address the challenges of Black males require the Pentecostal church to get involved in multifaceted approaches that encompass education reform, criminal justice reform, economic development, and healthcare access improvements tailored to the needs of Black males in inner-city communities.

Addressing the male/man crisis in the Black community is essential to empowerment. Community reformation must include correcting the missing man and the ill-equipped Black man syndrome; this cannot be said enough. Upon examination, we discover that many cultures have traditionally been patriarchal, where men occupy dominant roles in social, economic, and political structures. These roles often include being the primary breadwinner, decision-maker, or leader within the family or community. Men are vital to the strength of the family and community—but this is not to slight the importance nor significance of women. Many women stand up for the community but cannot do it alone or without males. There are more Black females than males old enough to work

17. Waidmann et al., "State Variation in Black and White Life Expectancy and Evolving Disparities," 2–3.

18. Sells et al., "Excess Burden of Poverty and Hypertension."

19. DeAngelis, "Helping Black Men and Boys Gain Optimal Mental Health."

20. Shikany et al., "African American Men's Health."

(aged sixteen and up)—about 1.8 million more—where are they? However, most Black women work for lower-paying jobs than men.[21]

In other cultures, men often hold responsibilities related to maintaining and protecting the family structure. This may include providing for the family economically or serving as a moral or spiritual guide. Cultural expectations often dictate that men display qualities such as strength, bravery, and leadership. However, there is growing recognition and acceptance of fluid and evolving gender roles in the Black community that have been birthed, unfortunately, out of cultural necessity. In contemporary societies, traditional gender roles are shifting. Men are increasingly participating in roles like caregiving and are more actively engaged in household responsibilities. Male representation in leadership positions often varies by culture and ethnicity, influenced by systemic factors such as education and opportunity disparities. However, Black men struggle educationally, which impacts their opportunities to function in those leadership roles. This affects their economics and self-esteem. Any attempt to restore and reform the Black community that doesn't have a plan of attack to address the men is futile.

Even in the animal kingdom, males are responsible for competing for mates and territories in many species. This often involves physical displays to showcase strength and dominance. Some species rely on males for specific reproductive roles, such as impregnating as many females as possible (e.g., many mammals). In contrast, sometimes males may participate in parental care, as with many bird species. In some species, males participate extensively in raising offspring. For instance, male seahorses carry and nurture young in a special pouch until birth.

In certain animal groups, males form coalitions or hierarchies that influence mating opportunities and resource access (e.g., wolf packs and lion prides). Male animals often play a critical part in protecting their group or territory from rivals or predators, ensuring the safety of mates and offspring. In both human and animal societies, males can hold significant positions of power and influence based on their roles, capabilities, and societal norms. Biological, cultural, and social factors influence the roles of men and males. In humans, these roles are increasingly dynamic, responding to cultural shifts towards equality and shared responsibilities, whereas, in animals, roles are often more constant and dictated by evolutionary needs.

21. BlackDemographics.com, "Black Men/Women."

COMMUNITY EMPOWERMENT: THE BLACK FAMILY

Black community empowerment must include the restoration of the Black family. If we help the Black man, we help the Black family and its socioeconomic status. Current thought is that Black men and Black women are not as responsible as it relates to their families as other ethnic groups are. The devastating state of the Black family is not due to the historical significance of the Black family but the impact of the transatlantic slave trade. The European slavery of Africans has had profound and lasting effects on Black families, reshaping their structure, dynamics, and positions within society. These impacts are deeply interconnected and have reverberated across generations. Because of slavery:

- Families were often forcibly separated as individuals were sold to different owners. Enslaved people were considered property, and their family ties were not recognized or respected, leading to the widespread fragmentation of family units.[22]
- The forced movement across continents severed connections to African homelands, erasing much of the cultural and familial heritage that would have been passed down through generations.[23]
- Slaves did not have legal rights, including the right to marry or maintain family units. Relationships were non-recognized and could be easily disrupted by the whims of slave owners.[24]
- The prolonged trauma of separation, subjugation, and dehumanization had profound psychological impacts on the Black family. However, African slaves often displayed incredible resilience, maintaining cultural and familial bonds where possible.[25]
- Enslaved individuals often formed substitute kinship networks or "fictive kinship" to replace fragmented families, creating communities of support where biological families were absent.[26]

22. Gutman, *Black Family in Slavery and Freedom*, 5–7.

23. Manning, *African Diaspora*, 45–48.

24. Blassingame, *Slave Community*, 75–77.

25. Gutman, *Black Family in Slavery and Freedom*, 3–10.

26. Carson, "How Independent Churches in Select Areas Are Reaching Young Adult African American Males," 154.

- Gender roles within families were altered, as both men and women were subjected to hard labor and abuse. Women's roles were heavily impacted, with them often being subjected to sexual exploitation.[27]
- Slavery deprived Black families of economic resources. Owning property or accumulating wealth was largely impossible, and it has had lasting socioeconomic impacts that contribute to wealth disparities today.[28]
- The systemic restrictions of slavery hindered any wealth-building opportunities, forcing subsequent generations into cycles of poverty that persisted even after emancipation.[29]
- The process of "seasoning" or integrating slaves into colonial society often involved stripping away cultural identities, languages, and traditions, creating profound identity crises for displaced individuals.[30]
- Despite this erosion, slaves were able to synthesize African traditions with new influences, resulting in unique cultural expressions in religion, music, dance, and language.[31]

Clearly, then, the challenges that the Black family faces today are rooted in the harsh realities in the wake of the devastation of slavery. The Black family today is experiencing the long-term effects of slavery. After emancipation (Reconstruction), families faced enormous challenges in reuniting and rebuilding. Laws such as Black Codes and Jim Crow further inhibited family stability and social progress. Systemic racism and discrimination continue to affect Black families, leading to disparities in education, employment, housing, and justice from the post-emancipation era through the present day. Continued struggles for equality, exemplified by the civil rights movement, have shaped modern Black family dynamics and the ongoing quest for social justice and equality.[32]

The legacy of the transatlantic slave trade and slavery deeply influenced the structure, dynamics, and struggles of Black families. And while the condition of the Black family has verified roots in the dark history of

27. White, *Ar'n't I a Woman?*, 27–35.

28. Darity Jr. and Mullen, *From Here to Equality*, 45–50.

29. Darity Jr. and Mullen, *From Here to Equality*, 55–60.

30. Patterson, *Slavery and Social Death*, 38–45.

31. Raboteau, *Slave Religion*, 68–75.

32. Carson, "How Independent Churches in Select Areas Are Reaching Young Adult African American Males," 170–73.

America, it is our responsibility to address inherited problems. Despite these profound challenges, resilience and adaptability have characterized the Black family experience, contributing to a rich cultural legacy and ongoing movements for justice and equity, such as the Black Lives Matter movement.

Historically, the Black church has played a central role in the African American community, often serving as a spiritual, social, and political hub for community and healing. The Black church has played a tremendous role in supporting and restoring the family, providing spiritual and moral guidance that has been a stabilizing force for many Black families. The Black church often serves as a place for community support, offering programs that address various social needs such as food banks, financial assistance, and educational support. Churches have historically been at the forefront of civil rights and social justice movements, advocating for equal rights and opportunities for Black families. The church is a repository of cultural heritage and traditions, playing a significant role in preserving and promoting African American culture.

The role and impact of the church on Black families have been the subject of extensive study and analysis over the years. When we consider some of the data concerning the impact of religious engagement on the Black family, we can see the positive effects the church can have on the Black family. Surveys (e.g., by Pew Research Center) have shown that African Americans are one of the most religiously observant groups in the US, with a high percentage regularly attending religious services and believing in God.[33] Research suggests that couples participating in religious services may have stronger marital bonds.[34] The shared community and values promoted by the church contribute to family stability. Churches often run or support educational programs, youth activities, and scholarship funds, impacting the education and personal development of Black children.

However, the twenty-first century has brought challenges and obstacles that must be overcome. Ongoing discussion exists about how the Black church can remain relevant to younger generations, which may not engage with traditional church structures as their predecessors did. Black families tend to face significant economic challenges, which the church often addresses through community support programs; however, these

33. Pew Research Center, *Religious Portrait of African-Americans.*

34. Wilcox and Wolfinger, *Soul Mates*, 45–52.

challenges also limit the resources the church has at its disposal. Changes in family structure and dynamics, such as single-parent households, affect how churches support families and children.[35]

Yet, the power of the Holy Spirit can assist the family and each member through personal empowerment to achieve and excel. The church must increase its involvement in family restoration and rescue. Churches can expand their role in providing social services, especially in areas like mentorship, education, and job training. The church's involvement in social justice movements remains crucial in advocating for systemic changes that directly benefit Black families. By leveraging technology, churches can better engage with and support families, particularly the younger demographic.

I am convinced that God has not forgotten about the broken and fragmented Black family that was programmed and structured for failure, allowing other families to prosper from their tragedy. The power of the Holy Spirit can assist men and women in understanding who they are. Matthew 3:17 is a pivotal verse in the Newer Testament, occurring during the baptism of Jesus by John the Baptizer. It serves as a significant moment of validation and empowerment for Jesus before he began his ministry. Note that after the baptism of Jesus and the descension of the Holy Spirit in the form of a dove, we hear the voice of God affirming who Jesus was and who he was connected to. The verse reads: "And lo, a voice from heaven, saying, 'This is My beloved Son, in whom I am well pleased.'" It is my contention that in this one statement, Jesus was empowered by the Spirit to face the wilderness. This statement provides several layers of meaning regarding Jesus' sense of acceptance, belonging, security, identity, and affirmation:[36]

- Acceptance—The voice from heaven represents God's acceptance and approval of Jesus, confirming his role and mission as central to God's plan. The baptism marks the beginning of Jesus' public ministry. This divine proclamation affirmed that he had been chosen and was ready to fulfill his mission.
- Belonging—The declaration "This is My beloved Son" established a profound sense of belonging. It highlights Jesus' relationship with God, affirming he is part of the divine family. Through the act of baptism, Jesus aligned himself with humanity. The divine

35. Pinn, *Black Church in the Post-Civil Rights Era*, 22–28.

36. Carson, *Kingdom Vision*, 46–47.

affirmation showed that while he is one with God, he shares in human experience and community.

- Security (or divine backing)—Knowing that one's actions and life path have divine approval provides ultimate security. It assured Jesus that his mission was supported by God's power and presence. The declaration suggested ongoing divine support and care, offering Jesus assurance as he faced the challenges of his ministry.
- Identity—The verse explicitly identifies Jesus as God's "beloved Son," providing him with a clear understanding of his unique identity and role within God's redemption narrative. It confirmed traditional Jewish expectations about the Messiah, helping Jesus and those present understand his true divine identity.
- Affirmation—The phrase "in whom I am well pleased" was a powerful affirmation of Jesus' character and mission. It publicly acknowledged God's delight and satisfaction in him. This affirmation presented Jesus as an example of a life pleasing to God, offering a model for ethical and spiritual living. Before Jesus lifted one finger in his ministry, he was affirmed in his essence. Affirmation allows one to embrace the value of their personhood.

The Holy Spirit established Jesus' identity, assured him of divine support, and tangibly conveyed acceptance, belonging, and affirmation. It was the Person of the Holy Spirit that led Jesus into the wilderness, it was the presence of the Holy Spirit that sustained him through the wilderness experience, and it was the power of the Holy Spirit that empowered him after the wilderness (Luke 4:14). Then, the Holy Spirit anointed him to help others (Luke 4:18–20). For believers, this passage also illustrates the intimacy and approval available through a relationship with God, mirrored in Jesus' example and inspired by the Holy Spirit. Thus, the Holy Spirit can give the Black family a sense of acceptance, belonging, security, identity, and affirmation, as he did with Jesus.

Black male identity is a complex and multifaceted concept that encompasses aspects of race, gender, culture, and personal experiences. It involves understanding oneself in relation to societal expectations, family dynamics, cultural heritage, and personal beliefs. In the Black culture and community, many of our young men who become older men suffer from an identity crisis. They have a difficult time understanding and embracing who they are. In various ethnic groups, men undergo specific rites of passage to transition into adulthood. These may include ceremonies, trials, or social rituals that affirm their roles as men in their community. Ceremonies and events like these contribute heavily to male identity and function. Unfortunately, among Black men of the diaspora, these types of events don't exist, and their rite of passage is a pass to the prison system. Thus, developing a Black male identity aligned with biblical teachings involves integrating faith with personal development, community engagement, and social awareness. We must engage in a biblical strategy that helps build identity in our Black males.

The following are some of the ways in which we can assist Black males to develop of identity and character from a biblical perspective:

(1) Recognizing and appreciating one's African American heritage and history is an essential aspect of identity. This includes an understanding of the struggles and triumphs of their ancestors, as well as the cultural expressions that shape one's self-understanding.

(2) Identity is also shaped by personal ideals, ethical beliefs, and spiritual convictions, which can be fortified through biblical principles.

(3) Central to a biblical understanding of identity is recognizing oneself as made in the image of God. This perspective affirms inherent dignity and worth irrespective of societal challenges. Ephesians 2:10 also emphasizes the uniqueness and purpose that God gives to every individual.

(4) Scripture encourages the pursuit of knowledge and wisdom (Prov 4:5–7). A biblically oriented identity involves seeking wisdom through prayer, meditation on God's Word, mentorship, and community involvement.

(5) Galatians 5:22–23 outlines the fruit of the Spirit, including love, joy, peace, patience, kindness, and self-control, which can guide Black males in shaping a character that reflects Christ.

(6) Biblical justice emphasizes caring for the marginalized and advocating for fairness (Mic 6:8, Isa 1:17). Black males can develop identity by engaging in activities promoting justice and equity within their communities.

(7) Healthy identity development fosters relationships built on mutual respect and biblical love (1 Cor 13). This includes family, friendships, and community relationships.

(8) Use biblical figures to model strength, resilience, and perseverance. Biblical figures, such as Joseph and David, exemplify resilience in the face of adversity. Romans 5:3–5 speaks to the development of perseverance and character through challenges.

(9) Jesus demonstrated leadership through service (Mark 10:45). Black male identity can be nurtured by adopting a servant-leadership model in different spheres of life, whether in the workplace, community, or church.

(10) Develop a rites of passage program that helps men to identify the expectations of manhood, the definition of manhood, and the execution of the basic requirements of manhood.[37]

By integrating these biblical principles into the understanding and development of black male identity, men can cultivate a sense of purpose and direction that is deeply rooted in faith. This development not only strengthens their personal and spiritual journey but also helps positively impact their families and communities.

As we endeavor to develop men who have gone through some sort of rite of passage, we must create intentional leadership pipelines that help us replace the missing male leadership that creates a void in our communities. For example, I personally head what I call a "Young Prophets" program, where I mentor fifteen to seventeen young Black men between the ages of fourteen and eighteen. They come to my house one weekend a month on Friday after school, and their parents don't retrieve them until Sunday after morning worship. I mentor them in biblical knowledge, Black and cultural history, financial literacy, social justice and the impact of racism, academics, personal hygiene, Black male brotherhood, and interpersonal skills.

After they complete my Young Prophets program, they enter into an apprentice program where I continue to mentor them through college and their professional careers. They, in turn, assist me with the existing young prophets as coaches. This program is doing phenomenally well! And the young men are all doing well, growing and maturing as young men of God. They have become a part of my leadership pipeline for the church; I will raise them up as young deacons and eventually elders. The church is the one place we can be very intentional about raising up Black

37. Carson, "How Independent Churches in Select Areas Are Reaching Young Adult African American Males," 255–56.

leadership. My wife does a similar program with young ladies in the same age group. We do this as a Pentecostal church that believes in the presence and the power of the Holy Spirit, creating a vibrant environment where both young and old worship in an equalitarian community of protocol.

This leads me to our next discussion—men and women of God must be anointed to do good in the community as leaders. The issue of Black male church leadership is part of broader discussions about representation and leadership within religious communities, and it often reflects broader societal dynamics. There is a perceived underrepresentation of Black males in specific church leadership roles within broader Christianity, particularly in predominantly white or multiethnic congregations. Historically, the Black church in America has been a vital institution, providing leadership opportunities that may otherwise have been inaccessible due to societal discrimination. Figures like Dr. Martin Luther King Jr. emerged as leaders from this context.

Broader societal issues impacting Black men, such as educational disparities, economic inequities, and systemic racism, can influence their participation and leadership within church settings. Younger generations may have different perspectives on organized religion, impacting leadership demographics. Some studies suggest younger Black men might be less likely to see church leadership as central to social or community life than previous generations. However, initiatives within many denominational bodies aim to address leadership gaps, enhance diversity, and encourage the mentoring of younger Black males for future leadership roles.

For example, establishing strong mentorship and leadership development programs can be crucial in raising a new generation of Black male church leaders. Churches that focus on community issues and broader societal engagement can attract leadership from individuals invested in holistic community development. Churches that make concerted efforts to address cultural and racial inclusivity may see increased participation from diverse demographics, including Black men. Increasing access to theological education and training for Black men can prepare them for various leadership roles within church settings. Engaging with contemporary social justice issues may resonate with younger Black men who might see their faith and potential leadership roles as avenues for activism and change. There isn't a straightforward set of statistics to reveal the current state of Black male leadership in churches; these observations indicate ongoing challenges and opportunities. Addressing these issues requires a multifaceted approach that considers historical contexts, current social dynamics, and proactive inclusivity strategies within religious settings.

We cannot have community empowerment without Black male leadership empowerment and female respect. Please understand that empowering Black men does not involve disempowering Black females; it simply means we must address the most sensitive areas first and then address the next serious area. The area of missing male leadership in the family, church, and community is vital to the empowerment of the Black community.

We all know that Jesus respected women in his ministry more than anyone in biblical history; however, he chose twelve male disciples to train as his primary kingdom leaders. Was the choosing of the twelve a sexist act of male superiority? Of course not! Jesus was simply building a kingdom community, which involved developing men and respecting women. Did he honor the gifts, abilities, and significance of women? Of course he did! Women first experienced the reality of the resurrection at the tomb and were trusted with the gospel message that he had been raised from the dead. However, in terms of primary leadership, the challenge of taking the message from Jerusalem to the uttermost parts of the world was entrusted to the disciples. They had to be able to endure the brunt of martyrdom and consistent persecution. Yet, Jesus was intentional about male responsibility for the family and charged John to care for his earthly mother (John 19:26–27). I strongly contend that Jesus' kingdom theology was highly effective in honoring women, building manhood, and supporting the family.

7

The Revival of Black Pentecostal and Charismatic Churches in the Twenty-First Century

Upon review of twenty-first-century Christianity, we discover that the most fertile ground for church growth in Christianity is taking place among the Pentecostal and Charismatic movements across the globe. The fastest-growing segment of the body of Christ is in Africa, which boasts some of the largest churches in the world. In this chapter, I want to discuss the revival of Black Pentecostal and Charismatic churches from a Pentecostal African perspective vs. a traditional European perspective in the twenty-first century.

It is my prophetic and biblical belief that before the return of Christ, there will be a revival, a reformation of sorts that will sweep the world, providing one last opportunity for all to receive the gospel of the kingdom before the rapture of the church. My biblical belief is based upon the latter and former rain concept of the feasts of Israel. Israel celebrated seven annual feasts, or festivals, as commanded by God (Exod 23:17; 34:23; Deut 16:16). While there were seven feasts, there were only three journeys or pilgrimages, which nod to three ultimate experiences God wants every believer to have:

(1) Feast of Passover (*Pesach*)—Leviticus 23:5

  a. Feast of Unleavened Bread (*Hag Hamatzot*)—Leviticus 23:6
  b. Feast of Firstfruits (*Yom Habikkurim*)—Leviticus 23:10–11

(2) Feast of Weeks (*Shavuot*)—Leviticus 23:15–16

(3) Feast of Tabernacles or Booths

a. Feast of Trumpets (*Rosh Hashanah*)—Leviticus 23:24
b. Day of Atonement (*Yom Kippur*)—Leviticus 23:27

The first journey was Passover, celebrated with Unleavened Bread and Firstfruits. For the disciple of Christ, this experience is salvation. The second journey was a stand-alone feast, the Feast of Pentecost, celebrated fifty days after Passover. For the disciple of Christ, this experience is the baptism of the Holy Spirit. However, for the believer, the seven feasts and the three journeys lack completion. The third journey makes three feasts a prophetic anticipation and expectation for us. The third journey speaks to Israel, the Day of the Lord, accompanied by the blowing of the trumpets, and the Day of Atonement, which includes both the coming of Christ in the clouds and the coming of Christ on the Mount of Olives. Believers should be anticipating this return based on the feasts of Israel, which are eschatological by nature.[1]

Each journey corresponded with a literal harvest season; there was a harvest at Passover, Pentecost, and Tabernacles. Likewise, for the Christian, each experience corresponds to an ingathering of souls. I espouse a pre-tribulation view of the end times; I believe the church will be raptured before the tribulation period. Therefore, just before the rapture, there will be a last ingathering at the Feast of Trumpets.

I am very well aware that this is a controversial position; however, I am convinced that an end-time revival is coming. The words in Joel 2:28 and Acts 2:17 that move from "it shall come to pass" to "in the last days it shall come to pass" mean something. Jesus spoke about the end-time events at the Mount of Olives. And amid a dark world that is becoming more and more anti-Christ, the prophetic utterance of Jesus was this kingdom gospel shall be preached in all of the world, and then the end shall come. I believe that we are on the brink of a kingdom revival. The version of the gospel that Jesus preached will be preached around the world as a witness; men and women will submit their lives to the King, and then end-time events, beginning with the rapture, will take place.

The gospel of the kingdom is mentioned in Matthew 4:23; 9:35; 24:14, and Mark 1:14. This demonstrative pronoun states "this gospel," which suggests that there will be different versions of the gospel. However,

1. Carson, *One True King*, 146–48.

one of the end-time signs will be the emergence of the gospel of the kingdom that Jesus preached, manifested through preaching, teaching, and signs and wonders. It will be, in modern-day terminology, a Pentecostal expression. In North America, secular humanism and rationalism are quickly rising and becoming the norm inside the church. At the same time, we also see the dissipation of belief in signs and wonders, even in the church. But Jesus stated that this gospel of the kingdom would be preached around the world, not simply in North America.

Unfortunately, we tend to believe that whatever God is going to do must start in the US. However, when we take a panoramic view of what is happening in the church, we discover North America is no longer the beacon light of the Christian faith. Studies show us that the US is a post-Christian nation that can easily slide into neo-paganism. This is a necessary component for my firm belief in a post-Reformation or a post-Pentecost revival—a Third or Fourth Great Awakening, if you will. In addition, from a biblical and historical perspective and modern-day data, there is a high probability that revival will heavily involve the African continent and people of color.

I discussed the significance of Africa and its prophetic importance as it relates to the Pentecostal church. The disparagement of Africa and Africans has had such a devastating impact on Black perception worldwide that this possibility is unfathomable. Yet, Africa (and her descendants) will have a historical, existential, and future place in the kingdom of God related to Pentecostal and Charismatic revival in the twenty-first century. However, we must understand why Africa is so important to Pentecostalism and revival.

AFRICA PAST

In the book *The Kingdom, Globalization and You*, Trevor Grizzle shares his sentiments concerning Africa and its significance in the kingdom and world revival. He quotes Thomas Oden, who recognizes Africa's significance for salvation history and the kingdom of God. Oden eruditely noted that

> all three Abrahamic families—Jews, Christians, and Muslims—share a history of salvation that had its earliest beginnings right on the geologic seam of two continents: Asia and Africa—between Libya and Palestine. Just as primitive human history

> begins with the transition of migrant human populations from Africa to Eurasia, so does the history of salvation in the great monotheistic religions nest in the same nexus. Classic Christianity has its roots in the narrative history of peoples formed in the close linkage between two continents: Africa and Asia. The Sinai Peninsula connected them. This lively interface of continental plates has formed the backdrop for the most decisive events of salvation history.[2]

Grizzle also comments:

> This observation is important in exploring God's dealings with Africa in his redemptive plan. Regarding land mass and population, Africa is the second largest continent in the world. If not the cradle of human history, it vies for first place with the oldest civilizations. Its cultural, literary, architectural, mathematical, and scientific contribution to world history and civilization is incalculable, inescapable, and irrefutable. In the ancient world, Africa and black people endured no reproach as a continent and as a people but were highly regarded—even emulated. Negative views about Africa's history and peoples developed in Europe as a partial justification of the slave trade in which it was engaged and the subsequent colonial hegemony it held over the continent and its peoples. Unfortunately, such unexamined and unsubstantiated beliefs have not altogether gone away—even in the 21st century.[3]

Indeed, eighteenth-century Enlightenment philosopher David Hume had this to say of the African peoples: "I am apt to suspect the Negroes to be naturally inferior to the Whites. There scarcely ever was a civilized nation of that complexion, nor even any individual, eminent either in action or speculation. No ingenious manufacture among them, no arts, no sciences."[4] Grizzle comments, "Such bigoted and stereotypical ideas about Africa and its people die-hard and have echoed down the corridors of time, reinforcing the pejorative myth of the 'dark continent.' Even today, with all the modernizations, innovations, and technological advances on the continent, Hollywood's depiction of Africa as a wild,

2. Grizzle, "Importance of Africa in the Kingdom," 87, quoting Oden, *How Africa Shaped the Christian Mind*, 31.

3. Grizzle, "Importance of Africa in the Kingdom," 87.

4. "Africa Rediscovered," Ebony, February 1960, 96.

uncivilized, undeveloped 'Tarzan and the Apes' place prevails in the minds of many Westerners."[5]

Grizzle states this about this perception:

> It is incredible—no, unthinkable—that renowned British historian Hugh Trevor-Roper would say this in his university broadcast lecture on "The Rise of Christian Europe" in 1963:
>
> "Undergraduates, seduced, as always, by the changing breath of journalistic fashion, demand that they should be taught the history of black Africa. Perhaps, in the future, there will be some African history to teach. But there is currently none, or very little: there is only the history of the Europeans in Africa. The rest is largely darkness, like the history of pre-European, pre-Columbian America. And darkness is not a subject for history."[6] His statement suggests that any modicum of light in African history was brought there by Europeans—what a raving indictment! [7]

Trevor-Roper continues his mindless psycho-babble:

> "The new rulers of the world, whoever they may be, will inherit a position that has been built up by Europe, and by Europe alone. It is European techniques, European examples, European ideas which have shaken the non-European world out of its past—out of barbarism in Africa, out of a far older, slower, more majestic civilization in Asia; and the history of the world, for the last five centuries, in so far as it has significance, has been European history. I do not think we need make any apology if our study of history is Europa-centric.[8]

Grizzle reacts, stating, "Pitiful! Pathetic! Lamentable! Appalling! Can there be a greater display of untamed ignorance? But it unmasks not only the skewed, jaundiced, yet concealed perspective of a celebrated historian—one who should have had a more lucubrated and objective view of the world—but echoes the unvoiced, suppressed, and repressed sentiment of many in the West. How different is Thomas Oden's view of

5. Grizzle, "Importance of Africa in the Kingdom," 88.

6. Trevor-Roper, "The Rise of Christian Europe," quoted in Falola, *Nationalism and African Intellectuals*, 221.

7. Grizzle, "Importance of Africa in the Kingdom," 88.

8. Trevor-Roper, "Rise of Christian Europe," quoted in Falola, *Nationalism and African Intellectuals*, 220.

Africa: "Africa has been the most fertile seedbed of intellectual depth in Christian reflection on Scripture."[9]

Grizzle writes, "The idea 'Kingdom of God,' originating from the Hebrew—*malkuth Yahweh* and the Greek counterpart, *hē basileia tou theou*, describes the sovereign rule or reign of God, God's kingship (RSV), the exercise of God's kingly power over the nations and the world. Such exercise of supreme and absolute control began not with the coming of Christ and the establishment of the New Testament church but as early as the dawn of creation. God does not reign in an abstract or remote manner. Rather, he exercises his reign concretely and relationally—at times through nations (particularly Israel in the Old Testament), institutions (most notably the church in the New Testament), and through individuals, such the prophets and apostles and, by extension, the members of Christ's body. Africans are not excluded from this deliberate placement in God's divine will."[10]

Africa is a critical geography and people as it relates to the revival of Pentecostalism and charismatic revival. While Eurocentric views have spun negativity towards Africa and people of color, without Africa and Africans we could not have a complete picture of salvation history. Unfortunately, when we think about the concept of revival, we can only imagine the Eurocentric perspective. Why? We have been taught that Africa carries the curse of Ham, as seen by the reality of savage living. This cultural default is the mentality of watershed theology developed through years of eisegesis, not the exegetical study of Hebrew thought and culture. However, Africa is a significant part of the Bible, the church, its teachings, and a coming revival.

The Bible never portrays Blacks in a negative light. In fact, it presents a relatively favorable attitude towards Blacks. The fabrication of the "curse of Ham" is an unfounded myth that reflects not only ignorance of the biblical narrative but also of historiographical realities. As Cain Hope Felder has noted, "[P]ost-biblical misconstruals of biblical traditions have created the impression that the Bible is primarily the foundation document of 'the white man's religion.' The mistaken notion widely persists that the relation of black people to the Bible is a post-biblical experience."[11] "Such historical distortions are the work of Eurocentric

9. Grizzle, "Importance of Africa in the Kingdom," 89, quoting Oden, *How Africa Shaped the Christian Mind*, 31.

10. Grizzle, "Importance of Africa in the Kingdom," 89.

11. Felder, *Troubling Biblical Waters*, 15, quoted in Grizzle, "Importance of Africa

scholars and missionaries, resulting in much harm to blacks."[12] Speaking of Africa's crucial role in the Bible and in shaping the global Christian mind, Methodist scholar of African history and religions Thomas Oden, stated, "The global Christian mind has been formed out of a specific history, not out of bare-bones theoretical ideas. Much of that history occurred in Africa. Cut Africa out of the Bible and Christian memory, and you have misplaced many pivotal scenes of salvation history. It is the story of the children of Abraham in Africa; Joseph in Africa; Moses in Africa; Mary, Joseph, and Jesus in Africa; and shortly thereafter Mark and Perpetua and Athanasius and Augustine in Africa."[13]

The early history of the Hebrew people began in Africa—Egypt. Abraham and the family of Jacob were early and unwitting partners in God's kingdom program who found refuge in Africa. Israel was physically and mentally developed in Africa. There, Israel was molded into the people of God. The word "Africa" is not mentioned in the Bible, but several countries on the continent are. The three most frequently cited places are Ethiopia (Cush), Libya, and Egypt. Cush (Ethiopia) is referenced as early as Genesis 2:13—"The name of the second river is the Gihon; it winds through the entire land of Cush" (NIV); "the same is it that compasses the whole land of Ethiopia" (American King James Version). Ethiopia/Ethiopians is/are alluded to forty-three times in the Scriptures—all but once in the Older Testament. Moses' wife was from Ethiopia (Num 12:1); Ebed-Melech, who saved Jeremiah's life by lifting him out of a muddy cistern, was an Ethiopian (Jer 38:7–13).

Though still debated by some scholars, the Queen of Sheba (named Makeda), who visited Solomon (1 Kgs 13:1–13, 2 Chron 9:1–12), was from Ethiopia. Many modern Ethiopians believe the child born from their tryst (Menelik, aka Ebna la-Hakim) became the first king of Ethiopia. The sole reference in the Newer Testament to Ethiopia/Ethiopians is in Acts 8:27, where Queen Candace of the Ethiopians is mentioned. Candace (Greek—*Kandake*) was more a dynastic title (like Caesar or Pharaoh) than a name. Scholars suggest that Ethiopia here is Meroe, which is in the area of modern Sudan.[14]

---

in the Kingdom," 90.

12. Grizzle, "Importance of Africa in the Kingdom," 90.

13. Oden, *How Africa Shaped the Christian Mind*, 14, quoted in Grizzle, "Importance of Africa in the Kingdom," 90.

14. Yamauchi, *Africa and the Bible*, 164–65, quoted in Grizzle, "Importance of Africa in the Kingdom," 90–91.

According to Oden, "Libya was from time immemorial a crucial segment of the world arena in which God's providential purpose was being worked out, according to the Hebrew prophets."[15] Libya appeared in Hebrew history as Put, Ham's third son (Genesis 10:6). Acknowledged as a great nation from King Jeroboam to Herod, its history is intertwined with that of the Jews. Libya appears in the Newer Testament under its ancient name, "Cyrene." All three Synoptic Gospels record Simon of Cyrene carrying the cross of Jesus (Matt 27:32; Mark 15:21; Luke 23:26). Also, present at Pentecost were Cyrenians (Acts 2:10). Luke tells us that "men from Cyprus and Cyrene went to Antioch and began to speak to Greeks also, telling them the good news about the Lord Jesus. The Lord's hand was with them, and a great number of people believed and turned to the Lord" (Acts 11:19–21). Regarding the church at Antioch, Luke further informs, "Now in the church at Antioch there were prophets and teachers: Barnabas, Simeon called Niger, Lucius of Cyrene, Manaen (who had been brought up with Herod, the tetrarch) and Saul" (Acts 13:1). It is of interest that Lucius apparently worked with Paul (Rom 16:21).

Egypt is mentioned in the Bible some 155 times—the most of any nation other than Israel. It was the place of captivity for the Israelites for 430 years but also the place of provision for Jacob and his family during a time of severe famine. In Scripture, it serves the dual role of both the place of oppression and refuge, a place to flee to, and a place from which to escape. Famine drove Abraham there (Gen 12:10). Jeremiah and the young child Jesus found refuge there. Still, because of the oppression of the Hebrew people, the negative symbolism makes the name Egypt one that can hardly be forgotten.

> The Egypt/exodus motif in the Older Testament is echoed in the Newer Testament; Jesus was being called out of Egypt where He had found safety from Herod (Matthew 2:15), just as Israel was called as God's son out of Egypt's bondage (Hosea 11:1). Matthew further connects Jesus with the historic suffering of Israel. Like Moses, Jesus came out of Egypt, escaping the temptation of a life of leisure, luxury, and peace, choosing instead to follow God's will that would lead to the cross—dying a death Luke describes as an "exodus" (Luke 9:31), which would bring about spiritual deliverance from sin's captivity.[16]

15. Oden, *Early Libyan Christianity*, 21, quoted in Grizzle, "Importance of Africa in the Kingdom," 91.

16. Grizzle, "Importance of Africa in the Kingdom," 92.

According to Grizzle,

> The presence of large Jewish communities in Egypt for many centuries before Christ is a well-documented historical fact. One of the crowning and enduring gifts of Greek-speaking Jews in Alexandria, a city on the coast of Egypt, to the Jewish and Christian religions and the world is the Septuagint—the Greek translation of the Hebrew Older Testament. Not only was the Septuagint used by early Christians, but Paul himself made extensive use of it—it became his Bible of choice. Throughout the history of Bible translations and even in the modern period, the Septuagint has been a vital linguistic and literary resource. Archeological findings have proved that a full-fledged Jewish Temple existed from the seventh century BC on the Nile River Island of Elephantine. Similarly, Josephus in "Antiquities and Jewish Wars" has described in detail another Jewish Temple built in the second century BC at Leontopolis in the central delta region of Egypt.[17]

Cain Hope Felder has drawn attention to a linguistic connection between the Semitic and African people. He states, "It can no longer be taken for granted that Semitic languages necessarily originated in the Near East. Various attempts at placing the ultimate origin of the Semitic languages in the Fertile Crescent or in Arabia have not proven successful." To the contrary, "many serious scholars accept the view that the Semitic language group is a branch of a major family called Hamito-Semitic or Afro-Asiatic."[18]

> During the first three centuries of the Christian era, Africa was a major hub for Christian thought and endeavor. Five hundred years after John Mark's ministry in Alexandria, Christianity flourished there, the city becoming an intellectual and theological center and a magnet for all peoples in the known world. The Christian Church has had a continuous and growing presence in Africa since the time of Christ's apostles, yet few of the persons responsible for its growth are known.[19]

Through the conversion of the Ethiopian treasurer (Acts 8) in about 40 AD, not only did Africa receive the Christian gospel, but tradition

17. Grizzle, "Importance of Africa in the Kingdom," 92.

18. Felder, *Troubling Biblical Waters*, 28, quoted in Grizzle, "Importance of Africa in the Kingdom," 93.

19. Grizzle, "Importance of Africa in the Kingdom," 93.

says Queen Candace herself came to embrace the Christian faith.[20] Libya, which had representatives at Pentecost, became a force in evangelism. Thomas Oden has listed seven ways ancient Africa has influenced world Christianity:

(1) The birth of the European university was anticipated in African Christianity
(2) Christian historical and spiritual exegesis of Scripture first matured in Africa
(3) African thinkers shaped the very core of the most basic Christian dogma
(4) Early ecumenical decisions followed African conciliar patterns
(5) Africa shaped Western forms of spiritual formation through monastic discipline
(6) Neoplatonic philosophy of late antiquity moved from Africa to Europe
(7) Influential literary and dialectical skills were refined in Africa[21]

Oden's further observation is worthy of mention. "The normative early Greek and Latin Bibles before Jerome (the Septuagint and the Old Latin Bible versions) were both products of Africa. The perplexing relationship between the Old and New Testaments was studied with great philological precision by Christians from Africa in the first three centuries. These patterns of interpretation became decisive for later studies in Syriac, Greek, and Latin, and much later in German, French, and English exegesis."[22]

Some of the leading ancient African scholars and theologians were Tertullian, Clement of Alexandria, Origen, Athanasius, Augustine, Cyprian, and Didymus the Blind. Of them, Oden says, "The chief intellectual guides of North African Christianity have been studied by Christians all over the world, but seldom recognized as African. They have often been considered purely Hellenists and Byzantines, but not Africans. These writers have been studied and pondered for centuries. Their voices

20. Acts 8.

21. Oden, *How Africa Shaped the Christian Mind*, 85–87.

22. Oden, *Early Libyan Christianity*, 45, quoted in Grizzle, "Importance of Africa in the Kingdom," 94.

have echoed in every subsequent generation of Christians."[23] Of these spiritual, theological, and intellectual pioneers, it has been written:

> These Christian leaders and saints arose out of a distinctly African experience on African soil. They were born as Africans, struggled in the African setting, nurtured within untold generations of indigenous African cultures. They are not European imports. They felt the sweat and knew the thirst of African deserts and mountains. They understood the resistance of local religious practices and customs to the transformative message of the gospel. In response, they developed small learning communities and theological curricula, which formed participants intellectually, spiritually, and ethically to such a degree that, if called upon, they would be able to resist the pressures of local religious conformity even to the point of death. Intellectually, these writers played a decisive role of the formation of Christian culture from its infancy. They profoundly shaped world Christianity and were instrumental in the formulation of some of the most decisive intellectual achievements of Christianity. Contrary to common perception, the intellectual leadership of Christianity largely moved from Africa to Europe—south to north. Early African Christian leaders figured out how to best read the law and prophets meaningfully, to think philosophically, and teach the rule of faith, long before the patterns became normative elsewhere.[24]

AFRICA PRESENT

Africa has been much more significant than watershed theology has presented to the world with its Eurocentric prejudice. So, let's continue our discussion concerning the idea of a Pentecostal and Charismatic revival being associated with Africa. It's crucial and necessary that we represent a biblical worldview of Africa and its people who are a part of the African diaspora. When we discuss revival, Pentecostalism, and Charismatics in the twenty-first century, the thought that it would occur among Africans and on the African continent does not immediately register to the conscious nor subconscious mind due to the racial perceptions of Black

23. Oden, *Early Libyan Christianity,* 37, quoted in Grizzle, "Importance of Africa in the Kingdom," 94.

24. Oden, *How Africa Shaped the Christian Mind,* 43.

people. I have established a strong foundation for the validity and qualifications of Africa being on the radar of God's prophetic purpose.

Essentially, the question is, what is God doing on and with the continent of Africa today? Based on the data, God is already bringing in souls worldwide; revival is already happening on the continent of Africa! Grizzle said, "At the turn of the 20th century, Christianity was practically non-existent in many parts of Africa. Today, it is the preferred faith of the majority of Africa. More than two billion (2.5 billion) strong worldwide, Christianity is not only the world's largest religion; in some regions, it is fastest growing, with most of that growth occurring in the majority world, pejoratively termed the third world. It is a known fact among missiologists that since about 1970, the axis of Christianity has shifted southward."[25]

Noting this fact in an article in "Global Religions" in 2003, Harvey Cox asserted that "the majority of the world's 2 billion Christians are no longer to be found in old European and North American precincts of Christendom but in Asia, Africa, and South America."[26] Grizzle states:

> The shift of the center of gravity for Christianity toward the non-western majority world has revealed two astounding developments: the de-Christianization of the West and the Christianization of non-western countries. Most of Europe is now post-Christian—much of it, neo-pagan. On the contrary, the greater majority of Christians around the world are non-western. A positive spinoff of this is that Christianity needs no longer bear the "shame" of being the white man's religion. Further, with the increasingly "darkening complexion" (less white) of Christianity has come increased immigration of non-westerners into Europe and the United States, resulting in a de-Europeanization of Christianity.[27]

Revival is happening in Africa and wherever Africans are found. And Pentecostalism is the denomination experiencing the most growth. The late Nigerian scholar/historian Ogbu Kalu wrote, "Across Africa, Christianity is thriving in all shapes and sizes. But one particular strain of Christianity prospers more than most—Pentecostalism."[28] In their "His-

25. Juergensmeyer, ed., *Global Religions*, 17, quoted in Grizzle, "Importance of Africa in the Kingdom," 95.

26. Cox, "Christianity," 17.

27. Grizzle, "Importance of Africa in the Kingdom," 96.

28. Kalu, *African Pentecostalism*, 7.

torical Overview of Pentecostalism in Nigeria," the Pew Research Center shows that "renewalists," which include Charismatics and Pentecostals, constitute approximately three in ten Nigerians and that "roughly six in ten Protestants in Nigeria are either Pentecostal or Charismatic, and three in ten Nigerian Catholics surveyed can be classified as Charismatic."[29] So, we must begin this conversation with Africa when we discuss the revival of black Pentecostalism and Charismatic churches in a twenty-first-century context.

Another statistic has shown that "in 2010, over 60 percent of Africans were Christians, and 24 percent of the world's Christians were Africans."[30] Today, there are 360 million Christians in Africa, and this number is projected to swell to one billion by 2050. These projections point to a revival that is taking place in Africa, where God has done most of his strategic kingdom work. It is unimaginable and amazing to think that presently one out of four Christians in the world is an African, and the Pew Research Center estimates that figure will grow to 40 percent by 2030.[31]

Let's take a broad base look at some of the largest churches in Africa. The research reveals that they are predominantly Charismatic or Pentecostal in belief and practice, and the majority of them are in Nigeria. Recent studies from academic and journal sources indicate that the Deeper Christian Life Ministry's Lagos headquarters, led by Pastor W. F. Kumuyi, sees approximately 120,000 attendees on Sundays. The denomination claims over 800,000 members in Nigeria and has established thousands of churches in the country, as well as several thousand in forty other countries.[32] World-renowned pastor David Oyedepo, of Living Faith Church in Lagos, averages an attendance of 50,000 and runs a network of 300 churches in Nigeria. Led by world-renowned pastor Enoch Adeboye, Redeemed Christian Church of God in Lagos marks an attendance of 40,000 and connections with churches in nine countries. Adeboye conducts services that have seen physical attendance estimates exceeding 500,000 people in the purpose-built, open-air worship complex sprawling across thousands of acres.[33]

29. Pew Research Center, "Historical Overview of Pentecostalism in Nigeria."

30. Pew Research Center, *Global Christianity*, 9.

31. Pew Research Center, "Future of World Religions," 59–60.

32. Combrinck, "Case Study of Deeper Life Bible Church."

33. Grizzle, "Importance of Africa in the Kingdom," 97.

The National Temple of The Apostolic Church, which is more of a conference center than a single church edifice, accommodates 100,000, making it the largest capacity religious facility in the world. Situated in Lagos, it took twenty-five years to build. It has Gabriel Olutola as its pastor. The Lord's Chosen Charismatic Revival Church in Lagos has Lazarus Muoka as its leader and 30,000 attendees; Pastor Muoka also oversees a network of 222 churches in seventy-seven countries. Another Nigerian ministry on the move is Word of Life Church, with an attendance of 30,000 and shepherded by Ayo Oritsejafor. Jesus Celebration Center in Mombasa, Kenya, meanwhile, has a sanctuary that seats 30,000 and claims a membership of 15,000 with multiple weekly services. It is shepherded by Wilfred Lai. Led by Ray McCauley and his wife, Rhema Bible Church North in Johannesburg, South Africa, confirms a weekly attendance of 45,000. United Family International Church in Harare, Zimbabwe, pastored by Emmanuel Makandiwa, is a church of around 35,000 with thirteen satellite campuses. Bringing up the rear is Lighthouse Chapel in Accra, Ghana. One of many megachurches in the country, it is pastored by Bishop Dag Heward-Mills and has 20,000-plus attendees and thirty-five extension campuses.[34]

Grizzle writes:

> The reach and impact of African Christianity extend far beyond the continent. Europe's experience of steady migration from Africa over the past 30 years or so has resulted in a change in the religious landscape of that continent. Today, independent churches, large and small, founded mainly by Nigerians and Ghanaians, dot the landscape of Europe. It is no speculation to say that not only are immigrant churches, largely African ones, responsible for keeping the feeble-smoldering embers of the gospel alive in Europe but are the hope of keeping Christianity on the continent from dying out in the foreseeable future. Predictions are that without the immigrant churches, Christianity will disappear from most of Europe, which is now a neo-pagan continent. In essence, a form of revival among black Pentecostal and Charismatic churches has already begun to spark a revival in geographies where the churches were dead and dying.
>
> Unlike the global north, where traditional denominations are generally in decline, Nigeria's Anglican churches, for example, are experiencing startling resurgent growth and have announced that "in the next ten years, they will double their

34. Grizzle, "Importance of Africa in the Kingdom," 97–98.

> numbers." That is not a pipe dream, considering that they "doubled their numbers in the previous 15 years from about 8 million to about 17 million." With such a showing, they are now confidently saying they will exceed 30 million in 10 years.[35]

This revival of the dead is due to Black Pentecostal theology and the power and presence of the Holy Spirit.

Grizzle states, "Migration of African Christianity to Europe has brought about a volte-face [about-face] in ecclesiastical and missional duties. The reversal of roles and responsibilities this has brought about has led to polarization between African and European Christians." Gerrie Ter Haar noted, "The new reality does not comply with the stereotypes often attached to Africa, which, basically, is seen as a continent in need of help. Africans are traditionally represented as on the receiving end and Europe on the giving end, of a relationship characterized by unequal transfer."[36]

In England, where there has been an explosion of Black majority churches, the Redeemed Christian Church of God (Nigerian) has established 296 new churches in the last five years—the largest of any religious tradition.[37] In London, Nigerian Matthew Ashimolowo pastors Kingsway International Christian Centre, a church with over 12,000 members. Nigerians' aggressive approach to evangelism and church growth is again demonstrated in the Ukraine, where Sunday Adelaja founded the Embassy of God, which is recognized as the largest megachurch in Europe, with over 25,000 members. What is more, Adelaja has planted 450 churches around the world.[38] "Christianity does not just go from the West to the rest of the world; now it is coming back in the other direction. Global evangelism now has come full circle."[39]

An area often overlooked in showing Africa's connection to the ancient people of the Bible is Judaism's lasting impression and imprint on certain people groups and countries in Africa. Exodus 12:38 says that after 400-plus years in Egypt, the Israelites were accompanied by a "mixed multitude" in the exodus. Grizzle ponders questions concerning the mixed multitudes. "I have often wondered who constituted that

35. Grizzle, "Importance of Africa in the Kingdom," 98.
36. See Grizzle, "Importance of Africa in the Kingdom," 98.
37. Gledhill, "Church Attendance Has Been Propped up by Immigrants."
38. "Out of Africa."
39. Imtiaz, "New Generation Redefines What It Means to Be a Missionary."

mixed crowd. Joseph married an Egyptian wife who bore him two sons: Manasseh and Ephraim, injecting African blood into the Hebrew people. Were there blacks among the gift of menservants and maidservants Pharaoh gave to Abraham (Genesis 12:16)? Is there any veracity to the claim by many modern-day Ethiopians that the kingly line of Solomon runs through Ethiopia and the Ethiopian King Haile Selassie?"

"I was intrigued, and my interest greatly piqued a few years ago as I watched Tudor Parfitt's NOVA documentary on the 'Lost Tribes of Israel.' His journey through southern Africa to study the black African Bantu-speaking Lemba tribe, who claims Jewish ancestry, brought to light 'unusual traditions' of this black African group. They were Semitic in religious traditions and practices, and many bore Semitic-sounding names." He shares, "What is more startling is that DNA tests show that the Lemba people seemingly have 'an ancestral connection to Judaic populations,' the Y chromosome handing from father to son 'a living record of the past.'"[40]

Grizzle further explains:

> The roots of Judaism run deep in Ethiopia and may reach back as far as the First Temple period. Many aspects of Ethiopian life and culture still show evidence of Jewish influence. Nowhere is this more obvious than with the Abyssinian Church, which maintains the customs of circumcision, a form of Sabbath observance, Torah dietary laws, and other practices of ancient Judaism. The claim of the Falashas to be Jews and recognized by all religious and non-religious groups in the nation as such, is well-known. One legend holds that Solomon had a son, Menelik, with the Queen of Sheba. Menelik returned to his father in Jerusalem and later resettled in Ethiopia with many from the tribes of Israel, among them priests and Levites. He, at this time, also smuggled the Ark out of Jerusalem and took it to Aksum, the capital of Abyssinia (modern Ethiopia). This is only one of the unsubstantiated theories of how Jewish beliefs and practices have come to prevail among black African people, and one that does not seem to have an enormous amount of traction.[41]

Today, thousands of Black African Jews migrate to Israel, where they are, for the most part, accepted as Jews and given the full rights and privileges that identity represents. I have had the privilege of meeting

40. Parfitt, *Journey to the Vanished City*, 201–5.

41. Grizzle, "Importance of Africa in the Kingdom," 100.

Ethiopian Jews in Israel and Africa. I believe Africans have been planted by God all over the globe for worldwide revival.

AFRICA FUTURE

Traditional European churches are becoming more liberal and view Pentecostal doctrine as too restrictive and controlling and lacking in compassion, grace, and mercy. However, I believe African churches, with their spiritual dynamism, great missionary zeal, vibrant worship, and belief in the supernatural, will help spark another Great Awakening in America.

I believe that God will use Pentecostal churches pastored by Africans of the diaspora and/or those of African descent to spark revival worldwide before the *parousia*. Pentecostalism is sweeping across the globe with the power and the presence of the Holy Spirit, transforming countries, nations, villages, and communities. Surely, if Black Pentecostal churches tap into the power of the Holy Spirit, they too can transform the ghettos and inner cities of the US, which are composed predominantly of people of African descent.

A study by the Pew Research Center concluded that "Christianity will increasingly become an African religion. Africa is already the largest Christian continent, with slightly more Christians than North America. But by 2050, North America will have less than half of Africa's Christian population (1.12 billion vs. 516 million)."[42] There is every indication that Africa will continue its steady march across the globe, hoisting the crimson cross on the skyline of every city in its wake and bringing hope where there is hopelessness and light where there is darkness.

While we are very hopeful concerning black Pentecostalism and Charismatic revival, Grizzle notes, "There are some homespun, self-styled eschatologists that prognosticate a 'come back' of Africa to universal hegemony. That is, in their view, the time will come again when, just as Egypt held sway over the known world in the heyday of the Pharaohs, so it will be for Africa someday in the future because, as they claim, 'Africa shall rise again' in fulfillment of prophecy. No such prophecy exists or can be thus interpreted."[43]

However, in biblical eschatological schema, there are two Scriptures that come to mind that predict a role for Africa in end-time events: Isaiah

42. Pew Research Center, "Future of World Religions."

43. Grizzle, "Importance of Africa in the Kingdom," 101.

19:23–25 and Ezekiel 38:5. Most scholars interpret the former historically rather than eschatologically. The passage does have nuances that cannot be fully explained by the normal flow of history alone. So, how that prophecy will be played out is a secret known only to God. Ezekiel 38:5 brings some African states in coalition with other nations, but in conflict with God and his chosen nation, Israel, fighting an end-time losing battle where God's fury is poured out upon them.

The Black Pentecostal church and the gospel of the kingdom of God remain the potential catalyst for community empowerment in America. Pentecostalism is a vibrant and dynamic form of Christianity known for its emphasis on the experience of the Holy Spirit, spiritual gifts, and revival. As a global movement, it has impacted regions differently based on historical, cultural, and theological contexts. However, I believe that Africans and the descendants of the African diaspora hold a very important and prominent role in global evangelism.

8

Black Pentecostal and Charismatic Churches and the Spirit in the Twenty-First Century

Ethics and Morality

When I was a kid growing up on the South Side of Chicago in the Englewood District, we had several churches on every block. I remember the Baptist, Holiness, Pentecostal, Methodist, some independent churches, and a Kingdom Hall of the Jehovah's Witnesses. Oddly enough, even though the churches were a part of different denominational persuasions, I don't remember any church or denominational wars. In essence, each of the churches were respectful of each other. However, each had a particular style of worship that they were known for in the community. The three most popular churches were the Holiness churches, the Pentecostal churches, and the Baptist churches.

The Pentecostal and Holiness churches were known for their strong ethical position of upright or holy living, and they quoted, "Pursue peace with all people, and holiness, without which no one will see the Lord" (Heb 12:14). The Holiness church motto was "holiness or hell!" The Pentecostal church emphasized holiness as well, and they tended to be very legalistic and thought of themselves as meticulously following Scripture. So, they literally interpreted Paul's admonishment to the Corinthians that a woman must have her head covered. Therefore, the Pentecostal women were known for the white head coverings. Additionally, baptism in the name of Jesus was essential for the Pentecostals, and speaking in tongues was evidence of receiving the Holy Spirit.

On the other hand, the Baptists were known for being the inspirational church, characterized by what some would refer to as emotionalism. They referred to it as "catching the Holy Spirit," demonstrated by uncontrollable shouting, bucking, and dancing so demonstratively that people would have to watch them so they didn't hurt themselves. The Baptist church was also known for its inspirational choirs and singing. Even though the Holiness and Pentecostal churches were known for it too, it wasn't like the Baptists; they had more finesse. The Methodist church was a very conservative church, and the independent churches seemed to be like crossover churches; I guess I would refer to them as "Bapti-costal."

The Jehovah's Witnesses were seen as the ultra-conservative church, known for their high moral conduct and judgmentalism. The Jehovah's Witnesses were known as the weird people who knocked on doors and passed out their magazine, *The Watch Tower*, which explained how everyone other than the Jehovah's Witnesses were not going to heaven.

The Pentecostal church was active in the neighborhood but was known for its strict moral behavior, similar to the Holiness church, which I will refer to from this point on as Pentecostal because they embraced the vibrancy of the Spirit; the baptism of the Holy Spirit, evidenced in glossolalic speech; the gifts of the Spirit; the fivefold ministry gifts; and high moral behavior.

While I am arguing that Black Pentecostalism and the kingdom of God can be a catalyst that can empower inner-city Black and Brown communities today, I am well aware that Black Pentecostal churches have always existed in the Black community. However, I recommend a Pentecostal renewal that emphasizes the kingdom of God and the power of the Holy Spirit to transform communities and nations. It is my strong contention that many black Pentecostals were directly or indirectly impacted by colonial Christianity informed by the five watersheds of history and theology: Romanization, Europeanization, colonization, Westernization, and Americanization of the gospel.[1]

The teaching of the colonial church was influenced by the need for a theology to complement the transatlantic slave trade. The church of the plantation was given the so-called biblical interpretation to make their slaves better by the Society of the Propagation of the Gospel in Foreign Parts (SPG). The early teachings of Christianity in the colonies suggest

1. Carson, *Five Watersheds*.

that one could not hold a Christian as a slave and promoted an egalitarian system of religious brotherhood. However, when the SPG presented Christianity as a religious persuasion, it was feared that it would interrupt the prosperity and cultural productivity of slavery. Thus, it was initially rejected by the plantation holders. So, the SPG modified their offering and emphasized slave obedience and master superiority from a spiritual perspective to make the slaves more docile and obedient, not just racially but biblically. This teaching created a form of what I refer to as "Judeo-Christian Judaism," a Protestant form of legalism or salvation by works.

On the other hand, the Pentecostal movement has its beginning with the Methodist Holiness movement and John Wesley. The Holiness and Methodist church movements are closely connected through their historical development, theological emphasis, and key figures like John Wesley. Here's an outline of their connections. John Wesley, an eighteenth-century Anglican minister, Reformationist, and the founding figure of Methodism, emphasized the doctrine known as "Christian perfection" or "entire sanctification," which is central to both Methodist and Holiness theologies. Wesley believed that Christians could, through the work of the Holy Spirit, reach a state of holiness in this life, characterized by a heart fully devoted to loving God and neighbor. The Methodist movement began as a revival within the Church of England, emphasizing personal and social holiness, evangelism, and a methodical approach to spiritual disciplines. Wesley's itinerant preaching and organizational structure led to the rapid growth of Methodism.[2]

The Holiness movement emerged in the mid-nineteenth century as some Methodists sought a deeper emphasis on Wesley's teaching of entire sanctification. Influenced by preachers like Phoebe Palmer and events such as camp meetings, the movement advocated for a second work of grace beyond conversion that brought about complete holiness of heart and life. As the Holiness movement gained momentum, some adherents felt that the Methodist Episcopal Church (the primary Methodist body in North America) was becoming too conservative and losing its focus on sanctification.[3] This led to the formation of distinct Holiness denominations, such as the Church of the Nazarene and the Wesleyan Methodist Church. Both movements share a theological emphasis on holiness and the pursuit of sanctification.[4] However, while Methodism maintained

2. Carson, *Five Watersheds*, 164–65.

3. Dieter, *Holiness Revival of the Nineteenth Century*, 19–25.

4. Synan, *Holiness-Pentecostal Tradition*, 55–60.

a broader emphasis on social justice and personal piety, the Holiness movement focused intensely on the doctrine of entire sanctification as a defining characteristic.

As the Holiness movement developed, it adopted certain practices and theological interpretations that distinguished it from its Methodist roots, including a stronger focus on revivalism, personal experiences of sanctification, and often stricter codes of personal conduct. The Holiness movement's focus on revivalism and personal piety contributed to the formation of many denominations. It influenced the development of Pentecostalism, which emphasized the gifts of the Holy Spirit, including speaking in tongues. In summary, the Holiness movement grew from the Methodist tradition and Wesley's teachings on sanctification but evolved into a distinct religious movement with its own emphases and practices, influencing the broader landscape of American Protestantism and contributing to the rise of Pentecostalism.[5]

The Holiness movement emphasized entire sanctification or the "second blessing" as a transforming experience that purified believers from sin.[6] However, the Wesleyan Movement was birthed out of the theology of England, what I referred to as watershed theology, which was influenced and impacted by Romanization, Europeanization, and the colonization of the gospel.[7] Yet, just as the Wesleyan movement influenced the Holiness movement, the Holiness movement influenced and impacted the Pentecostal movement. The Holiness movement and the Pentecostal movement are closely linked through their historical development and theological emphases, particularly concerning the role of the Holy Spirit and the pursuit of sanctified or holy living. Thus, the Holiness movement provided fertile ground for the rise of the Pentecostal movement.[8]

At the beginning of the twentieth century, many who were part of the Holiness movement sought greater spiritual experiences. The Azusa Street Revival in Los Angeles (1906–1909), led by William J. Seymour, a holiness pastor, is known as the birth of the modern Pentecostal movement.[9] This revival popularized speaking in tongues (glossolalia) as evi-

5. Dieter, *Holiness Revival of the Nineteenth Century*, 240–45.

6. Synan, *Holiness-Pentecostal Tradition*, 1–5.

7. Carson, *Five Watersheds.*

8. Synan, *Holiness-Pentecostal Tradition*, 89–95; Anderson, *Introduction to Pentecostalism*, 30–35.

9. Anderson, *Introduction to Pentecostalism*, 35–41.

dence of the baptism in the Holy Spirit, marking a clear distinction from the Holiness movement. Both movements share a fundamental commitment to the doctrine of sanctification and the transformative work of the Holy Spirit. The Holiness movement highlights sanctification as a defined, post-salvation experience, while Pentecostalism extends this to include baptism in the Holy Spirit, as evidenced by speaking in tongues.[10] The Pentecostal movement emerged from the theological and experiential framework established by the Holiness movement, evolving to emphasize a fuller charismatic expression of Christianity with a particular focus on the gifts and power of the Holy Spirit. Both movements, though, are influenced by John Wesley's teaching on Christian perfection.[11]

While the Holiness movement generally emphasizes a second work of grace for entire sanctification, the Pentecostal movement often regards Spirit baptism as an empowering experience for greater spiritual victories and evangelism. While the Holiness movement focused largely on sanctification and moral rigor, the Pentecostal movement is characterized by a broader emphasis on spiritual gifts, such as healing, prophecy, and tongues, drawn from the Newer Testament, particularly the Acts of the Apostles.[12] Pentecostalism is known for its lively forms of worship, which include enthusiastic singing, dancing, and speaking in tongues. In contrast, the Holiness movement, though lively also, is more varied in these aspects and less uniformly focused on charismatic gifts.[13]

Together, the Holiness and Pentecostal movements have significantly shaped contemporary Christian worship, theology, and practice around the world, emphasizing a direct, personal experience of God through the Holy Spirit. The influence of both the Holiness and Pentecostal movements led to the development of the Charismatic movement in the mid-twentieth century, which saw charismatic practices spread beyond traditional Pentecostal denominations into mainline Protestant and even Catholic churches.[14]

10. Synan, *Holiness-Pentecostal Tradition*, 103–8; Anderson, *Introduction to Pentecostalism*, 40–45.

11. Synan, *Holiness-Pentecostal Tradition*, 1–5, 103–8; Anderson, *Introduction to Pentecostalism*, 30–35, 40–45.

12. Synan, *Holiness-Pentecostal Tradition*, 103–10; Anderson, *Introduction to Pentecostalism*, 40–46.

13. Anderson, *Introduction to Pentecostalism*, 46–50.

14. Synan, *Holiness-Pentecostal Tradition*, 219–25; Anderson, *Introduction to Pentecostalism*, 63–70.

When we consider the Black Pentecostal and Charismatic churches and their quest for moral purity or a walk of holiness, they are a moral affront to the secularization of Christianity and the contemporary moral stance of the world, especially in North America. Pentecostalism is known for its high moral standards, which I will call its "pneumatic ethos." The pneumatic ethos is the spiritual practices and beliefs that inform ethical behavior within Pentecostal communities. The pneumatic ethos establishes the framework for ethical decisions and social justice imperatives within Pentecostalism.[15]

Pentecostals' ethics reflect their pneumatological understanding of how the Spirit offers moral and ethical guidance and spiritual empowerment by helping us understand Christ's teachings. Pentecostals draw near to their heart the teachings of the Torah and the teachings of Paul that contain instruction for holy living, particularly the epistles to the Romans, Galatians, Corinthians, Philippians, and Colossians, but certainly not limited to them.[16]

The Key Moral and Ethical Stances of Black Pentecostal and Charismatic Churches	
Holiness and Personal Conduct	• Focus on holiness, personal purity, and sanctification is paramount. Ethical behavior is seen as a reflection of one's faith and commitment to living a life aligned with biblical teachings. • Moral imperatives include abstaining from sinful behaviors, such as substance abuse or sexual immorality, and embodying virtues like honesty, integrity, and humility.[17]
Community and Social Justice	• A strong commitment to community welfare and social justice is a hallmark, emphasizing the biblical mandate to care for the marginalized and oppressed. • Churches often engage in social advocacy, addressing systemic issues such as racial injustice, economic inequality, and healthcare access, viewing this as part of their ethical duty to manifest God's kingdom on earth.[18]

15. Anderson, *Introduction to Pentecostalism*, 271–76; Yong, *In the Days of Caesar*, 23–27.

16. Yong, *Spirit Poured Out on All Flesh*, 143–50; Yong, *Beyond the Impasse*, 92–96; Yong, *In the Days of Caesar*, 22–28.

17. Synan, *Holiness-Pentecostal Tradition*, 15–18, 110–15.

18. Anderson, *To the Ends of the Earth*, 210–15; Yong, *In the Days of Caesar*, 95–102.

Family and Relationships	• High value is placed on family structure, marital fidelity, and child-rearing practices rooted in traditional religious principles. • Ethical teachings often emphasize the sanctity of marriage between a man and a woman, valuing this relational construct as a divine institution.[19]
Empowerment through the Spirit	• Spiritual empowerment is key to ethical living, where personal and communal decisions are guided by prayer and discernment of the Spirit's leading. • There is a belief in the active role of the Holy Spirit in guiding personal ethics and empowering believers to live transformative lives.[20]
Spiritual Discernment	• The Holy Spirit is crucial for discerning right from wrong, guiding moral decision-making, and addressing ethical dilemmas.[21]
Health and Prosperity	• A significant segment of Pentecostal and Charismatic churches emphasize health and prosperity, often teaching that faithfulness can lead to spiritual and material blessings. • Ethical teachings often include responsible stewardship of resources and personal health, with expectations that believers will use their resources to support the church and community.[22]

While individual Black Pentecostal and Charismatic churches may vary in their specific emphases and applications of these moral and ethical teachings, they commonly reflect a commitment to scriptural interpretation, holiness, community involvement, and the transformative power of the Holy Spirit in believers' lives. In a very simplistic presentation, these are the fundamental moral and ethical beliefs and practices of the Black Pentecostal and Charismatic church but are not limited to Black Pentecostals. These practices and beliefs create a dynamic moral framework that is spiritually inspired and often flexible in application, reflecting a living relationship with God.[23]

19. Sanders, *Saints in Exile*, 61–75; Butler, *Women in the Church of God in Christ*, 105–20.

20. Yong, *In the Days of Caesar*, 95–110; Anderson, *Introduction to Pentecostalism*, 210–18.

21. Yong, *Spirit Poured Out on All Flesh*, 257–65, Anderson, *Introduction to Pentecostalism*, 210–15.

22. Anderson, *Introduction to Pentecostalism*, 284–90.

23. Butler, *Women in the Church of God in Christ*, 12–18.

The moral and ethical values of Black Pentecostal/Charismatic churches also come with significant challenges and critiques, such as:

- Balancing Diversity: These churches often face the challenge of balancing diverse viewpoints within their congregations, particularly as they navigate contemporary social and ethical issues.
- Criticism of Prosperity Theology: While the prosperity gospel has been influential, it has also attracted criticism for potentially overshadowing broader social justice concerns.[24]

Another challenge for the Black Pentecostal church as it endeavors to impact and empower the Black community is the rise of secular humanism and religious pluralism that does not necessarily, and in most cases, share Pentecostal values. What is secularism, secular humanism, and religious pluralism? And how do they pose a threat or a potential stumbling block to Black Pentecostalism and community empowerment? These three distinct concepts cannot be ignored if the Pentecostal church will be impactful in empowering Black communities. [25]

Secularization refers to the process by which religion loses its influence and significance in societal and cultural spheres. It involves declining religious beliefs, practices, and institutions in favor of secular values, such as individualism, science, and rationality.[26] Secularization can result in a decreased role of religion in public life, a decline in religious adherence and participation, and a shift towards more secular worldviews and ideologies. Societies experiencing secularization may prioritize secular laws and governance over religious principles, leading to the separation of church and state and the promotion of secular values in public institutions and policies.[27]

Note that secular humanism and secularization are two distinct concepts, although both relate to secular, nonreligious approaches to life and society. Secular humanism is a philosophical and ethical stance that emphasizes human values, reason, and the pursuit of knowledge without reliance on religious beliefs. It advocates for a worldview that focuses on human welfare and happiness, using reason, science, and ethics as guides. Some of the critical characteristics of secular humanism include:

24. Bowler, *Blessed*, 9–11.

25. Sanders, *Empowerment Ethics for a Liberated People*, 87–94.

26. Berger, *Sacred Canopy*, 107–14.

27. Casanova, *Public Religions in the Modern World*, 19–39.

- Rational Inquiry: Secular humanists prioritize reason, critical thinking, and empirical evidence in determining the truth and making decisions.
- Ethics and Morality: Morality is derived from human needs and interests rather than divine commands. Ethics are concepts that can be evolved and refined through discussion and consensus.
- Human Potential: Emphasis is placed on human potential and the belief that humans can lead meaningful and ethical lives independent of religious doctrines.
- Free Thought: Encourages skepticism of dogmas and embraces open inquiry.
- Global Community and Equality: Promotes human rights, equality, and secular governance free from religious interference.[28]

When we consider the fact and reality of the presence of secularization and secular humanism, they stand in direct contrast to the religious mindset that prioritizes worship of God, adherence to his doctrine and practices, and participation in his church. We call this a biblical worldview. We must understand what a secular worldview is because it is the mentality of those who we are trying to empower who have not become fully immersed in God and a biblical worldview. So, let's dig into the concept of a secular worldview, which is the opposite of a biblical worldview.

A secular worldview is a perspective on life and the universe that is not based on religious or spiritual beliefs. Instead, it relies on reason, empirical evidence, and scientific understanding to explain the nature of reality, morality, and human existence. A secular worldview tends to be built upon the following:

(1) Naturalism: Belief that everything can be explained by natural causes and laws without invoking supernatural or divine elements.

(2) Humanism: Emphasis on human values and concerns, asserting that humans have the capacity and responsibility to lead ethical lives and improve the human condition through reason and compassion.

28. Kurtz and Wilson, eds., *Humanist Manifesto II*, 6–12.

(3) Skepticism: A questioning attitude towards knowledge, facts, or beliefs that are taken for granted, especially those held by religious traditions.

(4) Ethical Relativism: The idea that moral principles are not universally fixed but can vary based on culture, society, or personal circumstances.

(5) Separation of Church and State: Advocacy for the distinct and independent functioning of religious and governmental institutions.

(6) Empiricism: A focus on knowledge derived from sensory experience, experimentation, and observable evidence.

(7) Secular Ethics: Developing moral frameworks based on human well-being and rational thinking rather than religious doctrines.

(8) Progressive Values: Often associated with progressive attitudes toward social change, equality, and scientific advancement.[29]

A secular worldview doesn't necessarily oppose personal spirituality or religious freedom, but advocates for keeping religious doctrines separate from public policies and social institutions.

There are slight differences between secular humanism and secularization. Secular humanism is a specific worldview or philosophy focusing on humanist principles, while secularization is a broader sociocultural process affecting the role of religion in society.[30] Secular humanism proactively advocates for a life guided by human reasoning and ethics without religious considerations. At the same time, secularization describes a widespread societal trend where religious practice and belief may decline in importance. Secular humanism directly influences individuals' philosophical and ethical perspectives, whereas secularization impacts social institutions, traditions, and overall societal norms toward religion. Secular humanism is intentional and prescriptive, advocating for particular values and approaches. In contrast, secularization is often seen as a descriptive, organic outcome of modernizing influences like industrialization, education, and communication.

Another challenge to Black Pentecostal/Charismatic churches is religious pluralism. Religious pluralism refers to the coexistence of multiple religious traditions, beliefs, and practices within a society. It recognizes

29. Kurtz, *Courage to Become*, 15–25.

30. Taylor, *Secular Age*, 423–30.

and affirms the diversity of religious worldviews and allows for the peaceful coexistence of different faiths without privileging one over the other.[31] Religious pluralism promotes tolerance, respect, and dialogue among various religious groups, fostering interfaith understanding and cooperation. We have seen our societies become increasingly pluralistic, thus embracing religious diversity as a source of enrichment and engagement, encouraging individuals to express their religious beliefs freely while fostering social harmony and inclusivity.

This is the world and challenges that Pentecostalism must be aware of. The church must be prepared to apologetically defend the faith with a sound, biblical, hermeneutical, and exegetical foundation, yet operate in a highly ecumenical environment. Unfortunately, many Blacks have adopted a way of secular thinking in the twenty-first century. However, Black believers remain among the most faithful to an active religion in the US and the world. Black individuals, particularly in the US, tend to show higher levels of church attendance and religious participation compared to other racial and ethnic groups. This observation is supported by several studies and surveys:

(1) Pew Research Center: A 2018 survey found that 79 percent of African Americans identify as Christian, higher than the national average. Additionally, the survey reported that Black Americans are more likely to attend religious services on a regular basis and say religion is very important in their lives compared to the general US population.[32]

(2) Gallup Polls: Consistent Gallup polling has shown that Black Americans report higher weekly attendance at religious services compared to other racial and ethnic groups in the United States.[33]

(3) General Social Survey (GSS): Data from the GSS over the years has illustrated that African Americans are more likely to belong to a church or have higher church membership rates than other ethnic groups.[34]

31. Eck, *New Religious America*, 4–7.

32. Pew Research Center, *Faith Among Black Americans.*

33. Gallup, "Just Why Do Americans Attend Church?"

34. Davis, Smith, and Marsden, *New Compendium of Trends from the General Social Survey*, 45–47.

The research reports that African Americans have higher participation in religious life for the following reasons:

- Historical Role of the Church: Churches have historically served as crucial centers for community, leadership, and social action in Black communities, especially during and after the civil rights movement.
- Cultural Importance: Religion and faith traditions are often woven into cultural and familial identities in Black communities.
- Community Support: Black churches frequently provide social services, support networks, and leadership opportunities, linking personal and communal identities to church participation.[35]

The affinity for the spirituality of the Black community makes for a great probability that the Black community is more open to the gospel and Pentecostalism than the rest of the culture in the US. This fact is the foundation of my hope that Black Pentecostalism and the kingdom of God for empowerment can have a tremendous effect on minority communities. Black people, in general, tend to have more of an aptitude for spiritual things and the gospel than other ethnic groups. It appears to be something almost in our genes that imbues our desire for the Spirit of God in America and worldwide.

On a global scale, statistics on Black populations' religious participation outside the US are more varied and depend significantly on the specific cultural and regional context. Factors such as colonial history, local religious traditions, and cultural context play a role. However, many African nations report high levels of religious participation due to cultural and societal norms, with Christianity and Islam being dominant religions in various regions. While statistics can vary, many Caribbean and Latin American countries with significant Black populations also report vibrant religious traditions, which often blend Christianity with local religious practices. The higher level of religious involvement among Black Americans is well-documented in multiple survey sources, as we have seen. While societal resilience and cultural factors drive these statistics within the US, globally, the picture is more mixed and context-dependent based on historical and cultural influences. However, when we examine the concepts of secularization, secular worldview, secular humanism, and religious pluralism, we discover that our society has

35. Taylor, Chatters, and Levin, "Religious Participation Among African Americans."

varying moral constructs and ethical patterns. In this mix, Blacks have a greater propensity to be drawn to the gospel, the church, and Christ than other nationalities.

The moral ethics of Black Pentecostal and Charismatic churches are often derived from a deeply rooted spiritual worldview centered around scriptural teachings, the movement of the Holy Spirit, and a community-driven sense of responsibility. The Pentecostals/Charismatics' morals and ethics tend to differ from the nation's ethics and morality. Biblical texts and spiritual revelation primarily shape black Pentecostal and Charismatic ethics. In contrast, national liberal stances may lean more toward secular humanism, emphasizing reason, individual rights, and empirical evidence as moral guides. Hence, this results in different foundational priorities and interpretations of life, sexuality, and human rights.

While liberal ethics may prioritize individual autonomy and personal freedom, Pentecostal ethics often emphasize community welfare and responsibilities, viewing these as interconnected rather than opposing forces. Ethical decisions are usually made with a community-oriented mindset, prioritizing collective well-being.[36] On social issues such as LGBTQ+ rights, reproductive health, and gender roles, Black Pentecostal churches hold more conservative views compared to liberal perspectives that advocate for broader personal freedoms and inclusion. Pentecostals will advocate for freedom, but freedom in Pentecostal ethics often involves liberation from sin and a pursuit of divine justice.[37] This may contrast with the liberal notion of freedom, which pertains more to personal choice and expression. Justice is perceived differently, not only as a legal or socioeconomic matter but as a spiritual and moral one, requiring adherence to divine standards for true societal flourishing.[38]

The ethics of Black Pentecostal and Charismatic churches provide a unique perspective that blends spiritual fervor with practical community engagement. Differences with the national liberal stance highlight the diversity of thought in navigating contemporary ethical challenges, contributing to a broader discourse on morality in society. Balancing the world's liberal stance on morality and ethics with the often more conservative viewpoints of the Black Pentecostal and Charismatic churches requires careful dialogue, mutual respect, and an understanding of

36. Benyah, "Pentecostal/Charismatic Churches and the Provision of Social Initiatives."

37. Barnes, "Functions of Religion among Young Black Members."

38. Keller, *Generous Justice*.

common goals. While in some cases there is a gulf that exists between liberal vs. Pentecostal ethics and morality, we must have a dialogue with those who oppose our conservative moral views.

Here are just a few suggestions as we attempt to engage in community empowerment with a high percentage of non-Bible reading individuals:

- We must encourage open dialogue between church communities and liberal groups to understand each other's perspectives better. This involves active listening and a genuine effort to understand the values and concerns of both sides.
- We must approach discussions with empathy, respecting the sincerity and validity of each position, even when disagreements arise. Building relationships based on trust can pave the way for more productive conversations.
- We must focus on common ethical values such as compassion, justice, and community service. Both groups often prioritize helping the marginalized and advocating for social justice, providing a foundation for collaboration.
- We must collaborate on community projects that address issues like poverty, education, and healthcare, areas where both groups can agree on practical solutions despite differing philosophical or theological backgrounds.
- We must organize events that educate both church members and liberal groups about the diverse ways ethics and morality can be interpreted and applied. These can include historical contexts, theological explanations, and secular perspectives.
- We must promote an understanding of the cultural and religious traditions that shape each group's moral standpoint. Instead of seeking overwhelming changes, identify smaller steps that lead toward meaningful progress, fostering gradual acceptance and understanding of diverse viewpoints. This "literacy" will help dispel stereotypes and misconceptions. The extra time taken to explain Christian stances can open the door to the acceptance of the gospel of the kingdom.
- We must use adaptive problem-solving techniques where parties agree to experiment with solutions, assess outcomes, and adjust

strategies as needed, supporting a more flexible approach to ethical challenges.

- We must establish forums where individuals feel safe to express their perspectives without fear of judgment or retribution, enabling honest and constructive interaction.
- We must encourage inclusive policy-making that considers religious sensitivities and secular perspectives, ensuring that the public sphere respects and accommodates diversity in ethical views.
- We must encourage individuals to engage actively in their communities, promoting personal agency within ethical frameworks that respect both religious convictions and personal freedoms.
- We must support leadership within both groups who can bridge divides, acting as mediators who can articulate concerns and aspirations to broader audiences.

By focusing on unity and understanding where possible and respectfully managing differences, a balanced approach can help integrate liberal stances on morality and ethics with the traditional views of Black Pentecostal and Charismatic churches, in order to partner for community empowerment. This approach will facilitate a more harmonious coexistence where diverse ethical cultures enrich society and provide multiple avenues for fulfilling the common good.

The church has to approach a reformation of communications in a less radical way to provide the most amenable environment for others to open their minds and hearts and hear the voice of God that can break down any wall of resistance. When we're not sensitive to what God desires to do, we become insensitive to what God is doing. The transformation of communities requires diplomacy and discipline that can lead to spiritual discipleship.

9

The Kingdom of God, Empowerment, and the Black Community

THE KINGDOM RENEWAL

It's very important that we delve deeper into the concept of the kingdom of God. Unfortunately, it's become a buzzword in the church, yet no one *really* knows what it is. A review of the Bible shows us that the gospel of the kingdom of God was a message that John the baptizer preached, Jesus taught and preached, and Paul preached. However, the message they preached is not the message being preached in our churches today. For many, the kingdom of God is where you go when you die. We discussed the ministry of the Holy Spirit in the last chapter. It is the point of variance for many in evangelical theology because of this very topic. Thus, many of the teachings on the kingdom of God in the contemporary church are based upon a solely *future* eschatological reality of the kingdom of God with some present-day supernatural phenomena (miracles, tongues, the gifts of the Spirit) dismissed as existential side effects. Many of our historical and modern theologians view the kingdom from an eschatological perspective, emphasizing the kingdom's future consummation.

I'm arguing that the kingdom of God is a critical tool within the Pentecostal experience and the Black church for community empowerment. But we must first ask ourselves—what is the kingdom of God? The kingdom of God is the rule and reign of God in eternity and over his people in time.[1] I have spent more than thirty-five years studying and

1. Carson, *Kingdom Theology*, 124.

writing about the kingdom in its Jewish context. While I still have much to learn about the Jewish context, my study of the kingdom has been fruitful. I have written nearly 275 books, booklets, Bible study guides, and curricula focusing on the kingdom of God in its original context. Most importantly, I desire to teach the gospel of the kingdom around the world as a witness (Matt 24:14).

The discussion of the kingdom of God is very ambiguous in the church world because it requires an examination of the Bible in its authentic context. I often say to my seminary and Bible college students in all three classes—hermeneutics, exegesis, and homiletics—that when you approach the biblical text, you must do so through the lens of a biblical detective. This means you must sniff the text until you can smell it and then chew it until you can taste it.[2] There is more than meets the eye when you preach, teach, and comprehend the word of God.[3]

While the theme and focus of Jesus was the kingdom of God and the kingdom of God was the expectation of both Older Testament Jewish believers and intertestamental Jewish believers, the church has not historically given the kingdom of God enough focus and consideration as a relevant entity to transform communities, not just individuals.[4] Jesus stated that he came to deliver the good news of the kingdom. The gospel of the kingdom was good news to Jews, gentiles, women and men, slaves, and the wealthy. The kingdom of God was good news because when one submits their will to God, giving over the reins of their life to God, the benefits are enormous, regardless of one's past. The kingdom was God's answer to Israel and the world.

Yet, understanding the kingdom is rarely taught in churches, seminaries, and Bible colleges. Why? Often, we confuse the church and the kingdom and consider them to be one in nomenclature. In most modern theology, we perceive the kingdom as only otherworldly and irrelevant in our everyday lives. We attempt to interpret the kingdom through our cultural lens, which causes us to greatly misunderstand the message of Jesus and the kingdom of God. Most modern and contemporary theologians interpret the kingdom of God mainly as that which is to come or from a purely eschatological perspective.

2. Carson, "Gospel of the Kingdom Masterclass."

3. Carson, *What Meaneth This?*

4. See Rauschenbusch, *Christianity and the Social Crisis*, 12–25.

In my book *The Five Watersheds of History and Theology*, I attempt to tackle why I believe we misunderstand the kingdom message of Jesus.[5] The message, mission, and ministry of Jesus the King and his kingdom were uprooted from its cultural context and misinterpreted through the lens of a new, non-Jewish context—the Roman Empire. I expound on how Romanization, then Europeanization, colonization, Westernization, and Americanization of the gospel have replaced the Jewish context, changing its message, mission, and ministry. This change in context impacted our understanding of the kingdom of God and our ability to seek after it, like a mother who has lost her child. So, I will discuss the different views of the kingdom of God historically by some leading scholars and authors and examine the kingdom perspective of Jesus. This perspective transformed the world and the Jewish people. I contend that in order to understand the kingdom of God, we must study the kingdom of God in its original Jewish context.

THE KINGDOM OF GOD: JEWISH EXPECTATION

Jesus was the Yeshua Hammachiach—the Messiah, the fulfillment of Jewish prophecy about the coming King. Jesus was born a Jew, lived according to the Jewish law, studied the Torah and the Mishnah as a child, celebrated the Jewish feasts, adhered to the Jewish Sabbaths, and died as a Jew upon a Roman cross that bore a sign that read "King of the Jews."[6] Yet, Jesus' mission was to set the captives free, including Jews and gentiles. His priorities were to emancipate the world from the domination of Satan, beginning with Israel or the Jewish people, which he referred to as his own (John 1:11). The Gospels teach that the primary focus of Jesus was the kingdom of God. Jesus proclaimed, explained, and demonstrated the power and the presence of the kingdom of God among humanity.[7] Ultimately, Jesus provided access to the kingdom through his redemptive acts at the cross as the Lamb of God who came to take away the sins of the world. Jesus was on a mission of reconciliation for the world as a whole. However, the Jewish culture was the culture and people God decided to use to save the world. Jesus was called to lift an oppressed people who had a turbulent history filled with slavery and oppression that damaged

5. Carson, *Five Watersheds of History and Theology*.
6. Carson, *Jesus the Jewish Messiah and His Kingdom Ministry*, 48, 101.
7. Carson, *Jesus the Jewish Messiah and His Kingdom Ministry*, 106.

their self-esteem and impacted their holistic well-being, while inspiring global defamation. How did they remain hopeful? By believing in the Day of the Lord.

The Day of the Lord is a powerful Jewish concept that creates hope for the Jewish people regardless of Jewish pain and suffering. The Jewish people believe they have both a right and a reason to exist; they consider themselves the authentic representatives of God.[8] Though today, Jewishness is regarded by some as an ethnic group, Israel or the Jewish people are a group of people not predicated upon geography and culture but upon covenant and Torah, which is the yoke of the kingdom. The Day of the Lord provides Jews with hope and inspiration. What is the Day of the Lord? The Day of the Lord is a significant concept in Christian and Jewish theology, representing a time of divine intervention in human history. It is often described with themes of judgment, redemption, and the establishment of God's kingdom.[9]

According to the Hebrew Bible, prophets frequently mention the Day of the Lord, including Isaiah, Joel, Amos, and Zephaniah. It is depicted as a time when God will enact judgment on the nations and restore justice on behalf of Israel and the Jewish nation. This day is often associated with darkness, destruction, and upheaval, signaling divine retribution against the wicked. At the same time, it promises hope and restoration for those who are faithful to God. In Jewish theology and thought, the Day of the Lord is often connected to themes of Messianic expectation and the ultimate redemption of Israel. It is seen as a day of divine judgment and a day when God's sovereignty will be unequivocally recognized. In Jewish symbolism, the Day of the Lord often reflects hopes for peace, justice, and rebuilding Jerusalem, which align with ultimate redemption.[10]

The intertestamental period brought a slight modification or rethinking of the interpretation of the Day of the Lord, due to the evil persecution of Israel by the Hellenized leader, Antiochus Epiphanes, referred to as "Mad Dog." The Day of the Lord began to take on an "otherworldly" understanding because of how evil times had become upon the earth for the Jewish people.[11] During the intertestamental period, which spans roughly from the end of the Older Testament writings to the beginning of

8. Carson, *Jesus the Jewish Messiah and His Kingdom Ministry*, 89.

9. Carson, *Journey Through the New Testament*, 251.

10. Craigie, "Day of the Lord in the Book of Amos."

11. Carson, *Journey Through the New Testament*, 65.

the Newer Testament era, the concept of the Day of the Lord continued to develop in Jewish thought along those lines. This period was marked by significant religious, political, and social changes, including the influence of Hellenism and the rise of various Jewish sects, such as the Pharisees, Sadducees, Essenes, and Zealots.[12]

Notably, the intertestamental period saw the rise of Jewish apocalyptic literature, such as the books of Enoch, Jubilees, and Baruch. These texts often expanded on themes from the Hebrew Bible, portraying the Day of the Lord as a cosmic event marked by divine intervention, judgment, and the overthrowing of evil forces. This literature portrayed vivid imagery of battles between good and evil, often involving angelic and demonic forces, reflecting the current political struggles and a longing for divine deliverance.[13] Just as in the Older Testament, the Messianic expectation was still a prominent theme of the Day of the Lord. The anticipation of a messianic figure or king to lead the Jewish people to redemption became more pronounced during this time. Thus, the Day of the Lord was associated with the coming of this Messiah, who would defeat Israel's enemies, restore the nation, and reign as a righteous king.

The Jewish people had gone through Egyptian slavery, which had profound effects on their Israelite culture, as seen in the Exodus narratives. Israel eventually was granted their own promised land; however, she compromised her values and ethics and violated the parameters of God, desiring to be like the kingdoms of this world rather than the kingdom of our God. Biblical history records that Israel was commanded to live strict, disciplined lives that differed from the other nations of the world. Yet, due to their disobedience to the Torah, compromised behavior, and neglect of their relationship with God, he allowed them to experience exile. As a result, Israel's northern kingdom, which represented 10.5 of the twelve tribes of Israel, found herself in eighth-century Assyrian exile (721 BC). The Southern Kingdom did not learn a lesson from the Northern Kingdom and found herself (Judah) in Babylonian exile (586 BC). Israel then fell into Medo-Persian exile, followed by the cultural extermination of Greek Hellenization.[14]

Yet, despite their unfaithfulness toward God, they knew they were God's covenant people and believed in the Day of the Lord. Thus, the Day of the Lord continued to be linked with themes of judgment against both

12. Carson, *Journey Through the New Testament*, 64–76.

13. Collins, *Apocalyptic Imagination*, 53–78.

14. Kaiser Jr., *History of Israel*, 281–305.

foreign oppressors and the unfaithful within Israel. It held the promise of purification and restoration for the faithful remnant, aligning with the hope for a renewed covenant relationship with God. In their history, Israel experienced tumultuous Egyptian bondage, then the exilic experiences of Assyrian, Babylonian, Persian, and Greco-Roman domination. During the times of Jesus, Israel was still under the dominion and political control of the Roman Empire. These political realities often influenced the interpretation of the Day of the Lord, as Jews longed for divine intervention to free them from Greco-Roman oppression.[15]

In addition to messianic hope, the interpretation of the Day of the Lord evolved within a context of apocalyptic expectation. George Ladd espouses understanding the Day of the Lord from a prophetic, eschatological perspective. His view is that different prophets express the form of the future kingdom differently.[16] Scholars see two distinctly different kinds of hope in the Older Testament. The true Hebraic prophetic hope expected the kingdom to arise out of history and be ruled by a descendant of David in an earthly setting (Isa 9:11). However, after their return from exile, the Jews lost hope of a kingdom in history. In its place, they looked for an apocalyptic inbreaking of God in the person of a heavenly Son of Man with a wholly transcendent kingdom, one beyond history (Daniel 7).

THE TRANSCENDENT KINGDOM OF GOD

The kingdom of God is a central theme of the Bible; the Day of the Lord was the hope and expectation of the Jews. Jesus was the expected Messiah that the Older Testament prophets foresaw. An examination of the ministry of Jesus by any exegete worth their weight in salt will agree that the central theme in the ministry of Jesus was the kingdom of God. And I contend that it should be the central focus of every believer. Jesus proclaimed the kingdom, he explained the kingdom, and then he demonstrated the kingdom with signs, wonders, and miracles. Jesus utilized the supernatural power of the Holy Spirit to overturn the works of Satan. Then Jesus provided access to the kingdom through the atoning works of Calvary and his resurrection from the dead.

15. Wright, *Jesus and the Victory of God*, 180–85.

16. Ladd, *Presence of the Future*, 65–70.

Jesus was kingdom-centered and inaugurated the kingdom in his personhood. Kingdom theology is rooted in the Older Testament.[17] Its form and structure can be seen in the garden of Eden before the fall. God is King eternal, who created all things and ruled and reigned over them, including the garden, Adam, Eve, and the serpent. There has never been a time when he was not King, and there will never be a time when he ceases from being King. God is the sovereign King in the Older Testament, who established his kingdom in the realm of time, with Abraham in Jewish thought as the first kingdom citizen.[18] God formally introduced himself for the first time as Melchizedek, which means in Hebrew "King (*melek*) of righteousness (*tsedeq*)." Thus, God's first theophanic or Christophanic appearance was given to Abram as the King of Righteousness, which suggests that righteousness is both the character and property of God; he owns and has a monopoly on righteousness as King.[19]

God then introduced himself to Moses as King, the I AM, the Omnipotent One, who can be, and do whatever is needed; he is the King of kings. The Scriptures teach that God introduced himself to the tribes of Israel as King. Through the mechanism of covenant, Israel embraced him as King after he first demonstrated his royal ability by overcoming the ten gods of Egypt, the power and strength of Pharaoh and his army, and the Red Sea. Israel then became the corporate community of the citizens of the kingdom through Abraham and covenant. When they embraced God as King, God acknowledged them as a royal priesthood or a kingdom of priests (Exod 19:6). The covenants of God are kingdom covenants, blood covenants between the King and his citizens.

Older Testament history provides insights into the perpetual relationship of God and Israel and their betrayal or breaking of the terms of the covenant and compromise of the parameters of the covenant. They went whoring after other gods and behaved like those who did not have a covenant with God (they did not subscribe to his system of values or laws). Israel suffered consequences for their rebellion and disobedience to the covenant of God and experienced a series of exilic experiences. They had to live under the dominion and authority of pagans until the day God would ultimately bring them back under the authority of the kingdom of God.[20] The prophets declared that the kingdom of God

17. Ladd, *Gospel of the Kingdom*, 57–62.

18. Carson, *Kingdom Theology*, 141.

19. Carson, *Kingdom First*, 104–5.

20. Ladd, *Presence of the Future*, 69–73.

would be a day in which men and women would live together in peace and where social indiscretions would be solved and evil would pass away, commonly known and discussed earlier as the Day of the Lord.

What and where is the kingdom? The kingdom is multidimensional; it is past, present, and future, earthly and heavenly, temporal and eternal. On one occasion, when the Pharisees came and asked Jesus when the kingdom would come, he responded, "The coming of the Kingdom of God is not something that can be observed nor will people say, 'Here it is,' or 'There it is,' because the kingdom of God is in your midst" (Luke 17:20–21, NIV). Paraphrasing, Jesus was saying to them, "I am the embodiment of the kingdom." Jesus was and is the center, sum, substance, and circumference of the kingdom of God.[21] He initiated the present reign of God in the world. As King, he has defeated the renegade king, Satan, who usurped God's authority in the garden of Eden, led a rebellion against God, and subjected the human race to death, disease, destruction, and other painful consequences of sin. Paul tells us that as King, Jesus "must reign until He has put all His enemies under His feet. The last enemy to be destroyed is death" (1 Cor 15:25). Amidst the conflict, chaos, and confusion happening around us, Jesus reigns. He's on the throne. One day, He shall trample all of his enemies under his feet.

The kingdom of God in the Newer Testament is the central message and ministry of Jesus. The Synoptic Gospels—Matthew, Mark, and Luke—are filled with the proclamation, explanation, and demonstration of the kingdom of God in the life of Jesus, the Jewish Messiah. They often summarize the material on the kingdom. For example, Mark illustrated, "Now after John was put in prison, Jesus came to Galilee, preaching the gospel of the kingdom of God, and saying, 'The time is fulfilled, and the kingdom of God is at hand. Repent, and believe in the gospel'" (Mark 1:14–15). Matthew summarized in a very similar fashion to Mark. However, Matthew went to great lengths to establish the lineage of Jesus as the seed of David and described Jesus through forty-two generations. Matthew succinctly expressed the threefold kingdom ministry of Jesus in terms of proclamation, explanation, and demonstration of the kingdom (Matthew 4:23; 9:35). Jesus summarized the message of the kingdom and gave his disciples instructions to preach the gospel of the kingdom, while healing the sick, casting out demons, and raising the dead (Matthew 10:5–15). Luke used similar language when he recorded Jesus sending

21. Luke 17:20–21; Matt 12:28.

out his disciples, but he added the testimony of the disciples after they completed their assignment. Luke records that the disciples were ecstatic about the response they received when using his name (Luke 10:17–19).

The term "kingdom" was constantly on the lips of Jesus and represented his core message. Jesus published or announced the readiness of the kingdom and taught people how to enter the kingdom and the type of people who inherit the kingdom of God (Matthew 5–7). Jesus' works authenticated the kingdom as a present reality as he cast out demons (Matt 12:28). His parables presented us with the mystery of the kingdom (Matthew 13). In prayer, he modeled what we should desire in our hearts—to see the kingdom come and God's will be done on earth as it is in heaven (Matt 6:10). His death, burial, and resurrection provided us with access to the kingdom in order to carry on his kingdom ministry of proclamation, explanation, and demonstration of the kingdom of God through the power of the Holy Spirit (Acts 1:8). His second coming promises the consummation of the kingdom (Matt 25:31).

While the kingdom of God is the focus of the Scripture, the message of the kingdom was a very obscure discussion in the patristic, Reformation, and contemporary schools of theology. The church fathers attempted to discuss the kingdom of God in a Romanized context. Athanasius (293–373) wrote in his statement of faith that Jesus ascended into heaven, which at that time was synonymous with the kingdom of God, "having been created as the beginning of ways for us," and that he showed us "a way up into the heavens, whither the humanity of the Lord . . . entered as a precursor for us."[22] It is believed that Athanasius spoke of heaven as the kingdom of God.

John Chrysostom (347–407) usually spoke of the kingdom as synonymous with heaven, as seen by his antithesis of "hell" and "the kingdom." But he added another element. In *The Kingdom of God in the Writings of the Fathers*, Henry M. Herrick writes the following about Chrysostom:

> But in his thought of the Kingdom, he is profoundly evangelical, and the burden of his splendid eloquence from first to last is, "Realize the Kingdom here!" and "Make earth a heaven!" He has reached the social view of the Kingdom as the redeemed society on earth, as it were by way of heaven, where Christ dwells and reigns. He thinks but little of the return of Christ to earth, the primitive eschatological view of the Kingdom having almost faded from sight. Placing the essence of the Kingdom in

22. Athanasius, *On the Incarnation of the Word*, 37–80.

> character, in a life well-pleasing to God, his strenuous ethical tone almost obliterates the boundary between things present and future.[23]

One of the most profound thinkers and writers about the kingdom of God, who has had the most influence on the subject, is Augustine (354–430). Herrick writes of him: "The chief works of Augustine have about 1,300 references to the Kingdom, nearly one-third of the whole number in the patristic writings under consideration. In the vast range of his works, the evangelical view of the Kingdom as the community of souls born anew through the gospel is ever dominant. In Augustine, this view takes its most characteristic form—in his explicit, though carefully modified, identification of the Kingdom with the church, which is found in several of his treatises, most fully expressed in 'De Civitate Dei [The City of God]' and in his 'Tractates on the Gospel of John.'"[24] This view, occasionally traceable in patristic thought from the time of Hermas, is nevertheless found in close connection with a clear distinction between the church and the kingdom, showing that the kingdom is generic, and the church is its only distinctive organized form. Augustine also considered the kingdom the celestial abode, but time and place are incidental and uncertain; to be in a state of salvation is to be in the kingdom of God. "The reign of God in the soul is always assumed of the members of the Kingdom, but the social idea receives the greater emphasis."[25]

Though the church fathers wrote of the kingdom, when we explore the kingdom of God in its original context, we do not find an overarching emphasis on it in that era. The patristic writers were captives of their history and contemporary theology, which was significantly impacted by their immediate context. The scope of this book will not allow me to discuss kingdom thoughts among the Reformers and contemporary thinkers in detail. However, I thoroughly investigate the kingdom of God throughout history in my book *The Kingdom Then, Now, and to Come.*[26]

In summary, the kingdom of God is the rule and reign of God in the hearts of persons that manifests the powers of the age to come in the now! Trevor Grizzle defines the kingdom as God's kingdom and God's power at work in his people. His definition highlights the power of the

23. Herrick, *Kingdom of God in the Writings of the Fathers*, 142–43.

24. Herrick, *Kingdom of God in the Writings of the Fathers*, 147–48.

25. Herrick, *Kingdom of God in the Writings of the Fathers*, 151.

26. Carson, *Kingdom Then, Now, and to Come.*

kingdom to change anyone's life that submits to God's sovereign rule and reign. God rules and reigns over Satan, sin, sickness, situations, and the saints. Brad Young, a first-century Hebrew scholar from Hebrew University and Professor of Semitic studies and Old Testament Theology at Oral Roberts University, and my mentor/friend, states that the kingdom of God is simply "God doing whatever he wants to do and his people doing what he says."[27]

The kingdom of God focuses on the redemption, restoration, and reconciliation of fallen humanity. When people live in the kingdom of God, they live under the rule or the crown of God, not simply the cross of God. The cross is the way to the kingdom; thus, it is a means to the end—the kingdom. To live in the kingdom, one must understand the royal decrees of the kingdom (the Scriptures). The reason many people are oppressed, such as in our Black and Brown communities, is due to a combination of factors that include individual responsibility, socioeconomic conditions, or both external and internal conditions. However, when God begins to reign in the heart and life of an individual, the individual can rise above external conditions through the power of the Holy Spirit.

God can lift anyone out of their condition. The Bible shows us how God lifted the Gadarene demoniac when Jesus operated in kingdom power. He was delivered from what we would refer to as mental illness; after an encounter with kingdom power, the Bible declares, "he was clothed and in his right mind" (Mark 5:15). The power of the kingdom and the Pentecostal experience can prove to be a force to be reckoned with. In order to understand the kingdom of God, the message of the kingdom, the model of kingdom ministry, and the mission of the kingdom, we must interpret it within the kingdom's original context and see its existential relevance and power.

THE GOSPEL OF THE KINGDOM

The preaching of the message of the kingdom of God has an eschatological edge. Jesus declared in his Olivet Discourse that the gospel of the kingdom would be an end-time message. Matthew 24 is often called the "Olivet Discourse" because Jesus delivered it to his disciples on the Mount of Olives. It addressed events that would occur before his second

27. Carson, *Crown and the Cross*, 28.

coming (*parousia*) and the end of the age. It states that false teachers and prophets will arise, along with wars, famines and earthquakes, and the persecution of God's people. The increase of wickedness will herald the events that will take place at the end of the age and the return of Christ.

What is the *parousia*? The term *parousia* comes from the Greek word παρουσία, which means "coming" or "presence." Christian theology refers it specifically to the second coming of Jesus Christ. This is an anticipated event in which Jesus is expected to return to earth to fulfill remaining biblical prophecies. Matthew 24, 1 Thessalonians 4:13–18, and the book of Revelation discuss the return and reign of Jesus Christ, describing the signs and significance surrounding the event. It is seen as the culmination of God's salvation plan, where he will establish his kingdom in totality, renew creation, and consummate history. During the *parousia*, it is believed that Jesus will judge the living and the dead, determining the eternal destiny of all people. This event includes the resurrection of the dead and is often associated with apocalyptic imagery.

Yet, it's against the backdrop of (partially) bad news that Jesus declared, "And this gospel of the kingdom shall be preached around the world, and then shall the end come." For many Pentecostals, this signals an end-time revival or a latter rain (Matt 24:14). The gospel of the kingdom appears in the Olivet Discourse amidst dark and evil times and the prophetic reality of the dark events that will plague our world. Yet, the gospel of the kingdom offers hope. It encourages living a life of faithfulness and readiness in expectation of Christ's imminent return. It also provides hope for our world, communities, and families right here and now.

Jesus' gospel of the kingdom was preached in the power of the Holy Spirit, accompanied by signs and wonders. In the time of Jesus and his disciples, it was believed that "gospel" was any news that came from the residence of the emperor in Rome, especially the birth of a son to him. "Gospel" means good news, not good views. God sent his Son, and Christ brought salvation, deliverance, and restoration to humanity—that was the good news. Thus, despite what church people traditionally think is the good news—Jesus' death, burial, and resurrection—Jesus pointed out a particular and specific gospel that should be preached. He called it "this gospel" of the kingdom.

Not every sermon you hear is "this gospel." Not every preacher preaches "this gospel." Many preach what Paul calls "a different gospel . . . which is no gospel at all" (Gal 1:6–7). Jesus began his ministry by preaching the good news—Greek *euaggelion* (gospel) of the kingdom (Matt

4:23; Mark 1:14)—and concluded his ministry on the same note. The kingdom of God, kingdom of heaven, and equivalent expressions appear eighty times in the Gospels. Trevor Grizzle asserts, "The gospel of the Kingdom was all Jesus ever preached. It was the theme and watchword of His ministry. In preaching, He declared the presence of the Kingdom. In teaching, He illustrated what it was and how it worked via parables. Through His healings and miracles, He demonstrated its power in the world. The gospel of the Kingdom was the message the apostles preached. It's a timeless message the church is mandated to preach today."[28]

We read in Matthew 4:17, "From that time on, Jesus began to preach, 'Repent, for the kingdom of heaven is near.'" Luke informs us that "Jesus traveled about from one town and village to another, proclaiming the good news of the kingdom of God" (8:1). "I must proclaim the good news of the kingdom of God to the other towns also, because that is why I was sent," Jesus told a crowd that was looking for him (Luke 4:43). When Jesus commissioned his disciples, "He sent them to preach the kingdom of God" (Luke 9:2). Luke records that it was this very message Jesus taught during his last meeting with his disciples before ascending into heaven. "He also presented Himself alive after His suffering by many infallible proofs, being seen by them during forty days and speaking of the things pertaining to the kingdom of God" (Acts 1:3).

The gospel of the kingdom was all the earliest followers of Christ knew. "Day after day, in the temple, courts and from house to house, they never stopped teaching and proclaiming the good news that Jesus is the Messiah" (Acts 5:42, NIV). When Philip went to Samaria, "they believed [him] as he proclaimed the good news of the kingdom of God and the name of Jesus Christ" (Acts 8:12, NIV). From prison in Rome at the end of his ministry, Paul witnessed "from morning till evening, explaining about the kingdom of God" (Acts 28:23, NIV) and was "preaching the kingdom of God and teaching the things which concern the Lord Jesus Christ" (Acts 28:31).

We are commissioned to preach the good news of the kingdom of God. The good news of the kingdom is God's defeat of the rogue king, Satan, and the restoration of what Adam lost in Eden. Christ's present rule of grace in people's hearts and lives will culminate in his reign in glory. The gospel of the kingdom is "the gospel of Jesus Christ" (Mark 1:1)—the good news that is all about him, the good news that he preached, that no

28. Grizzle, *Unpublished Notes on Matthew 24:14*, 1.

matter what things look like, God is in control; that Jesus died for our sins according to the Scriptures (1 Cor 15:3); that he is Lord; that he reigns, saves, delivers, and heals; and is coming again. These truths constitute the *kerygma*—the gospel the early apostles preached.[29]

The gospel is about Jesus—what he has done, is doing, and will do for those who believe in him. The good news is also the demands he makes on those who will follow him. If what we preach is not about Jesus, his lordship over our lives, his saving work, and our obedience to his commands, it is not the gospel. Paul tells us we must preach "the message of truth, the gospel of your salvation" (Eph 1:13). We must preach "the gospel of the grace of God" (Acts 20:24). We must preach the good and joyful news of salvation that Jesus created a new order and a new people (2 Cor 5:17), and that he will establish a kingdom on earth where there will be perfect peace and righteousness (Rev 21:1–5). The kingdom message we must preach is that Jesus offers forgiveness, and through repentance from sin and being born again, we enter his kingdom (John 3:5).

THE PURPOSE OF THE KINGDOM OF GOD

The question of "*When* is the kingdom of God?" requires us to examine the ultimate purpose of the kingdom of God. We must acknowledge again that the kingdom is a present reality and a future hope, suggesting that neither perspective lessens the significance of the other.[30] As mentioned, many of our modern and contemporary theologians have wrestled with this aspect of the kingdom of God. Grizzle states, "Since the future has already penetrated the present, it denotes any teaching about ultimate reality."[31] Two basic ideas are implied in eschatology, which is that the present evil age will end and be replaced by a new perfect order established by God. The transitions between these two ages are considered imminent and are summed up in the ideology of the kingdom being "already-not-yet," or the two-age motif. Embedded in the faith of Israel was both a realized and futuristic aspect of God's kingship and sovereignty.

The "two-age motif" is a concept found in Jewish and Christian apocalyptic literature that divides history into two distinct periods: "this

29. Carson, Gospel of the Kingdom Masterclass.

30. Ladd, *Presence of the Future*, 218–22.

31. Grizzle, *Unpublished Notes on Matthew 24:14*, 5.

age" and "the age to come."[32] This framework is particularly evident in apocalyptic texts and is central to understanding the eschatological (end times) expectations within these traditions. Let's begin by discussing this present age, considered the Adamic age or the age of the fall of humanity. "This age" is characterized by sin, suffering, evil, and the present world order. It is often depicted as a time of moral decay and societal corruption, dominated by forces opposed to God (2 Cor 4:3–4). Believers are seen as living amidst trials, persecution, and spiritual warfare during this period. It's a time of waiting and endurance for those who trust in God. Despite its dark portrayal, "this age" is not eternal; it's seen as temporary and will give way to a transformative event ushered in by God's intervention—the Day of the Lord.[33]

"The age to come" signifies the arrival of God's kingdom, characterized by righteousness, peace, and divine justice. It is the fulfillment of God's promises and the complete realization of his rule. This period involves the restoration of creation, the resurrection of the dead, and the establishment of a new heaven and a new earth, as described in texts like Revelation. Unlike "this age," "the age to come" is depicted as eternal, with no end to the peace and joy that it brings. It is the time of ultimate fulfillment and harmony. The two-age motif is a very important intertestamental period concept that appears in the Newer Testament but first in the Older Testament (Daniel).

These two ages are sharply contrasted in apocalyptic literature, such as the books of Daniel and Revelation. The texts prophesy about a cosmic battle between good and evil, where the forces of darkness appear to dominate "this age" but are ultimately vanquished with the arrival of "the age to come."[34] Apocalyptic writings often depict a dramatic intervention by God that decisively closes "this age" through a cataclysmic event, commonly referred to as the Day of the Lord, culminating in the initiation of "the age to come." Rich symbols and visionary experiences affirm the hope of restoration and victory for God's covenant people, who will be vindicated in the coming age. The two-age motif encourages believers to live with an eternal perspective, maintaining hope and faith amidst present difficulties in anticipation of transformative and redemptive events that usher in the "age to come." It offers assurance that present adversities

32. Ladd, *Presence of the Future*, 127–35.

33. Ladd, *Presence of the Future*, 135–38.

34. Collins, *Apocalyptic Imagination*, 75–79.

are temporary and will ultimately give way to God's triumph and the renewal of all things.

When approaching the end of the days from a biblical perspective, we must examine the subject matter of the messianic promise (a theology of hope) and the prophetic future of Israel. Eschatology, in its raw essence, is a kingdom of God perspective that culminates with Israel and the second coming of Christ. While the kingdom was a present reality in the ministry of Christ, after his ascension and establishment of the first-century church, many different interpretations of the kingdom of God entered the church. After the early church, the message of the kingdom of God became murky, and people's understanding of the message of the kingdom was unclear. Today, the message of the kingdom of God has been interpreted from different perspectives, from being a future reality of heaven and eschatological kingdom to a charge for social renovation.

The kingdom has been understood in diverse ways based upon the theological camp one resides in, whether that be liberal, conservative, fundamentalist, or evangelical. Grizzle, in *The Kingdom, Globalization, and You*, writes, "While some believe that the Kingdom is a present reality that has been suspended or the Kingdom is here, but not yet, one thing is for sure, the Kingdom of God was one of the dominant topics of Newer Testament study in the 20th century because it was the central theme of the ministry of Jesus."[35]

(1) The twentieth century marked a new era of interest in what was meant by Jesus' message of the kingdom of God and how his message impacts the church today. Two of the theologians who fueled the flame of interest in discussions concerning the kingdom of God were Johannes Weiss and Albert Schweitzer. These German theologians of the early twentieth century made their case that Jesus' teaching was profoundly Jewish and was deeply entrenched in intense eschatological hope. Thus, their view of the kingdom differed from nineteenth-century views, which focused more on the moralization of the kingdom, which made it more palatable to modern taste. This moralizing view argued that the kingdom was merely an expression of ethical sensitivity raised in the heart. However, Weiss and Schweitzer argued that Jesus' presentation of the kingdom anticipated God's intervention in the very near

35. Grizzle, "Kingdom of God in a Globalized World," 329.

future, which would reshape creation. Their view became known as "consistent or imminent eschatology."[36]

(2) For Weiss, the kingdom was purely religious, not ethical; it was not present in any form but was purely future. His consistent eschatology theory held that God's final miracle would be Jesus functioning as the Messiah, for in the understanding of Jesus, he believed that one day he would become the Son of Man. Grizzle explains:

> Schweitzer's position of the Kingdom posits that Jesus expected the end to come at first in His ministry. As He sent out the twelve in mission (Matthew 10:23), He believed before they finished their tour of the cities of Israel, the Son of Man would come and bring the Kingdom. Its appearance would mean the end of the present age, and He would be transformed into the Son of Man. When the disciples returned from their mission without this taking place, Jesus' hopes of the end changed. It would take suffering, His own suffering, for the Kingdom to come. His death would bring the Kingdom.[37]

(3) Though very different from Schweitzer, the oldest dispensationalists argued for the Jewish roots of kingdom hope. They associated it with the hope of Israel's Scriptures, placing the kingdom strictly in the future and referring to it as the kingdom of heaven. Because this understanding of the kingdom of God was considered one of the most thoughtful positions of that time, especially in a Jewish context, it created some interpretations that ignored other contextual understandings concerning the kingdom of God or the kingdom of heaven.[38]

(4) The kingdom of God (θεοῦ) and the kingdom of heaven (οὐρᾰνός) are synonymous in nomenclature. The kingdom of God is commonly used in all the Synoptic Gospels except the Matthean Gospel, which only uses it a few times. Matthew leaned towards using the phrase "kingdom of heaven." Matthew is the most Jewish of all the Gospels; thus, he shied away from using the name of God, which was held in extremely high regard among the Jewish

36. Weiss, *Jesus' Proclamation of the Kingdom of God*, 1–3; Schweitzer, *Quest of the Historical Jesus*, 346–52.

37. Carson, *Kingdom, Globalization and You*, 330.

38. Blaising and Bock, *Progressive Dispensationalism*, 32–36.

people. Even when translating the Septuagint, the Jewish scribes would put down their writing instruments when they came to the Hebrew word "Yahweh" or "God" and would bow in worship and simply say "the name" or *hashem*. The Jewish people were careful not to take the Lord's name in vain, the second of the Ten Commandments. Therefore, the scribes would employ what is referred to as the "tetragrammaton," which removes all the vowel markers to make it impossible to pronounce the name of God. So, when we explore the Gospel of Matthew from a Jewish perspective, we discover that there is no definitional difference between the kingdom of God and the kingdom of heaven, just Jewish preference.[39]

(5) Dispensationalism is a theological framework within evangelical Christianity that often distinguishes between the "kingdom of God" and the "kingdom of heaven." However, this distinction varies among theologians and is not universally accepted among all interpreters. Here's a general overview of how dispensationalists might differentiate between the two concepts:

(6) Kingdom of God: The term "kingdom of God" is typically interpreted as the universal reign of God, encompassing his sovereign rule over all creation, spiritual matters, and redemptive purposes. Dispensationalists might emphasize the spiritual and moral dimensions of the kingdom of God, highlighting its present reality in the hearts and lives of believers and how it encompasses all of God's purposes in history and eternity. The kingdom of God is often seen as transcending time and space, not limited to earthly or ethnic particularities. It pertains to the overall divine realm and authority.[40]

(7) Kingdom of heaven: A term predominantly used in the Gospel of Matthew, as previously mentioned. Dispensationalists often view this kingdom as referring specifically to God's rule from heaven, particularly in relation to the earthly aspect of God's dominion associated with the messianic reign. Some dispensationalists suggest that the kingdom of heaven has a more specific Jewish context, often tied to the fulfillment of Hebrew prophecies concerning the Messiah and the nation of Israel. It is sometimes perceived as reflecting Matthew's focus on Jesus as the Jewish Messiah who fulfills

39. Carson, *Journey Through the New Testament*, 252–53.

40. Blaising and Bock, *Progressive Dispensationalism*, 34–38.

Older Testament expectations. In dispensational eschatology, the kingdom of heaven might be associated with the future millennial reign of Christ, where Christ physically rules on earth for 1,000 years, which will fulfill promises made to Israel.[41]

(8) Dispensationalists observe the usage of these terms in specific contexts within the Newer Testament, arguing their different emphases. While these terms are sometimes used interchangeably in traditional interpretations, dispensationalists argue for nuances based on their distinctive roles in God's plan. Biblical history is divided into distinct periods or "dispensations within the dispensational framework."[42] The use of these terms can reflect different expectations about how God administers his authority and unfolds his plan through these dispensations, the kingdom of God and the kingdom of heaven. It's important to note that not all dispensationalists agree on these distinctions. However, this is one instance of how we can misunderstand the ministry of Jesus and miss what God is trying to say to us if we do not study the Scriptures in their original Jewish context.

The study of the kingdom of God produced different schools of thought about what Christ meant when he proclaimed the kingdom of God. While the theme of the kingdom of God has been the topic of discussion in many seminary classes around the globe, to date, this discussion has not been communicated to the church with any depth. The ongoing discussion in the schools of theology is whether Christ's kingdom is a part of active history or merely pertains to the end times. Over time, all the many views on the kingdom of God have congealed into certain major areas. Christ's teachings about the last things are inseparable from Christ's kingdom teachings; the kingdom will always be viewed from the perspective of the end of time. Debates on the kingdom of God continue to take place, mainly between those who hold to consistent eschatology, realized eschatology, inaugural eschatology, dispensationalism, and most recently, dominion theology (non-charismatic Reconstructionism and Kingdom Now Charismatic Theology).

We will look at the four main schools of thought plus a more recent view so that you can begin to understand the historical conclusions of scholarship about the kingdom of God. Here are the four theological

41. Ryrie, *Dispensationalism*, 167–72.

42. Ryrie, *Dispensationalism*, 29–44.

camps on the kingdom of God (as stated by Trevor Grizzle, one of my mentors and my former New Testament and Greek professor):[43]

(1) Consistent Eschatology—Spawned from the idea that any interpretation of Jesus' understanding of the kingdom of God must be consistent with the prevailing view and expectation of first-century Jewry, this approach states that the kingdom expected in the generation of Jesus never took place, and Jesus died disappointed that he was unable to bring it about. Proponents of this view are Johannes Weiss, Albert Schweitzer, and Rudolf Bultmann.[44]

(2) Realized Eschatology—Championed by C. H. Dodd[45], but also embraced by Rudolf Otto, realized eschatology proposes that the kingdom is here, and that all the people of God hope for in the second coming of Christ is already given. Challenged by his scholarly counterparts for the inadequacy of his perspective, Dodd modified it to incorporate elements of the future.

(3) Inaugurated Eschatology—This view is sponsored by R. H. Fuller, Herman Ridderbos, and J. A. T. Robinson and maintains that the kingdom is a present reality and future hope.[46] The people of God live in the tension of the new phase of the kingdom—Jesus' death and resurrection initiated the "already" kingdom, whose consummation will come in the future (the "not-yet" kingdom). Darrel Bock and R. H. Fuller argue that this view of the kingdom has both present and future elements.[47] This became known as the "already/not yet" view of the kingdom, or "eschatology in the process of realization." Joachim Jeremias, in his conclusion to his volume on the parables, closes this way: "In attempting to recover the original significance of the parables, one thing above all becomes evident: it is that all the parables of Jesus compel His hearers to come to a decision about His person and mission. For they all are full of 'the secret of the Kingdom of God' (Mark 4:11), that is to say, the

43. Grizzle, "Kingdom of God in the New Testament and Eschatology," 46.

44. See Grizzle, *Kingdom Advancing*; Weiss, *Jesus' Proclamation of the Kingdom of God*; Schweitzer, *Quest of the Historical Jesus*; Bultmann, *Jesus and the Word*.

45. Dodd, *Parables of the Kingdom*; Dodd, *Apostolic Preaching and Its Developments*.

46. Fuller, *Mission and Achievement of Jesus*; Ridderbos, *Coming of the Kingdom*; Robinson, *Jesus and His Coming*.

47. Bock, "Kingdom of God in New Testament Theology"; Fuller, *Mission and Achievement of Jesus*.

recognition of 'an eschatology in the process of realization.' The hour of fulfillment is come, that is the urgent note that sounds through them all."[48] This view was made famous in evangelical circles by George E. Ladd. In *The Presence of the Future*, Ladd attempted to define the kingdom by arguing the presence of the future. He suggested that the kingdom that will come has already begun acting upon the hearts of men and establishing the reign of God until the fullness of the eschatological manifestation. It is probably the most prominent view currently in Newer Testament circles at large, both conservative and critical. It is known as "inaugurated" eschatology because the kingdom was inaugurated or was dawning in Jesus.

(4) Dispensationalism—Dispensationalism teaches that there is a difference between the kingdom of God and the kingdom of heaven. The former has to do with what God is doing in the world today through the church—the latter, the millennial reign and Israel. Darrell L. Bock cites Blaising's observations of the four aspects of dispensationalists on the kingdom and its coming. Blaising notes four distinct approaches to the question among revised dispensationalists. The four approaches represented in this revised period are: (1) Alva McClain and Stan Toussaint (no mediatorial kingdom today, but a limited, interim rule; McClain interacts with Schweitzer and Weiss and stands closest to a consistent eschatological view); (2) Charles Ryrie (a spiritual, invisible kingdom today [the church] within a mystery of the kingdom to come in its cosmic fullness [which entails Christendom]), (3) John Walvoord (spiritual form of the kingdom is the church), and (4) Dwight Pentecost (the kingdom today is part of the present theocratic kingdom, a part of God's ongoing theocratic kingdom program). Where the first three approaches stress discontinuity with the past and future kingdoms, the last option is an attempt to articulate continuity in that program. Dispensationalism has never been as monolithic as its proponents and critics have contended.[49]

As to the present reality of the kingdom, Dwight Pentecost offers the following based upon what he calls the mystery of the kingdom, arguing

48. Jeremias, *Parables of Jesus*, 230–31.

49. See Bock, "Kingdom of God in New Testament Theology," citing Craig A. Blaising.

that it has nothing to do with the Davidic kingdom as prophesied by the Older Testament prophets. Here he is on Matthew 13:[50]

> This period includes the time from Pentecost, in Acts 2, to the rapture; that is, the age of grace (which we also call the age of the Holy Spirit or the church age). Although this period includes the church age, it extends beyond it, for the parables of Matthew 13 precede Pentecost and extend beyond the rapture. Thus, these parables do not primarily concern the nature, function, and influence of the church. Rather, they show the previously unrevealed form in which God's theocratic rule would be exerted in a previously unrevealed age, made necessary by Israel's rejection of Jesus Christ.[51]

THE EFFECT OF THE KINGDOM OF GOD

Historically, we have wrestled theologically with what effects the kingdom of God has on society. I often reflect back on some of my former seminary discussions over books such as *Christ and Culture*, by H. Richard Niebuhr.[52] This book is a seminal work in Christian ethics that explores the relationship between Christianity and society. Published in 1951, the book examines how Christians have historically approached the cultural dimensions of their faith and how they should engage with the secular world. Niebuhr proposes five distinct paradigms or approaches that Christians have taken in relation to culture:

(1) Christ Against Culture: This perspective advocates for a clear and unambiguous separation between Christ and the secular world. It often emphasizes the inherent sinfulness of worldly institutions and insists that Christians should avoid cultural engagement to maintain spiritual purity.[53]

(2) Christ of Culture: This view sees Christ as fundamentally compatible with the best aspects of culture. It often leads to an accommodation with cultural norms and values, suggesting that the

50. Matt 13.

51. Pentecost, *Things to Come*, 145.

52. Niebuhr, *Christ and Culture*.

53. Niebuhr, *Christ and Culture*, 45–82.

teachings of Christ can be realized within the existing cultural paradigm.[54]

(3) Christ Above Culture: This stance holds that while culture has its own validity, it is ultimately subordinate to the divine truth revealed in Christ. There's a hierarchical relationship where human culture is fulfilled and perfected by Christian revelation.[55]

(4) Christ and Culture in Paradox: According to this perspective, Christians live in a dualistic tension, acknowledging the secular world's values while maintaining that ultimate allegiance belongs to Christ. It emphasizes the continuous struggle and paradox inherent in trying to live faithfully in a fallen world.[56]

(5) Christ Transforming Culture: This approach encourages Christians to actively engage in and transform culture through the power of the gospel. It holds an optimistic view that Christian principles can and should permeate and reform societal structures.[57]

Niebuhr doesn't prescribe one model as the definitive Christian response to culture. Instead, he examines the strengths and weaknesses of each approach, recognizing that different contexts may call for different responses. His objective is to offer a comprehensive framework for understanding varying Christian engagements with culture, urging a reflective and discerning approach. This work speaks to the challenge of understanding the role of the kingdom, the church, and Christians in society.

Are we called to make an impact in our world or simply tolerate it until the *parousia* of Jesus? My perspective on the kingdom of God offers a dynamic vision that seeks to bring about tangible change in the world by fully embodying the teachings and implications of the kingdom message. Through my ministry, I call for an engaged and active faith that impacts the church and the broader community at multiple levels.

While the Scriptures discuss God's kingdom eternally, historically, prophetically, and eschatologically, the Gospel of Matthew helps us to understand the Jewish background of Jesus and the kingdom more than

54. Niebuhr, *Christ and Culture*, 83–101.

55. Niebuhr, *Christ and Culture*, 116–41.

56. Niebuhr, *Christ and Culture*, 149–52.

57. Niebuhr, *Christ and Culture*, 190–229.

any of the other biblical writings. In the Matthean Gospel, we discover four things about the kingdom of God:

(1) The kingdom of God is the rule and reign of God with both an existential and eschatological focus, beginning with John the baptizer and from the time of Jesus' Galilean ministry and the power of the future being experienced in the present.

(2) The kingdom is here, but not yet. The two-age motif of this age and the age to come comes to full expression.

(3) The kingdom is inaugurated in Christ Jesus' coming and will be consummated in his return.

(4) The kingdom was a present reality through the power of the Holy Spirit in the ministry of Jesus, manifesting in the proclamation, explanation, and demonstration of the kingdom of God.

The effect of the kingdom of God in society lies within key factor #4. The kingdom of God is the power of God expressed throughout the Scriptures, beginning with the book of Acts. They show us that the power of God remains a present reality in the presence of the Holy Spirit. Power is associated not simply with Jesus in the early church but with the Holy Spirit (Acts 1:8; 4:33; 6:8; 7:22; 8:10; 10:38). The Holy Spirit was the power source of Jesus that made the kingdom a present reality and a force against the power of Satan.

Paul refers to the gospel of the kingdom as the power of God unto salvation (Rom 1:16; 15:13,19; 1 Cor 1:18, 24; 2:41, 51; 4:20; 5:41; 2 Cor 4:7; 6:7; 12:9; 13:4; Eph 1:19; 3:16, 20; 1 Thess 1:5; 2 Thess 1:11; 2:9; 2 Tim 1:8). Paul and the early church accessed the power of the Holy Spirit when operating in kingdom ministry. The book of Acts begins with a query about the consummation of the kingdom, and Jesus states, "times and seasons are in the Father's hand, but you shall receive power after the Holy Spirit shall come upon you" (Acts 1:6–8). The book of Acts begins with the disciples asking about the kingdom and ends with Paul preaching the kingdom of God and things concerning the Lord Jesus Christ (Acts 28:31).

The Pentecostal experience in Acts 2 and the power of God at work represent the true intentions of God to break and destroy barriers that oppress people. As mentioned in the writings of Luke in Acts 10:38, Jesus was described as being a man from Nazareth who was anointed by the Holy Spirit and with power, who went about healing all who were oppressed by the devil.[58] However, Luke wrote that Jesus "went around," not just in affluent neighborhoods but in poor, disadvantaged communities, and he healed those oppressed by the devil.

When we talk about the kingdom of God, the Black Pentecostal church, and community empowerment, the work of Jesus serves as a model for the Black Pentecostal church not simply to engage in glossolalic speech but to heal the oppressed. The word "oppressed" in Acts 10:38 is the Greek word καταδῦναστεύω (transliterated as *katadunasteuó*), which means "to oppress" or "to exploit." It involves exercising power over others in a harsh or unjust manner, often leading to the suffering or marginalization of those under that power.[59] Luke states that the kingdom ministry of Jesus was focused on addressing the conditions of the marginalized by the power of God.[60] The Greek suffix -κατα denotes "ill" and δῦναστεύω means "to rule." The word is used in the present tense, which suggests continual action; it represents a simple statement of fact or reality occurring in actual time. The word is also a passive participle, which means another is doing the action upon a recipient of the action, and the mood is a participle used like a verb.

The devil is the ultimate oppressor, and the people are the victims of oppression. The Greek word "devil" is διάβολος, which means "slanderer, backbiter, accuser." It is often used in the Newer Testament to refer to the adversary or Satan, who seeks to deceive and oppose God's will. In Acts 10:38, Peter refers to Jesus of Nazareth being anointed by God with the Holy Spirit and power, going about doing good and healing all who were oppressed by the devil (διάβολος), for God was with him. So, the oppressive forces—metaphorically or spiritually—are attributed to the work of the devil. Jesus' ministry is shown as counteracting and liberating people from those oppressive influences, highlighting his role in freeing people from physical and spiritual forms of oppression.

This connection emphasizes the broader theme of liberation and empowerment through Jesus' actions, counteracting the negative forces represented by διάβολος. It underscores the significance of confronting and overcoming various forms of oppression—systemic, spiritual, or personal—aligned with the biblical portrayal of Jesus' mission. The term καταδυναστεύω (*katadunasteuo*) is a critical term as it relates to

58. Acts 10:38.

59. Acts 10:38.

60. Acts 10:38.

the kingdom of God, the Black Pentecostal church, and empowering the Black community. In the context of empowering the Black community, understanding and addressing καταδυναστεύω is crucial. It is no secret that the devil is oppressing inner-city Black and Brown communities in the forms of racism, classism, sexism, and egotism. And history has shown that various forms of systemic and institutional oppression have impacted Black individuals and communities for hundreds of years

When Jesus spoke of the kingdom, he did not speak simply of the kingdom as otherworldly; he spoke of the kingdom as invading this present age, which is under the sway of Satan (2 Cor 4:3–4). Jesus ushered the kingdom of God into the kingdom of this age, creating a clash of the kingdoms. On earth, this present age and the age to come converged; however, the power of the kingdom of God prevailed over the power of this present age. This present age, or the kingdom of darkness, which is under the influence of Satan, is ultimately responsible for the evil, oppression, and division in our world. But the kingdom ministry of Jesus prevailed over the power of this present age; it invaded the kingdom of darkness. Jesus stated that if he casts out demons by the Spirit of God, the kingdom has come unto you (Matt 12:28).

So when we see the ministry of Jesus beginning in the ghetto-like conditions of his time, he was sent to a people who had a debt to pay both to God and humanity, while being disregarded and discriminated against for their natural heritage. One can only imagine the effects slavery, oppression, and social injustice must have had upon them. The Jewish people of Jesus' era suffered from economic deprivation, poor access to healthcare, limited access to capital, and poverty crimes such as thievery, robbing, and mugging. They were in need of spiritual renewal, social reformation, and economic and community development.

Jesus' kingdom mission was to bring spiritual renewal and provide holistic deliverance that involved both the internal person and their external conditions. Jesus' ministry was the ministry of empowerment, not enablement. Enablement teaches one how to be cared for by another, but empowerment teaches one how to be responsible for oneself. Jesus required personal discipline and ethical behavior combined with the working of the Spirit. Jesus made his Holy Spirit experience relevant to the culture and the people by demonstrating and modeling kingdom behavior based upon the power of the kingdom, which the Holy Spirit gave.

When I think about the Jewish experience as an African American who is disconnected from his history and the slavery of his ancestors, I often liken our experience to the Jewish experience. While there are some strong similarities between the African experience and the Jewish experience, one of the most significant differences is that the Jewish people's history is well documented in the Scriptures. They were able to maintain their ancestry even during the exiles and the Holocaust. Though they are in the minority, they are inspired to become the preferred people of the Yahweh. Messianic Jews believe the Messiah came through their lineage, while more traditional Jews still expect the Messiah to come through their lineage. This creates a hopeful theology that can do nothing but inspire people even when they are being persecuted. They still clearly understand that they have a covenant with God. It is that hope that assists them in thriving and striving to maximize themselves in a context that threatens their existence daily as one of the smallest nations on earth.

The Day of the Lord, or the manifestation of the expected King, ignites faith, hope, and perseverance for those who put their ultimate confidence in God. It is my firm opinion that hope can inspire tenacity, perseverance, and courage to face tomorrow while expecting a better future. Jesus utilized the concept of hope and the power of the Holy Spirit to lift a people with a long history of oppression. Today, Israel is one of the wealthiest financial groups on the earth. If Jesus used the good news of the kingdom, the Holy Spirit, and personal transformation to lift a people whose history included Egypt, Assyria, Babylon, Persia, and Greco-Roman oppression, empowered them to withstand the devastation of the Jewish Holocaust, and defend their homeland against greater military powers, surely the gospel of the kingdom, hope, purpose, and the Holy Spirit can lift the Black community.

There are many semblances between the Jewish experience and the Black experience. Both were enslaved people for over 400 years. Each of these groups has gone through systemic racism and oppression while being economically frustrated due to lack of opportunity. But while they are similar, they still have some differences. One of the most incredible things that happened to Israel was that her national identity was restored in 1948. As promised by God, Israel reclaimed her homeland, her history, and her heritage. There is a huge difference in African oppression; millions of slaves were displaced without any connection to their tribes, families, culture, language, etc. Because of this important factor of historical disconnections to culture and tribes, it left Blacks as international nomads. However, if the similarities between the two people can be examined, I believe they would be an excellent start to lift and empower Black people.

Jesus stated that he came for the lost sheep of Israel (Matt 15:24). He said he was not here for the gentiles in a conversation but was asked for the crumbs of the children's bread (Matt 15:26–27). Jesus was able to lift Jewish people because he had a focus on Jewish people without being seen as discriminatory or racist. When African Americans give attention to African Americans, it is seen by the larger population of Christians as liberation theology, a part of the Black Lives Matter social justice movement, or some other name that carries a negative connotation. I believe that the body of Christ should support African American church leaders in making changes in the Black community. Some church leaders will lend their support to the Black community through proposals birthed from the unhealthy perspective of racism and paternalism; thus, their efforts never touch the Black community's actual needs. Their humanitarian efforts are sometimes trusted more than credible Christian leaders; that should not be.

Jesus' ministry touched people from Jerusalem, Judea, Samaria, and to the ends of the earth. When he commissioned the Twelve, Jesus gave specific orders for them to go to the lost sheep of Israel. We must learn from the ministry methods of Jesus how to address the marginalized, oppressed, and neglected. The condition of a person creates the mentality of a person, not the mentality of the person creating the condition of the person. We are all products of our geographical demographics and nurturing DNA. Jesus overcame "Nazareth" because he didn't have a Nazareth spirit (he did not look down on his community). He constantly referred to what he heard the Father saying and doing (John 5:19; 14:31).

The kingdom ministry of Jesus provided Jewish empowerment through a direct focus on the people and the power of the Holy Spirit. Jesus teaches us that empowerment requires focusing on those we have come to empower. The Scripture declares he had compassion for Israel because they were scattered like sheep without a shepherd (Matthew 9:35–37). As Jesus visited the devastated communities of the Jewish people, he was moved to do something. But what and how? What can you possibly do for people who are suffering from social rejection and societal oppression that creates low-level communities?

Jesus was piloted by the presence and power of the Holy Spirit. Jesus was born of the Spirit (Luke 1:35), he was baptized by the Spirit (Luke 3:21–22), he was led by the Spirit (Luke 4:1), and he was empowered by the Spirit (Luke 4:14). He went about doing good, healing everyone oppressed by the devil (Acts 10:38). Luke is clear that Jesus did what he did as a man, empowered by the Spirit of God. Jesus, as a full citizen of the kingdom of God, utilized what we would refer to as Pentecostalism to change an oppressed people in first-century Palestine and can do the same in twenty-first-century America and abroad.

As we consider the impact of Jesus in the lives of all people, but especially the poor, the term καταδυναστεύω (*katadunasteuó*) tells us that he came to heal those who were oppressed by the devil. He attacked the infrastructures that held people back and down. The Bible states that he went around doing good. The Greek term for "to do good" is εὐεργετέω, which means "to confer benefits." The outcome of his doing good was that the people were healed. Jesus went about doing good as a regular course of life for benefitting others. This passage highlights the positive and benevolent actions of Jesus. It emphasizes his proactive approach to bringing about positive change and helping others. This "good-doing" is associated not only with moral or ethical actions but is also practical, shown by his acts of healing and providing relief to those under various forms of oppression. Overall, the term εὐεργετέω captures the essence of Jesus' compassionate ministry and his mission to heal, restore, and uplift those in need. It underscores the kindness and tangible acts of goodness that he demonstrated throughout his life.

This clearly demonstrates how the Pentecostal church, through kingdom ministry, can empower the Black community. When we consider the word "oppressed" and what it means, we can see the opportunity to do urban or inner-city ministry. Jesus' ministry identified and dismantled systems of oppression, thus serving as practical models for the Pentecostal church involvement. We can allow Jesus' acts of alleviating the oppressive power of Satan upon the poor and neglected to be a model for us as we recognize the structures and practices that perpetuate inequality and work to change them. This involves challenging discriminatory laws, policies, and practices—key acts of empowerment.

Overturning oppression also involves ensuring that the narratives, experiences, and leadership of Black individuals are heard and respected. Encouraging diverse representation and participation in decision-making processes is vital. Combatting καταδυναστεύω includes creating avenues for economic growth, equitable resource distribution, and access to quality education. This helps rectify disparities that have resulted from systemic oppression. Building strong networks and partnerships within and outside the Black community can help resist oppressive forces. Solidarity movements can bring about changes through collective action and advocacy. Addressing the effects of past and present oppression also involves healing through restorative justice, acknowledging historical wrongs, and working toward reconciliation and empowerment. By actively challenging and overcoming the forces described by καταδυναστεύω, the Black community can move towards greater empowerment, equality, and recognition on multiple societal levels.

I believe that it is important not just to understand the works that Jesus did but also to understand who he was; he was and is a healer. Peter stated as an eyewitness that Jesus went around healing all who were oppressed by the devil, for God was with him. Jesus healed because he is a healer, not just of some people but all people. Regardless of their illness or condition, he cares and can heal. The Greek word ἰάομαι (*iaomai*) means "to heal" or "to cure." In the context of Acts 10:38 it describes one of the primary actions that Jesus undertook during his ministry—healing those who were afflicted or oppressed.

In this passage, ἰάομαι highlights the miraculous and compassionate nature of Jesus' actions. It emphasizes his role as a healer whom the Holy Spirit anointed to cure physical illnesses and liberate individuals from spiritual and demonic oppression. This healing aspect was a significant part of his ministry and demonstrated his authority and the presence of God's kingdom. I believe that it is important for the church to realize that the use of ἰάομαι here underscores Jesus' mission to bring wholeness and restoration to people's lives, both physically and spiritually. It speaks to the transformative impact of his presence and power among those who are suffering.

Jesus taught that the coming of the kingdom was also the coming of power. In our contemporary church, we have lost the dependence on and expectation of the power of God, a loss that cripples our faith. The kingdom may include speaking in tongues and flowing in the gifts of the Spirit, but it is also operating in the power of God to fight back the forces of evil that oppress people all over the world. Jesus taught that when he performed the miraculous acts of the Holy Spirit, it was a manifestation of the existential presence of the kingdom of God (Matt 12:28, by the Spirit; Luke 11:20, by the finger of God). The supernatural power of God is present existentially and eschatologically. The kingdom of God is an answer to the transformation of communities and peoples. God is reigning right now, and there are things we can receive from God now!

The kingdom was present in Jesus, and now the kingdom continues to be present in the Holy Spirit.

Matthew's Gospel provides a very powerful and, I believe, one of the most misunderstood narratives found in Scripture. Read Matthew 11:12: "And from the days of John the Baptist until now the kingdom of heaven suffers violence, and the violent take it by force." Many church leaders have traditionally taught that the kingdom of God was under siege or attack, suffering violence. However, a closer linguistic look at this text provides us with other options of interpretation. The word *biazó* (traditionally translated in the passive voice, "the kingdom is under violent attack") is a deponent verb that can be translated with either the middle voice or passive voice. However, linguistically, one must know that the deponent verb is passive in form but active in meaning Βῐάζω (Pres. Act.).[61]

The deponent stresses the active force of the kingdom of heaven, breaking its way forward. The active meaning of the verb βιάζομαι is used in the Septuagint. If we were to interpret it solely as passive, the kingdom would be under attack, which suggests "the use of property without the owner's consent" or "to acquire the kingdom by force." If interpreted in the middle voice, it suggests movement and forceful advancement from within for oneself. The Hebrew Heritage Bible, the NIV (1984), and N. T. Wright's translation render this word as a deponent verb, which is translated in the active voice.[62]

A better translation using the active voice of this deponent verb would give us this wording: "The kingdom of heaven is powerfully advancing, and people breaking out with its power are seizing hold of it." The NLT translates it "The kingdom of heaven has been forcefully advancing." The KNT translates, "The kingdom of heaven has been forcing its way in." David Flusser argued for the active voice based upon the verb's connection to Micah 2:13, where we see the Hebrew word (צַרָפּ—*paratz*), which is the equivalent of the Greek word βιάζομαι. The Hebrew word *paratz* describes sheep forcefully breaking out of a makeshift pen corral in ancient Israel.[63]

The breaker (*poretz*) forcefully opens the way by breaking down the makeshift wall, and the sheep follow the one who leads them forward.

61. Carson, *Five Perspectives of the Kingdom, Part 6*, 32.

62. Robinson, *Hebrew Heritage Bible Newer Testament*; Barker, ed., *NIV Study Bible*; Wright, *Kingdom New Testament*.

63. Carson, *Kingdom Then, Now, and to Come*, 515–16; Flusser, *Jesus*, 18–20.

The breaker is John the baptizer, and the King is the branch of David. E. Pocoke, an imminent linguist, made a similar observation in the seventeenth century in his commentary on Micah 2:13. The context and analysis require the active meaning of *biazó*.[64] In early Jewish thought, based upon rabbinic thought, Matthew 11:12 is a direct reference to messianic interpretations of Micah 2:13, where Elijah comes and prepares the way for the scion of David. Some powerful words in this text that suggest the kingdom is advancing with power are βῐαστής (noun), meaning "the one who advances forcefully," and ἁρπάζω (Pres. Act.), meaning "they do so with its power; to grab or snatch."

The kingdom is advancing! So, when you see evil being torn down and its effects reversed, that is the kingdom at work! This was the kingdom ministry of Jesus and must be the kingdom ministry of the church—we have the power to transform communities! The church is a powerful force transforming societies, and the church is a powerful force that is growing and growing. We must not limit our view of the church from a Western perspective. We must envision a world where the church is transforming communities.

64. Carson, *Kingdom Then, Now, and to Come*, 515–16; Pococke, *Commentary on the Prophecy of Micah*, 42–44.

10

A New Model for a Kingdom-Minded, Twenty-First-Century Pentecostal and Charismatic Church

THIS BOOK ADDRESSES SOME of the most relevant issues concerning the Black Pentecostal and Charismatic church, the kingdom of God, and empowerment. As we survey the issue of empowerment through the renewal of the Jesus model of kingdom ministry, we will discuss some very poignant and relevant concepts that I believe can serve as a model for the Black Pentecostal and Charismatic church.

Kingdom theology within the context of Second Temple Judaism is a framework for understanding the nature and expectations of God's kingdom as anticipated by Jewish thought leaders and texts from roughly 516 BCE to 70 CE. This theological perspective profoundly influenced the teachings of Jesus and early Christianity. Examining the kingdom teachings of Jesus from a Jewish context, not a European context, provides us with profound insight concerning the kingdom message of Jesus. It helps us to hear like they heard when we understand the Holy Writ in their context, which is the context in which Jesus taught the kingdom.

A kingdom theology formulated in Second Temple Jewish concepts includes the following:

- Messianic Expectation—The Jewish people expected the arrival of a Messiah, an anointed king who would usher in God's kingdom, restore Israel, and rule with justice and righteousness.[1]

1. Wright, *Jesus and the Victory of God*, 207–15.

- Restoration of Israel—Kingdom theology often included hopes for Israel's political and spiritual restoration, liberation from foreign oppression, and reestablishment as a sovereign nation under God's rule.
- Apocalyptic Vision—Many Second Temple Jewish writings contained apocalyptic elements, portraying God's kingdom as coming through divine intervention that would end the present evil age and inaugurate a new divine order.
- Judgment and Renewal—These texts frequently emphasize themes of judgment, where wickedness would be vanquished, and a new era of peace and justice would be established.
- God's Sovereignty and Rule—Central to kingdom theology is the belief in God's ultimate sovereignty. Even when the literal kingdom of Israel was not politically realized, God was still viewed as the supreme ruler over the universe.
- Rule through the Law—Acceptance of the Torah, or God's law, is a covenant sign of his kingdom rule, providing a guideline for living under God's sovereignty.[2]
- Community and Covenant—The community of Israel viewed itself as God's chosen people, tasked with upholding his laws and covenant in anticipation of his full reign.
- Ethics and Social Justice—Kingdom expectations included themes of social justice, where ethical living and care for the poor and oppressed were vital to preparing for the kingdom.[3]
- Divergent Interpretations—Within Second Temple Judaism, there was a diversity of thoughts regarding how and when God's kingdom would arrive. Different sects (e.g., Pharisees, Sadducees, Essenes) held varying interpretations and expectations.[4]
- Spiritual vs. Political Kingdom—While some groups expected a literal, earthly kingdom, others, such as the Essenes, emphasized a more spiritual or eschatological interpretation of God's coming reign.

2. Sanders, *Judaism*, 180–204.
3. Wright, *Jesus and the Victory of God*, 207–15.
4. Cohen, *From the Maccabees to the Mishnah*, 132–58.

- Influence on Early Christianity—Many of these Second Temple Jewish concepts were carried into early Christian thought, particularly through the teachings of Jesus, who proclaimed the arrival of God's kingdom in a manner that was both continuous with and transformative of these Jewish expectations.
- Jesus' proclamation of the kingdom of God blended apocalyptic expectations with ethical teachings, emphasizing repentance, the internalization of God's law, and renewal of the covenant—all influenced by Second Temple Jewish theological currents.

One of the most powerful aspects of Jesus' kingdom teaching concerned the existential reign and rule of God that broke into this age with power over the enemy, accompanied by the manifestation of signs, wonders, and miracles. The discussion of signs and wonders is a very controversial topic in Western civilization. Many churches and denominations adamantly teach that miracles have ceased, though miracles and the supernatural are experienced frequently around the world. Denying the existence of physical manifestations of the Spirit is known as "cessationism," which argues that Charismatic and Pentecostal theology and their practices regarding the "gifts of the Spirit" (healing, miracles, speaking in tongues, etc.) are not for these times. But what are signs and wonders? Are they the same thing? What is their purpose? How do they occur? The Scriptures hold the answers to these and many other questions regarding these supernatural phenomena.

Released by Touchstone Pictures in August of 2002, the science fiction sleeper *Signs* achieved international success, grossing $400 million during its cinematic run.[5] While *Signs* was born out of the imagination of its director and the existence of life on other planets is still a myth, its premise was sound. Truly, a world exists beyond humanity's natural ability to perceive it. These demonstrations occur in the form of signs and wonders, which characterize the life of Spirit-filled believers who exist in the kingdom of God and have committed themselves to following Christ.

We define the supernatural as "anything above or beyond the laws that govern the natural, material, and observable world in which we exist."[6] It is the term used by humans in an attempt to comprehend the magnitude and depth of God's infinite power and ability. Conduct a quick survey of the Bible, and you will discover that the word

5. Carson, *Signs, Wonders, and Miracles*, 49.
6. Carson, *Signs, Wonders, and Miracles*, 49.

"supernatural" does not appear. However, the Scriptures repeatedly refer to the numerous supernatural acts performed in the Older Testament and conducted by Christ, the disciples, and the apostles as signs and wonders.

The Older Testament recounts how God sovereignly chose a man (Moses) from which to create a nation of people to be his own special people. God chose and distinguished Israel from the other people of the world by commanding Israel to worship him, *Yahweh El Elyon*—the Most High God. He then provided the means by which Israel was delivered, preserved, prospered, and became a mighty fighting force.

- And I will harden Pharaoh's heart, and multiply My signs and My wonders in the land of Egypt.—Exod 7:3
- Or did God ever try to go and take for Himself a nation from the midst of another nation, by trials, by signs, by wonders, by war, by a mighty hand and an outstretched arm, and by great terrors, according to all that the Lord your God did for you in Egypt before your eyes?—Deut 4:34
- You have set signs and wonders and wonders in the land of Egypt, to this day, and in Israel and among other men; and You have made Yourself a name, as it is this day.—Jer 32:20

As used in these Older Testament, "sign" is the Hebrew word *oth*, and "wonder" is the Hebrew transliteration *mopheth*. Other Hebrew transliterations are used to describe a wonder, like *pele* and *temah*; however, *mopheth* is used more frequently.

Signs and wonders are referred to repeatedly throughout the Older Testament—their primary purposes being:

- To provide proof of the existence of God (Exod 7:17, Deut 4:35, Dan 3:28–29)
- To demonstrate the power of God (Exod 4:3–4; 7:10–12)
- To redeem Israel (Exod 7:16; 14:22)
- To preserve Israel (Exod 16:4–31; 17:5–6, 2 Kings 20:9–11)
- To demonstrate God's choice for leadership (Num 17:1–9, Josh 3:1–7)

Thus, in the Older Testament, signs and wonders are most commonly associated with demonstrations of God's omnipotence that establish his supremacy—Israel's deliverance from the land of Egypt and the rule of Pharaoh and God's establishment of Israel as his covenant people.

As found in the Newer Testament, the Greek transliteration for "signs" is *semeion,* and the Greek transliteration for "wonder" is *teras.* Each of these words is closely related to their Hebrew counterpart and refer to supernatural demonstrations of God's power.

- But He answered and said to them, "An evil and adulterous generation seeks after a sign, and no sign will be given to it except the sign of the prophet Jonah."—Matt 12:39
- For false christs and false prophets will rise and show great signs and wonders to deceive, if possible, even the elect.—Matthew 24:24

One could safely surmise that signs and wonders were a hallmark of Jesus' ministry. It's important that we consider the impact of signs and wonders in kingdom theology and ministry to understand their relevance to the ministry of Jesus today. The signs and wonders performed by Jesus did not simply provide proof to men that he was the Christ, the Son of the living God. They also:

- Caused the masses to marvel and be greatly astonished at the ministry of Jesus (Matthew 9:8; Mark 2:12; 5:42; 6:51; Luke 5:9, 26; Acts 3:10; 13:12).
- Caused people to believe in God (John 2:11, 23; 4:53; 7:31; 10:37–38; 11:45; 20:30–31; Acts 9:42; 13:12)
- Aroused the fear of God in humans (Matthew 14:26; Mark 6:49–50; Luke 5:26; 7:15–16)
- Caused the throngs of people who followed Christ to increase (Luke 5:15; 6:17; John 6:2; 12:9)
- Were demanded by onlookers to solidify their belief (John 4:48; 6:30)

Signs and wonders were the primary distinguishing features of Christ's ministry—a fact attested to by the Pharisee, Nicodemus, who came to Jesus by night and said to him, "Rabbi, we know that you are a teacher come from God; for no one can do these signs that You do unless God is with him" (John 3:2). In fact, the kingdom of God and the supernatural was commonplace in the ministry and message of Jesus. Jesus himself was raised from the dead; thus he overcame the great enemy of death.

Brad Young states, "The reality of the sovereignty of God means that everything is possible to the one who believes."[7]

Before Pentecost, Jesus sent out the disciples with the instructions to teach, heal, force out demons, and proclaim that the kingdom of heaven had arrived. Then, after Pentecost, the disciples were empowered with the Holy Spirit to go to the ends of the earth and to be witnesses concerning everything that they had learned from the teachings of Jesus. They were taught to use the power of the kingdom of God as a force of healing in a hurting world. The apostle Paul taught us that the same Spirit that raised Jesus from the dead lives in us to give life to our physical beings in the present time (Rom 8:11).

In Jesus' career, the teachings about the kingdom were accompanied by miracles of healing; the miracles were teaching tools. The most neglected aspect of the miracle episodes of the Gospels is the proclamation of the force of divine sovereignty. Often, people read Gospel stories of miracles without an awareness that the miracles teach a message. First and foremost, the miracles proclaim the present reality of the kingdom as suffering people receive relief and healing. Four elements of the healing narratives must be kept in clear view.

(1) One must recognize the character of God. Miracles begin with God.

(2) One must acknowledge the role of faith.

(3) One must define a miracle.

(4) One must hear the teaching message that accompanies the miracle.[8]

Comparing the miracles of Jesus with other healing stories from first-century Judaism gives fresh meaning and application. The message of the miracle events gains greater clarity. Within this supernatural context, Jesus was placed within first-century Jewish life, fulfilling his mission and purpose.

Newer Testament scholar Graham Twelftree observed, "Jesus' understanding is better reflected by saying that where the Spirit is operative in Jesus, there is the kingdom."[9] Indeed, the parallel in Matthew 12:28 mentions the Spirit instead of the finger of God. I believe that the Jewish background supports the "finger of God" reading as the actual words

7. Carson, *Kingdom, the Culture, and You*, 25.

8. Carson, *Signs, Wonders, and Miracles*, 25.

9. Twelftree, *Jesus the Exorcist*, 218.

of Jesus, while Matthew brilliantly finds meaningful application in the reference to the Spirit.[10] Significantly, both Matthew and Luke witnessed to the kingdom message of a miracle. The kingdom was actualized in the work of Jesus. The supernatural had become natural.

When Jesus desired to affirm his identity to John, he gave a message to John's disciples to "Go and tell John the things which you hear and see: the blind see and the lame walk; the lepers are cleansed and the deaf hear; the dead are raised up, and the poor have the gospel preached to them" (Matt 11:4–5). The answer Jesus gave iterates the very things Scripture predicted the Messiah would do. It is an answer in the affirmative because "Jesus is conscious that He now breaks the power of the devil and his angels because He is the One in whom the dominion of God is present on behalf of humanity."[11]

Trevor Grizzle postulates that Jesus was both the fulfiller and bearer of God's kingdom in the new era. The supernatural power at work during this period fills nearly every page of the Gospels.[12] So, as we consider a new model of kingdom ministry, the Pentecostal church must engage in a renewal of our understanding of the kingdom through the existential lens of the first-century ministry of Jesus. Grizzle conjectures, "The supernatural that attended the message and ministry of Jesus also accompanied that of His disciples, whom He sent out with the commission, 'Go into all the world and preach the good news to all creation. . . And these signs will accompany those who believe: In my name, they will drive out demons; they will speak in new tongues . . . ; they will place their hands on sick people, and they will get well'" (Mark 16:15, 17–18).[13]

Peter may be used to represent the apostles when he carried out this command: by healing the paralytic Aeneas and raising Dorcas from the dead in seemingly quick succession (Acts 9:32–42). But laymen also got into the act: "When the crowds [in Samaria] heard Philip and saw the miraculous signs he did, they all paid close attention to what he said. With shrieks, evil spirits came out of many, and many paralytics and cripples were healed" (Acts 8:6–7).

When we understand the message of the kingdom of God, at its roots it is victory over spiritual conflict that was present in both Testaments. Grizzle opines, "Israel's victories over her enemies were not

10. Luke 11:20.

11. Carson, *Kingdom, the Culture, and You*, 44.

12. Carson, *Signs, Wonders, and Miracles*, 41.

13. Carson, *Signs, Wonders, and Miracles*, 41.

achieved by sheer military might but by the power of her God. The wars of Israel against her pagan neighbors were the visible expressions of two kingdoms in collision; two opposed spiritual powers arrayed against each other in the supernatural world, the kingship of God overcoming that of Satan. Israel's triumphs represented Yahweh's defeat of the gods of her pagan foes."[14]

It is worth noting that God's first act of deliverance of Israel was attended by miracles. Grizzle argues, "The ten plagues in Egypt were God's judgment upon its pagan gods, but served as a vehicle of deliverance and salvation of the Israelites. God's involvement in guiding and shaping the history of Israel differentiates that nation and her history from the other nations of the world. Israel's history is holy because it is a catalog of the acts of God—punctuated with Yahweh's supernatural interventions. The ten plagues that struck Egypt were indicative of the supernatural hand of God and signaled God's future relationship with Israel. Crossing the Red Sea, the forty-year trek in the wilderness, crossing the Jordan, and conquering the Promised Land were all displays of the supernatural in the life and history of the people of God—Israel."[15]

Grizzle continues, "In his exhaustive two-volume work on miracles, Craig Keener has cogently demonstrated that 'all of the many ancient sources that comment on the issue [miracles] agree that Jesus and His followers performed miracles.' Drawing upon human and documentary sources, Christian and non-Christian, the Gospels through Acts, the epistles through Revelation, and up to the contemporary scene, he has shown, incontrovertibly, the important role of miracles in the life of Christ, His disciples, and the Christian church up till today. The God who littered Israel's history with supernatural displays of power continued to do so through Jesus. Jesus' miracles served a redemptive purpose, just as in the OT."[16]

Frank Stagg, commenting on the kingdom of God and Jesus, says, "The very power of God which came to expression in these mighty acts . . . is now at work in Jesus. This is the kingdom of God overcoming the kingdom of Satan. The miracles are signs of the kingdom already having been inaugurated. And the writer of Hebrews exhorted that the Father, who bore witness to the Son by signs and miracles (John 5:36–37), also

14. Carson, *Signs, Wonders, and Miracles*, 35.

15. Carson, *Signs, Wonders, and Miracles*, 35–36.

16. Carson, *Signs, Wonders, and Miracles*, 36–37.

worked with the apostles and others, confirming the gospel they preached by similar signs and wonders and gifts of the Holy Spirit (2:4)."[17]

The force of the kingdom demonstrates the supernatural in action. The kingdom, as a new model, is God ruling and reigning. He is ruling and reigning, and he will rule and reign. Thus, it is important as we approach the kingdom of God as a transformative answer to the social, political, and economic ills that plague the inner cities of America and the ghettos of the poor worldwide. As referenced earlier regarding the two-age motif and the clash of the kingdoms, the Messiah broke into human history, and God became flesh and dwelt among us. Jesus ushered in or inaugurated the kingdom in his personhood through the power of the Holy Spirit, who was responsible for his birth, affirmation at baptism, personal empowerment, and anointing to deliver and proclaim Jubilee. Paul wrote that the same Spirit that raised Christ from the dead would also quicken our mortal bodies (Rom 8:11). Essentially, the kingdom was ushered in through the virgin birth of the Messiah, borne by the Spirit, and continues today by the same Holy Spirit.

God is reigning as the King eternal over all creation, but he is reigning "in the Now"—in the present kingdom age that is manifesting every time the chains of darkness are broken, and people are delivered from the power of Satan to the power of God (Colossians 1:13, Acts 26:18). Jesus said that if he cast out demons by the finger of God then the kingdom "has come unto you" (Matt 12:28). And as discussed earlier, the kingdom of God is forcefully advancing and those who are laying hold of it are breaking out with its power (Matt 11:12). Jesus, as the breaker of Micah 2:13, has released the captives into a new, profound reality of kingdom power. God is ruling and reigning now in the hearts of men and women who submit themselves to the power of the Holy Spirit and the Word of God.

While the message of salvation is proclaimed in the evangelical movement, the kingdom of heaven is conceived as a future event following the church age. In the meantime, many mainline denominations accept the teachings of Rudolf Bultmann, who advocated a demythologizing of the text of Scripture for modern society.[18] Hence, the church no longer believes in the supernatural. It believes that the miracles of Jesus are myths that may be explained away as an embarrassment to people

17. Stagg, *New Testament Theology*, 137.

18. Bultmann, *Jesus Christ and Mythology*, 15–16.

influenced by the Enlightenment. In a postmodern and post-Christian age, miracles are viewed as a superstition of primitive societies.

The culture of the Western world is said to be "post-Christian" and "postmodern." Steeped in a scientific and empirical worldview, it has little or no tolerance for the supernatural. The cynicism and skepticism that imbues such an orientation either stultifies biblical miracles as creations of a primitive imagination or attempts to explain them away with rational arguments. But as J. D. Spiceland has observed, "Belief in miracles lies at the heart of authentic Christian faith. . . . Understanding the role of miracles in the genesis and spread of our faith is an imperative for today's Christian."[19]

A famous Christian missionary leader who served the church in India, E. Stanley Jones, challenged Christian believers with the power of Pentecost. After the disciples experienced the force of God's kingdom at Pentecost, Jones noted, "The supernatural had become naturalized within the natural as well as within the spiritual. They were ready for anything."[20] Based on the teachings of Jesus, everything is possible. Miracles do happen. The kingdom of God is still present in the now and is still manifesting its authority over the powers of Satan.

Because of the existential reign of God, the supernatural is available as the power of God to transform and set the captives free. Young states:

> In studying the Kingdom and the supernatural, we must carefully examine the miracles of Jesus within Charismatic Judaism of the first century. The creation of the world, as described in Genesis, set in motion self-perpetuating miracles of nature that should amaze us just as nature inspired awe and wonder in the faith of ancient Israel. Faith begins with wonder. Science does not contradict scripture. Even if we have a scientific explanation for how the natural world functions, the explanation does not explain the origin of creation. The more I study science the more I stand in awe at the greatness of our Creator. Science cannot prove or disprove our Creator. This is a matter of faith. Through the eyes of faith, we must recognize the Master Designer in the wonders of the world. In ancient Israel, God is known as the ultimate cause of all that is. The fact that the earth revolves around the sun results from the original miracle of creation. We must develop a sense of the universe tingling with the Divine Presence. Jewish scholar Abraham Joshua Heschel teaches us

19. Jones, *Christ of Every Road.*

20. Jones, *Christ of Every Road*, 164.

> that radical amazement opens our hearts to the experience of faith."[21]

When we look at the hardships of the Black community, it is apparent that even after having an African American US President, we need something more than simply socioeconomic and political change that impacts education and economics. We need deliverance ministry, which takes place on the back of the presence and the power of the Holy Spirit in kingdom warfare and sets the captives free. Deliverance ministry is not novel to the Black Pentecostal church; it just needs to be revisited and renewed.

Deliverance ministry is a key aspect of Pentecostal practice, focusing on the expulsion of evil spirits that are believed to influence individuals through various forms of spiritual attack, oppression, or possession. The theological basis for deliverance is:

(1) Victory Over Evil—Central to deliverance ministry is Christ's victory over evil, as depicted in verses such as Colossians 2:15, where Jesus triumphs over evil powers.

(2) Authority of Believers—Pentecostals hold that Christians possess authority over demonic forces, as shown in Mark 16:17, where Jesus states that believers "will cast out demons."

(3) Spiritual Warfare—Deliverance is often seen as a form of spiritual warfare against powers and principalities, emphasized in Ephesians 6:12–18. Deliverance ministry usually involves discernment and diagnosis (1 John 4:1), prayer and fasting (Matthew 17:21), standing in authority, or using the name of Jesus (Acts 16:18). An illustrative biblical example is found in Mark 5:1–20, where Jesus encounters a man possessed by a legion of demons. The demons recognize Jesus' authority; through his command, they are expelled and transferred into a herd of pigs.

Keith Warrington states the following concerning Pentecostalism and deliverance ministry: "Pentecostalism and its deliverance ministry form a significant facet of contemporary Christianity, combining fervent worship, spiritual gifts, and practices deeply rooted in scriptural interpretations. Through deliverance, Pentecostals believe they can witness God's supernatural power, furthering their faith and solidifying the transformative role of the Holy Spirit in overcoming evil. This vibrant practice

21. Carson, *Signs, Wonders, and Miracles*, 24.

continues to attract those seeking profound spiritual experiences and divine intervention in personal and communal struggles against spiritual oppression."[22] Warrington addresses deliverance ministry as an integral aspect of Pentecostal spiritual practice, emphasizing its connection to the experiential and supernatural elements of Pentecostal theology.

Deliverance ministry involves praying for individuals to be freed from demonic influence or oppression, reflecting the Pentecostal belief in the ongoing spiritual battle between good and evil. Warrington emphasizes the role of the Holy Spirit, a biblical foundation, experiential theology, community support, and the connection to holistic healing, saying, "Deliverance ministry is closely linked to Pentecostal beliefs in divine healing, reflecting a holistic view of salvation that encompasses physical, emotional, and spiritual well-being. It is viewed as part of God's redemptive work, restoring individuals to wholeness."[23] Warrington acknowledges the critiques that deliverance ministry can sometimes face, including concerns about psychological implications and potential misuse or harm. He stresses the importance of pastoral care and guidance to ensure that deliverance practices are conducted ethically and responsibly. His exploration of deliverance ministry within Pentecostal theology underscores its significance as a spiritual practice that highlights Pentecostalism's dynamic engagement with the supernatural, the experiential nature of faith, and the empowerment of the Holy Spirit in overcoming evil.[24]

Guy P. Duffield and Nathaniel M. Van Cleave affirm, in their book *Foundations of Pentecostal Theology*, the significance of deliverance ministry. The book also advises caution and pastoral care, ensuring that such practices are conducted with wisdom and sensitivity to individual needs. They state that deliverance should be approached with a balanced understanding, integrating biblical teachings, pastoral concerns, and the guidance of the Holy Spirit.[25] *Unleashed! The C1–13 Integrative Deliverance Needs Assessment*, by Peter Bellini, provides an in-depth exploration of the theological and practical aspects of understanding demonic influence and the practice of deliverance ministry.[26] Bellini approaches the subject with a scholarly yet accessible style, aiming to offer a balanced perspective

22. Warrington, *Pentecostal Theology*, 223–28.

23. Warrington, *Pentecostal Theology*, 176.

24. Warrington, *Pentecostal Theology*, 178–79.

25. Duffield and Van Cleave, *Foundations of Pentecostal Theology*, 414–16.

26. Bellini, *Unleashed!*, 152.

that is theologically sound and practically applicable. He recognizes the complexity of differentiating between psychological issues and genuine spiritual oppression. Bellini outlines a robust theological framework for understanding the nature of demons and spiritual warfare. *Unleashed!* is a theological resource and a practical guide for those involved in or studying deliverance ministry. It advocates for a balanced understanding that respects both spiritual and psychological dimensions, all while anchoring the ministry in Scripture and the empowerment of the Holy Spirit.[27]

A twenty-first-century model of the kingdom of God and Pentecostalism must involve deliverance ministry, especially when we consider the rise of mental illness and embrace that some of the cases involve demonic oppression and possession and require spiritual warfare and deliverance ministry. We must take a fresh look at the kingdom of God and its relevance for the Black and Brown community not simply from a social justice perspective, which is vitally important, but from a supernatural perspective. Because of the psychological and social damage that has happened to the Black community through the lasting impact of slavery, the Pentecostal church model must be Bible-centered, Spirit-filled, community-minded, and kingdom-empowered. The supernatural power of the kingdom must be the foundation of the prescription for community empowerment, or we will just have another sophisticated social movement.

The kingdom of God is not just a teaching; it is an experience. Those who encounter the power of God are delivered from the power of Satan—that's supernatural. Additionally, deliverance ministry is key to releasing the captives from addiction, low self-esteem, a poverty mentality of co-dependence, etc. Young highlights the power of deliverance and states, "In the Beelzebub Controversy (Luke 11:14–23), Jesus proclaimed the realization of the Kingdom when a man, troubled by demonic influences, was set free. The critics of the times accused Jesus of forcing out demons through the help of Beelzebub, the leader of demon forces."[28]

Jesus answered the criticism by teaching that a house divided against itself goes to ruin. Satan does not cast out Satan. In fact, Jesus reminded the critics that their own followers also force out demons. On the one hand, Jesus was telling them that both he and their disciples who

27. Bellini, *Unleashed!*, 33–35.

28. Carson, *Signs, Wonders, and Miracles*, 29.

expel demons are on the same side. On the other hand, the words of Jesus challenge us because he accepted the spiritual leaders of his day who were ministering deliverance.

The miracle event in the Gospel narrative, in which the man, troubled by demons, was set free, constructs a foundation. A spiritual force of evil afflicted a man created in God's image. The kingdom of God overcame the kingdom of Satan; Jesus forced the demons out. Jesus declared that he had forced out the demons by the finger of God; the supernatural had been experienced. This terminology recalled the story of Exodus, in which Moses worked miracles by the finger of God. Therefore, Jesus performed miracles of redemption like the redemption from slavery in Egypt.[29]

As we move forward in kingdom-empowered ministry, we must increase our awareness of the supernatural in all of God's creation. We must accept and anticipate the miracles of the kingdom. Young says, "We must develop our faith to expect the goodness of God in our lives as we seek discipleship in action to love others and demonstrate love, acceptance, and forgiveness. The power of the Kingdom is experienced in the force of forgiveness. This is what Jesus taught the crippled man. Jesus can heal spiritual and emotional injuries just as He healed the physical body."[30]

So we must consider a new model for Pentecostalism and the kingdom of God in the twenty-first century. Young adds,

> We must cause our faith to arise within our hearts. We must believe in God: that is, learn the character of God. Consider His ways. We must develop faith: that is, faith grows in an intimate relationship with God. Faith flows from action. Know who God is. Know that you are important to God. We must expect miracles: that is, seek the God of miracles rather than the miracles of God. His mighty works are sure to follow. Stand in awe in His presence. Wonder at the works of God. We must listen to the teaching message of the miracles: that is, understand the practical application of the teachings of Jesus. The miracles teach a message. God is speaking to you through His signs and wonders. Stand in radical amazement and learn the message of the miracles. The Kingdom of heaven is realized in the supernatural realm as a force in your life.[31]

29. Carson, *Signs, Wonders, and Miracles*, 29–30.

30. Carson, *Signs, Wonders, and Miracles*, 31.

31. Carson, *Signs, Wonders, and Miracles*, 31

Trevor Grizzle states:[32]

> The fundamental, cognitive orientation of the ancient world was one that believed in the supernatural. As it is with the majority two-thirds of the world today, people perceived only a thin veil existed between the natural world and the supernatural. Spiritual beings were very present in this world as a "natural" and normal part of life and made their presence felt—for good or ill. Getting to know how to tap into the supra-cosmological world and harness the spiritual forces for one's benefit depended upon developed and time-tested procedures and protocols. That worldview invited, expected, and accommodated, without any difficulty, super-mundane forces, whether benevolent or malevolent, and believed that they manifested their power in the world, impinging on the lives and destinies of nations and individuals. Any belief to the contrary was an aberration. Suspicion of the supernatural, miracles, and the extra-normal found little or no reception—even among the intelligentsia.

Grizzle also states, as we consider the place of the supernatural in a new kingdom model for the twenty-first century, "This was true of the world of Israel in the Older Testament (OT) and the first-century world in which Jesus and the apostles lived and ministered. They accepted, as fact and reality, the world of the supernatural. Jesus and the apostles believed in a dualistic world, one in which Satan opposed God and his purposes. The beloved disciple says, "The whole world is under the control of the evil one" (1 John 5:19). Jesus called the devil the "prince of this world," whom he had come to drive out (John 12:31). The conflict to deliver humankind from the bondage of Satan colored the message and ministry of Jesus and the apostles in the Newer Testament (NT). They viewed the struggle "as one between a rogue king and his kingdom and the true King and Kingdom of God."[33]

I offer this new model for the Pentecostal/Charismatic church in the twenty-first century—a return to kingdom theology. While we maintain our commitment to high ethical standards and sound moral discipline, we understand that we are who we are by the grace of God, as Paul said, not because we fulfilled the law. Kingdom theology is not a return to Judeo-Christian Judaism, but neither is it a turn to lawlessness. During his kingdom ministry Jesus did not weaken or compromise the law

32. Carson, *Signs, Wonders, and Miracles*, 33.

33. Carson, *Signs, Wonders, and Miracles*, 34.

(Matthew 5:17–20), but he came to fulfill it. We see Christ upholding the Torah but having grace and mercy for the people. Even on the cross, as he fulfilled the law of Passover, He cried out, "Father, forgive them, for they do not know what they do" (Luke 23:34). I believe that a new model of Pentecostalism must not compromise the mandates of Scripture or Torah, but we must understand that we don't fulfill it but that we strive to keep it through the process of the sanctification, which is an act of the Holy Spirit.

A new model of Pentecostalism and the Charismatic church in the twenty-first century must be known for more than glossolalic speech and vibrant worship; we must be known for compassion for the lost sinner, the hurting, and the spiritually troubled. I want to offer a practical model for twenty-first-century Pentecostalism ministry, constructs I have been employing for nearly forty years—a kingdom-minded model of ministry. Let me begin by briefly explaining what I mean by kingdom-minded.

I am a systematic theologian who specializes in kingdom doctrine, and I developed the construct "kingdom-minded" with five P's: Protection through Covenant, Protocol through Leadership, Parameters through the Word of God, Provision through Faithful Stewardship, and Perpetuity through Evangelism and Discipleship. I draw this model from elements present in the garden of Eden, the ark of the covenant, and the ministry of Jesus. Thus, if one is kingdom-minded, one observes and participates in these five P's.[34]

With Adam, God established the covenant of obedience whereby God took care of Adam as long as he obeyed (the Protection of Covenant); however, the covenant was broken when he disobeyed—"the day you eat thereof you will surely die" (Genesis 2:17). The Protocol of Leadership was exemplified in Adam himself; he was God's chosen leader by divine appointment, signifying that God appoints leaders for his divine will. When God told Adam not to eat the fruit of the tree of the knowledge of God, that was the Parameter by the Word of God. Adam could freely eat of any other tree, and all the ground yielded for him, signifying Provision through Faithful Stewardship. Perpetuity through Evangelism and Discipleship is seen when Adam was commanded to be fruitful and multiply (Gen 1:28).

We also find this model present in the ark of the covenant. The mercy seat represents Protection through Covenant, Aaron's rod that budded

34. Carson, *Kingdom Theology*, 214–16.

represents Protocol of Leadership, the Ten Commandments represent Parameters by the Word of God, and the manna from heaven represents Provision through Stewardship. The mobility of the ark, since it was carried from nation to nation, represents Perpetuity through Evangelism and Discipleship.[35]

Finally, this model is present in the kingdom ministry of Jesus; he is the object of the Newer Testament covenant. He was divinely appointed, and he divinely appointed (Protocol of Leadership). He was the Word of God, and he taught the parameters of God that faithfulness to the kingdom would bring provisional favor (Parameters by the Word and Provision through Faithful Stewardship). He taught that this gospel is to be preached around the world as a witness (Perpetuity through Evangelism and Discipleship).[36] Jesus teaches us that in order to have an effective ministry, we should be clothed and empowered by the Holy Spirit (Luke 24:49; Acts 1:8).

A kingdom mentality, or being kingdom-minded, is one of being fueled by the presence and the power of the Holy Spirit, who drives us to be witnesses to what we have heard, seen, and experienced. The kingdom is not simply knowledge, but it is an experience. In fact, it is a life-changing experience that removes Satan from the throne of your heart and places Christ on the throne of your heart/soul as Lord, Savior, and King.

Unfortunately, in the contemporary church, we see Jesus as Savior but do not honor him as Lord. I contend it is due to the nature of a Savior vs. the nature of a Lord or King. Everyone can appreciate a helping hand, but not everyone desires to subjugate themselves to the wishes of another. In the Newer Testament, the word "Savior" is used eighteen times, yet the word "Lord" is used about 450 times. Saving is what Jesus does, but Lord is who he is! We must change or adjust our mentality to become a kingdom-minded church.

What does it mean to be a kingdom-minded church? "Kingdom-minded" is a term often used within Christian contexts to describe individuals or communities that prioritize the values, mission, and priorities of God's kingdom as central to their lives. It reflects a broad spiritual outlook in which believers view their lives and actions in the context of God's sovereign rule and purpose.

35. Carson, *Kingdom Theology*, 214–16.

36. Carson, *Kingdom Theology*, 214–16.

I believe that a kingdom-minded church is comprised of kingdom-minded individuals who practice the five P's. But what does it look like to be a kingdom-minded individual?

- Kingdom-minded people prioritize the spiritual, ethical, and missional teachings of Jesus about the kingdom of God. This includes living out values such as love, justice, mercy, and humility, as outlined in the Gospels.
- Kingdom-minded people actively participate in the Great Commission, seeking to spread the message of Jesus and the kingdom of God through power evangelism, service, and discipleship.
- Kingdom-minded people have an outlook that emphasizes eternal values over temporal gains, making decisions that reflect long-term spiritual outcomes rather than immediate personal benefits.
- They work towards unity within the body of Christ (the church) and embrace a community-oriented approach, supporting one another and addressing communal needs.
- Kingdom-mindedness includes concern for social justice, peacemaking, and advocating for the marginalized and oppressed, reflecting God's care for justice throughout biblical teachings.

A kingdom-minded church should act and do things differently than any traditional church. These churches, regardless of denomination, should espouse the five P's in their ministries to the glory of God:

- A kingdom-minded church emphasizes teaching and living in accordance with Jesus' teachings related to the kingdom of God. Preaching typically reflects themes about God's righteousness, mercy, and love as shared in the Newer Testament.
- It actively engages in local and global missions, intending to offer spiritual guidance and practical support to those in need. The aim is often to reflect God's heart for the world through words and actions.
- Such a church invests in its local community, striving to address issues such as poverty, injustice, and social disparity, often through various programs and partnerships.
- The church focuses on nurturing believers to grow in faith and maturity, often through small groups, Bible studies, and mentorship programs that emphasize living out kingdom values.

- Being kingdom-minded often involves creating an inclusive and welcoming atmosphere, accepting individuals of diverse backgrounds, and integrating them into the faith community, creating an authentic multicultural environment.
- These churches often look for innovative ways to reach people and adapt to cultural changes without compromising core doctrinal truths. This might include using technology for outreach, experimenting with service styles, or redefining traditional church roles.

Overall, a kingdom-minded church seeks to embody and manifest the reign of God in all its practices, reflecting both a commitment to Christ's teachings and active participation in his redemptive work in the world. Using my ministry efforts as an example, I suggest a ministry model that addresses the following areas:

(1) Education: Day care, private Christian school, after-school care program
(2) Evangelism/Discipleship Global Presence: Missional academy for children
(3) Exposure: Bringing in a broad variety of experienced guest speakers, field and mission trips
(4) Economics/Wealth-Building: Financial literacy classes and wealth-building seminars
(5) Social Support for Families, Males, and Females: Family ministries, mentoring programs for both males and females, and men's and women's ministry
(6) Entrepreneurship: Training and coaching
(7) Empowerment and Capacity Building: Empowerment seminars and classes
(8) Social Justice: Engagement in social justice for Black/Brown communities
(9) Theological Training: Training for laypeople and pastors; Bible college and seminary
(10) Leadership Development: Creating leaders through a leadership pipeline
(11) Business development: Incubate and launch successful businesses

These are some of the ways I have found to help transform Black and Brown communities for forty years around the globe! Selah!

Bibliography

Adenekan-Koevoets, B. "Nigerian Pentecostal Diasporic Missions and Missionary Churches in Europe." *MIST: Journal for Mission Studies* 38, no. 3 (2021) 424–42.

Adu-Ampong, Emmanuel Akwasi, and Ishmael Mensah. "African Diaspora Tourism: Concepts, Issues, and Prospects beyond Slavery-Oriented Heritage." In *Cultural Heritage and Tourism in Africa*, edited by Dallen J. Timothy, 184–99. Abingdon: Routledge, 2023.

"Africa Rediscovered." *Ebony*, February 1960, 96–97.

African Development Bank. *Feeding Africa: Strategy for Agricultural Transformation in Africa, 2016–2025*. Abidjan: AfDB, 2016.

———. *Investing in the Creative Industries: Culture as a Driver of Africa's Growth*. Abidjan: AfDB, 2018.

Akurang-Parry, Kwabena O. "Ghana's Year of Return and the Politics of Diaspora Engagement." *African and Black Diaspora: An International Journal* 14, no. 1 (2021) 1–15.

Alexander, Estrelda Y. *Black Fire: One Hundred Years of African American Pentecostalism*. Downers Grove, IL: IVP Academic, 2011.

American Civil Liberties Union. "School-to-Prison Pipeline." June 27, 2023. https://www.aclu.org/issues/juvenile-justice/school-prison-pipeline.

American Psychological Association. "Mental Health Disparities: African Americans." https://www.apa.org/pi/disability/resources/publications/african-american.

American University SOE Online. "Who is Most Affected by the School-to-Prison Pipeline." American University School of Education, February 24, 2021. https://soeonline.american.edu/blog/school-to-prison-pipeline/.

Anderson, Allan. *An Introduction to Pentecostalism: Global Charismatic Christianity*. 2nd ed. Cambridge: Cambridge University Press, 2014.

———. *To the Ends of the Earth: Pentecostalism and the Transformation of World Christianity*. Oxford: Oxford University Press, 2013.

Anderson, Robert Mapes. *Vision of the Disinherited: The Making of American Pentecostalism*. New York: Oxford University Press, 1979.

Anselm Ministries. "Montanus | Faith Seeking Understanding." https://faith-seeking-understanding.org/tag/montanus/.

Artiga, Samantha, Latoya Hill, and Anthony Damico. "Health Coverage by Race and Ethnicity, 2010–2022." Kaiser Family Foundation, January 11, 2024. https://www.kff.org/racial-equity-and-health-policy/issue-brief/health-coverage-by-race-and-ethnicity/.

Asamoah-Gyadu, Johnson Kwabena. *Sighs and Signs of the Spirit: Ghanaian Perspectives on Pentecostalism and Renewal in Africa.* Eugene, OR: Wipf and Stock, 2015.

Assemblies of God. "Our Statistics." https://ag.org/About/Statistics.

Athanasius. *On the Incarnation of the Word.* In *Nicene and Post-Nicene Fathers*, Series II, Vol. 4, edited by Philip Schaff and Henry Wace, 37–80. Peabody, MA: Hendrickson, 1994.

Atherstone, Andrew. *Hillsong Church: A Sociological Analysis of Contemporary Pentecostalism in Australia and Beyond.* London: Routledge, 2023.

Azusa Books. "The Azusa Papers." https://www.azusabooks.org/papers.shtml.

Baer, Hans A., and Merrill Singer. *African-American Religion in the Twentieth Century: Varieties of Protest and Accommodation.* Knoxville: University of Tennessee Press, 1992.

———. *African American Religion: Varieties of Protest and Accommodation.* 2nd ed. Knoxville: University of Tennessee Press, 2024.

Barker, Kenneth L., ed. *The NIV Study Bible.* Grand Rapids: Zondervan, 1984.

Barnes, Andrew. "Review: 'How Africa Shaped the Christian Mind: Recovering the African Seedbed of Western Christianity.'" *Church History* 77, no. 4 (December 1, 2008) 1108–10. https://doi.org/10.1017/s0009640708001984.

Barnes, S. L. "Functions of Religion among Young Black Members: Respectability, Morality, and Conservatism." *Religions* 14, no. 9 (2023) 1–19.

Barrett, David B., George T. Kurian, and Todd M. Johnson. *World Christian Encyclopedia: A Comparative Survey of Churches and Religions in the Modern World.* 2nd ed. Oxford: Oxford University Press, 2001.

Bartleman, Frank, and Cecil M. Robeck Jr. *How Pentecost Came to Los Angeles : The Story behind the Azusa Street Revival.* Springfield, MO: Gospel Publishing House, 2017.

Bauer, Walter, Frederick W. Danker, William F. Arndt, and F. Wilbur Gingrich. *A Greek-English Lexicon of the New Testament and Other Early Christian Literature.* 3rd ed. Chicago: University of Chicago Press, 2000.

Beasley-Murray, George R. *Jesus and the Kingdom of God.* Grand Rapids: Eerdmans, 1986.

———. *John.* Word Biblical Commentary. Waco, TX: Word, 1987.

Bellini, Peter J. *Unleashed! The C1-13 Integrative Deliverance Needs Assessment: A Qualitative and Quantitative Probability Indicator.* Eugene, OR: Wipf and Stock, 2018.

Bennett, Lerone. *Before the Mayflower: A History of the Negro in America, 1619–1962.* Chicago: Johnson, 1963.

Benyah, F. "Pentecostal/Charismatic Churches and the Provision of Social Initiatives such as Education, Health, Rehabilitation Services, and Poverty Reduction Programs." *Transformation: An International Journal of Holistic Mission Studies* 38, no. 4 (2021) 257–71.

Berger, Peter L. *The Sacred Canopy: Elements of a Sociological Theory of Religion.* New York: Anchor, 1967.

Berlin, Ira. *Many Thousands Gone: The First Two Centuries of Slavery in North America.* Cambridge: Belknap Press of Harvard University Press, 1998.

Berry, Mary Frances, and John W. Blassingame. *Long Memory: The Black Experience in America.* New York: Oxford University Press, 1982.

BlackDemographics.com. "Black Men/Women: Who Works and for How Much?" December 1, 2023. https://blackdemographics.com/black-men-women-who-works-and-for-how-much/.

Blaising, Craig A., and Darrell L. Bock. *Progressive Dispensationalism*. Wheaton, IL: Victor, 1993.

Blassingame, John W. *The Slave Community: Plantation Life in the Antebellum South*. Rev. ed. New York: Oxford University Press, 1979.

Bloesch, Donald G. *The Holy Spirit: Works & Gifts*. Christian Foundations. Downers Grove, IL: InterVarsity, 2000.

Blumhofer, Edith L. *Daughters of the Spirit: Women Leaders in the Early Pentecostal Movement*. Urbana: University of Illinois Press, 2002.

———. *Pentecost in My Soul: Explorations in the Meaning of Pentecostal Experience in the Assemblies of God*. Springfield, MO: Gospel Publishing House, 1989.

———. *Restoring the Faith: The Assemblies of God, Pentecostalism, and American Culture*. Urbana: University of Illinois Press, 1993.

Board of Governors of the Federal Reserve System. "2016 Survey of Consumer Finances." The Federal Reserve, September 2017. www.federalreserve.gov/econres/scf_2016.htm.

Bock, Darrell L. "The Kingdom of God in New Testament Theology: The Battle, the Christ, the Spirit-Bearer, and Returning Son of Man." In *Looking Into the Future: Evangelical Studies in Eschatology*, edited by David W. Baker, 28–60. Grand Rapids: Baker, 2001. https://bible.org/article/kingdom-god-new-testament-theology-battle-christ-spirit-bearer-and-returning-son-man.

Boles, John B. *Black Southerners, 1619–1869*. Lexington: University Press of Kentucky, 1983.

Bonilla-Silva, Eduardo. "Rethinking Racism: Towards a Structural Interpretation." Center for Research on Social Organization, October 1994. http://deepblue.lib.umich.edu/bitstream/2027.42/51290/1/526.pdf.

Bowler, Kate. *Blessed: A History of the American Prosperity Gospel*. New York: Oxford University Press, 2013.

Bradley, Anthony B. *Liberating Black Theology: The Bible and the Black Experience in America*. Wheaton, IL: Crossway, 2010.

Brendlinger, Irv A. "A Study of the Views of Major Eighteenth Century Evangelicals on Slavery and Race, With Special Reference to John Wesley." PhD diss., George Fox University, 1982. http://digitalcommons.georgefox.edu/cgi/viewcontent.cgi?article=1123&context=ccs.

Bright, Jake, and Aubrey Hruby. *The Next Africa: An Emerging Continent Becomes a Global Powerhouse*. New York: St. Martin's, 2015.

Brown, Raymond E. *The Gospel According to John I–XII*. Anchor Bible 29. Garden City, NY: Doubleday, 1966.

Bruce, F. F. *The Book of Acts*. New International Commentary on the New Testament. Grand Rapids: Eerdmans, 1988.

Bultmann, Rudolf. *Jesus and the Word*. Translated by Louise Pettibone Smith and Erminie Huntress Lantero. New York: Charles Scribner's Sons, 1934.

———. *Jesus Christ and Mythology*. New York: Charles Scribner's Sons, 1958.

Bundy, David. "Swedish (Pentecostal Movement)." In *The New International Dictionary of Pentecostal and Charismatic Movements*, rev. ed., edited by Stanley M. Burgess and Eduard M. van der Maas. Grand Rapids: Zondervan, 2002.

Bureau of Justice Statistics. *Prisoners in 2019 (NCJ 255115).* Washington, DC: U.S. Department of Justice, Office of Justice Programs, October 2020. https://bjs.ojp.gov/content/pub/pdf/p19.pdf.

———. *Prisoners in 2019.* October 2020. https://bjs.ojp.gov/library/publications/prisoners-2019.

———. *Prisoners in 2020.* Bureau of Justice Statistics, December 2021. https://bjs.ojp.gov/library/publications/prisoners-2020-statistical-tables.

———. *Prisoners in 2021.* Washington, DC: U.S. Department of Justice, December 2022. https://bjs.ojp.gov/library/publications/prisoners-2021-statistical-tables.

Butler, Anthea D. *Women in the Church of God in Christ: Making a Sanctified World.* Chapel Hill: University of North Carolina Press, 2007.

Bynoe, Yvonne. *Stand and Deliver: Political Activism, Leadership, and Hip Hop Culture.* Brooklyn: Soft Skull, 2001.

Cannon, Katie G. *Black Womanist Ethics.* Atlanta: Scholars, 1988.

Carroll, Charles. *The Negro: A Beast, or in the Image of God?* St. Louis: American Book and Bible, 1900.

Carson, Dana. *The Crown and the Cross: Understanding the Kingdom of God.* Houston: Dana Carson Kingdom Ministries, 2015.

———. *Five Perspectives of the Kingdom, Part 6: Kingdom Power.* Vol. 8. Houston: Kingdom Publishing and Printing, 2021.

———. *The Five Watersheds of History and Theology.* Houston: Kingdom Builders, 2001.

———. "The Gospel of the Kingdom Masterclass." PowerPoint presentation, International Leadership Conference, Orlando, Florida, May 5, 2023.

———. "How Independent Churches in Select Areas Are Reaching Young Adult African American Males Between the Ages of 14–35." DMin. diss., Boston University, 1995.

———. *Jesus the Jewish Messiah and His Kingdom Ministry.* Houston: Kingdom Publishing and Printing, 2018.

———. *A Journey Through the New Testament: Examining the New Testament in Light of the Kingdom of God.* Houston: Kingdom Publishing and Printing, 2013.

———. *Kingdom First.* Houston: Dana Carson Kingdom Ministries, 2018.

———. *The Kingdom, the Culture, and You.* Houston: Dana Carson Kingdom Ministries, 2014.

———. *The Kingdom, Globalization and You.* Houston: Dana Carson Kingdom Ministries, 2017.

———. *The Kingdom Then, Now, and to Come.* Houston: Dana Carson Kingdom Ministries, 2016.

———. *Kingdom Theology: An Introduction to Kingdom Doctrine.* Houston: Kingdom Publishing and Printing, 2023.

———. *Kingdom Vision.* Houston: Dana Carson Kingdom Ministries, 2018.

———. "Nicodemus and Jesus." Unpublished sermon manuscript.

———. *One True King: The Biblical Theology of the Kingdom.* Houston: Dana Carson Kingdom Ministries, 2023.

———. *Signs, Wonders, and Miracles and the Kingdom of God.* Vol. 1. Houston: Dana Carson Kingdom Ministries, 2018.

———. *What Meaneth This? Getting the Most out of the Text from a Biblical Perspective.* Unpublished manuscript, 2022.

Casanova, José. *Public Religions in the Modern World.* Chicago: University of Chicago Press, 1994.

Center for American Progress. *The Latest Poverty, Income, and Food Insecurity Data Reveal Continuing Racial Disparities.* Washington, DC: Center for American Progress, December 21, 2022.

Centers for Disease Control and Prevention. "Health, United States Spotlight: Racial and Ethnic Disparities in Heart Disease." U.S. Department of Health And Human Services. https://www.cdc.gov/nchs/hus/spotlight/heart_disease.htm.

———. *National Health and Nutrition Examination Survey (NHANES).* Hyattsville, MD: U.S. Department of Health and Human Services, Centers for Disease Control and Prevention, National Center for Health Statistics, updated 2023. https://www.cdc.gov/nchs/nhanes/index.htm.

Chesnut, Mary Boykin. *A Diary from Dixie.* New York: D. Appleton and Company, 1905.

Choi, Jung Hyun. "Breaking Down the Black-White Homeownership Gap." Urban Wire (blog), Urban Institute, February 21, 2020. https://www.urban.org/urban-wire/breaking-down-black-white-homeownership-gap.

Chopp, Rebecca S., and Mark Lewis Taylor. *Lifting the Curse of Babel: Language, Diversity, and the Church.* Nashville: Abingdon, 2004.

Clemmons, Ithiel C. *Bishop C. H. Mason and the Roots of the Church of God in Christ.* Lexington, KY: Pneuma Life, 1996.

COGIC Education Commission. "About Us—COGIC Education Commission." November 2, 2023. https://www.cogic.org/education/about-us.

Cohen, Shaye J. D. *From the Maccabees to the Mishnah.* 3rd ed. Louisville: Westminster John Knox, 2014.

Collins, Barbara J. "Teaching to Transform: The Legacy of African American Scholar-activists in Higher Education." *ScholarWorks*, January 1, 2000. https://scholarworks.umass.edu/cgi/viewcontent.cgi?article=1849&context=dissertations.

Collins, John J. *The Apocalyptic Imagination: An Introduction to Jewish Apocalyptic Literature.* 3rd ed. Grand Rapids: Eerdmans, 2016.

Combrinck, Johan. "Case Study of Deeper Life Bible Church." *Developing Country Studies* 3, no. 12 (2013) 1–7. https://iiste.org/Journals/index.php/JCSD/article/download/9156/9375.

The Concise Columbia Encyclopedia. "Great Awakening." 361. New York: Columbia University Press, 1983.

Cone, James H. *A Black Theology of Liberation.* Philadelphia: J. B. Lippincott, 1970.

Cox, Harvey. "Christianity." In *Global Religions: An Introduction*, edited by Mark Juergensmeyer, 13–32. New York: Oxford University Press, 2003.

———. *Fire from Heaven: The Rise of Pentecostal Spirituality and the Reshaping Of Religion in the Twenty-First Century.* Reading, MA: Addison Wesley, 1995.

Craigie, Peter C. "The Day of the Lord in the Book of Amos." In *The Book of Amos*, 105–21. Word Biblical Commentary. Dallas: Word, 1988.

Curtin, Philip D. *The Atlantic Slave Trade: A Census.* Madison: University of Wisconsin Press, 1972.

Darity, William A., Jr., and A. Kirsten Mullen. *From Here to Equality: Reparations for Black Americans in the Twenty-First Century.* Chapel Hill: University of North Carolina Press, 2020.

Davis, James A., Tom W. Smith, and Peter V. Marsden. *A New Compendium of Trends from the General Social Survey.* Social Change Report No. 64. Chicago: NORC at the University of Chicago, 2007. https://gss.norc.org/content/dam/gss/get-documentation/pdf/reports/social-change-reports/SC64%20A%20new%20compendium%20of%20trends.pdf.

Dayton, Donald W. *Theological Roots of Pentecostalism.* Studies in Evangelicalism. Grand Rapids: Baker Academic, 1987.

De Brey, Cristina, Jijun Zhang, and Mary Ann Fox Duffy. "Digest of Education Statistics, 2020." Washington, DC: U.S. Department of Education, National Center for Education Statistics, Institute of Education Sciences, 2021. https://nces.ed.gov/pubs2021/2021009.pdf.

DeAngelis, Tori. "Helping Black Men and Boys Gain Optimal Mental Health." *American Psychological Association Monitor on Psychology* 52, no. 6 (2024). https://www.apa.org/monitor/2021/09/ce-black-mental-health.

Dieter, Melvin E. *The Holiness Revival of the Nineteenth Century.* 2nd ed. Metuchen, NJ: Scarecrow, 1996.

Dodd, C. H. *Apostolic Preaching and Its Developments.* London: Hodder & Stoughton, 1936.

———. *The Parables of the Kingdom.* New York: Charles Scribner's Sons, 1935.

Douglas, Kelly Brown. *The Black Christ.* Bishop Henry McNeal Turner/Sojourner Truth Series in Black Religion 9. Maryknoll, NY: Orbis, 1994.

Duffield, Guy P., and Nathaniel M. Van Cleave. *Foundations of Pentecostal Theology.* Los Angeles: L.I.F.E. Bible College, 1983.

Eck, Diana L. *A New Religious America: How a "Christian Country" Has Become the World's Most Religiously Diverse Nation.* San Francisco: HarperSanFrancisco, 2001.

Economic Policy Institute. "The State of Working America: Wages by Race and Ethnicity." https://www.epi.org/publication/state-of-working-america-wages-race-and-ethnicity/.

"The Supreme Being in African Traditional Religion and Christianity." EduBirdie, October 10, 2023. https://edubirdie.com/examples/the-supreme-being-in-african-traditional-religion-and-christianity/.

Edwards, Bryan. *The History, Civil and Commercial, of the British Colonies in the West Indies.* Vol. 2. London: John Stockdale, 1793.

Eltis, David, and David Richardson. *Atlas of the Transatlantic Slave Trade.* New Haven: Yale University Press, 2010.

Ely, Danielle M., and Anne K. Driscoll. "Infant Mortality in the United States, 2019: Data From the Period Linked Birth/Infant Death File." NCHS Data Brief No. 395. Hyattsville, MD: National Center for Health Statistics, Centers for Disease Control and Prevention, March 2021. https://www.cdc.gov/nchs/products/databriefs/db395.htm.

Equal Justice Initiative. "Racial Justice." https://eji.org/issues/racial-justice.

Ervin, Howard M. *Conversion-Initiation and the Baptism in the Holy Spirit: An Engaging Critique of James D.G. Dunn's* Baptism in the Holy Spirit. Peabody, MA: Hendrickson, 1990.

———. *Spirit Baptism: A Biblical Investigation.* Peabody, MA: Hendrickson, 1987.

Europe Missions. "Sweden Northern Europe Missions." https://www.europemissions.org/sweden.

Evangelical Friends Alliance. "Evangelical Friend." October 1983. http://digitalcommons.georgefox.edu/cgi/viewcontent.cgi?article=1175&context=nwym_evangelical_friend.

Everett, David L. *The Future Horizon for a Prophetic Tradition: A Missiological, Hermeneutical, and Leadership Approach to Education and Black Church Civic Engagement*. Eugene, OR: Wipf and Stock, 2017.

Ezenwa, Chinedu Paul. "The Value of Human Dignity: A Socio-Cultural Approach to Analyzing the Crisis of Values among Igbo People of Nigeria." PhD diss., University of Würzburg, 2017. https://doi.org/10.25595/1351.

Faith Seeking Understanding. "Montanus: Faith Seeking Understanding." https://faith-seeking-understanding.org/tag/montanus/.

Falola, Toyin, and Niyi Afolabi, eds. *The African Diaspora: Slavery, Modernity, and Globalization*. Rochester, NY: University of Rochester Press, 2007.

———. *Nationalism and African Intellectuals*. Rochester, NY: University of Rochester Press, 2001.

Felder, Cain Hope. "The Impact of Christianity on the Black Race." *Journal of Black Studies* 15, no. 3 (1985) 327–43.

———. *Stony the Road We Trod: African American Biblical Interpretation*. Minneapolis: Fortress, 1991.

———. *Troubling Biblical Waters: Race, Class, and Family*. Maryknoll, NY: Orbis, 1989.

Fields, Bruce L. *Introducing Black Theology: Three Crucial Questions for the Evangelical Church*. Grand Rapids: Baker Academic, 2001.

Finley, Stephen C., ed. *Religion of White Rage: White Workers, Religious Fervor, and the Myth of Black Racial Progress*. Edinburgh: Edinburgh University Press, 2020.

Flusser, David. *Jesus*. Jerusalem: Magnes, Hebrew University, 1969.

Franklin, John Hope. *From Slavery to Freedom: A History of African Americans*. 7th ed. New York: Alfred A. Knopf, 1994.

Frazier, E. Franklin. *The Negro Church in America/The Black Church Since Frazier*. New York: Knopf, 1974.

Freeman Institute. "The Lemba—the Black Jews of Southern Africa." http://www.freemaninstitute.com/Gallery/lemba.htm.

Fuller, R. H. *The Mission and Achievement of Jesus: An Examination of the Presuppositions of New Testament Theology*. London: SCM Press, 1954.

Furnas, J. C. *The Road to Harper's Ferry*. New York: William Sloane Associates, 1959.

Gallup. "Just Why Do Americans Attend Church?" April 6, 2007. https://news.gallup.com/poll/27124/just-why-americans-attend-church.aspx.

Gavitt, Robin. "The Nature of Pentecostal Religious Commitment: Views From the Outside and the Inside." MA thesis, University of Rhode Island, 1983. https://doi.org/10.23860/thesis-gavitt-robin-1983.

Gee, Donald. *The Pentecostal Movement: Its Origin, Development and Distinctive Character*. Rev. ed. Springfield, MO: Gospel Publishing House, 1967.

Ginn, Craig Warryn Clifford. "Theological Authority in the Hymns and Spirituals of American Protestantism, 1830-1930." PhD diss., The University of Leeds, 2009. https://etheses.whiterose.ac.uk/12735/1/505058.pdf.

Gledhill, Ruth. "Church Attendance Has Been Propped up by Immigrants, Says Study." *The Guardian*, June 3, 2014. http://www.theguardian.com/world/2014/jun/03/church-attendance-propped-immigrants-study.

God's Kingdom First. "The Kingdom in the Early Church Fathers." http://godskingdomfirst.org/Fathers.htm.

Godwyn, Morgan. *The Negro's and Indian's Advocate, Suing for Their Admission Into the Church: Or, a Persuasive to the Instructing and Baptizing of the Negro's and Indians in Our Plantations, Etc.* London: 1680.

Goff, James R., Jr. *Fields White Unto Harvest: Charles F. Parham and the Missionary Origins of Pentecostalism.* Fayetteville: University of Arkansas Press, 1988.

Gordon, Laura W. "Back to Eden: A Practical Ecotheology and Entrepreneurial Endeavor." DMin diss., George Fox University, 2023. https://digitalcommons.georgefox.edu/cgi/viewcontent.cgi?article=1585&context=dmin.

Grizzle, Trevor. "The Importance of Africa in the Kingdom: Past, Present, and Future." In *The Kingdom, Globalization and You,* edited by Dana Carson, 87–98. Houston: Dana Carson Kingdom Ministries, 2017.

———. *Kingdom Advancing: Rethinking the Kingdom of God for the Twenty-First-Century Church.* Tulsa, OK: Harrison House, 2006.

———. "The Kingdom of God in a Globalized World." In *The Kingdom, Globalization and You,* edited by Dana Carson. Houston: Dana Carson Kingdom Ministries, 2017.

———. "The Kingdom of God in the New Testament and Eschatology." In *The Kingdom, the Church and You,* edited by Dana Carson, 39–51. Houston: Kingdom Publishing & Printing, 2013

———. *Unpublished Notes on Matthew 24:14,* January 10, 2023.

Gutiérrez, Gustavo. *A Theology of Liberation: History, Politics, and Salvation.* Translated and edited by Caridad Inda and John Eagleson. Maryknoll, NY: Orbis, 1973.

Gutman, Herbert G. *The Black Family in Slavery and Freedom, 1750–1925.* New York: Pantheon, 1976.

Hackett, David G. *Religion and American Culture: A Reader.* 3rd ed. New York: Routledge, 2015.

Hadden, Jeffrey K. "Pentecostalism." Religious Movements Homepage Project, University of Virginia. https://en-academic.com/dic.nsf/enwiki/14301.

Hall, Gwendolyn Midlo. *Africans in Colonial Louisiana: The Development of Afro-Creole Culture in the Eighteenth Century.* Baton Rouge: Louisiana State University Press, 1992.

Harrell, David Edwin, Jr. *All Things Are Possible: The Healing and Charismatic Revivals in Modern America.* Bloomington: Indiana University Press, 1975.

Harris, Jessica B. *High on the Hog: A Culinary Journey from Africa to America.* New York: Bloomsbury, 2011.

Heckman, James J., and Paul Lafontaine. "The American High School Graduation Rate: Trends and Levels." *The Review of Economics and Statistics* https://pubmed.ncbi.nlm.nih.gov/20625528/.

Heartland Center for Leadership Development. "Building Strong Leaders Through Programs for Community Vitality." https://heartlandcenter.info/wp-content/uploads/2015/03/HC-tri-fold-7-161.pdf.

Herrick, Henry M. *The Kingdom of God in the Writings of the Fathers.* Chicago: University of Chicago Press, 1903.

Hollenweger, Walter J. *The Pentecostals.* Minneapolis: Augsburg, 1972.

Hughes, Ray H. *Pentecostal Preaching.* Cleveland, TN: Pathway, 1981.

Humphreys, David. *An Historical Account of the Incorporated Society for the Propagation of the Gospel in Foreign Parts.* London: Joseph Downing, 1730.

Hunter, Harold D., and Cecil M. Robeck Jr. *The Azusa Street Revival and Its Legacy.* Eugene, OR: Wipf and Stock, 2009.

Hyman, Mark. *Blacks Who Died for Jesus: A History Book.* Philadelphia: Corrective Black History Books, 1983. Reprint, Nashville: Winston-Derek, 1988.

Idowu, E. Bolaji. *African Traditional Religion: A Definition.* London: SCM, 1973.

Imtiaz, Saba. "A New Generation Redefines What It Means to Be a Missionary." *The Atlantic,* March 8, 2018. https://www.theatlantic.com/international/archive/2018/03/young-missionaries/551585/.

Inman, Jimmy. "The Biblical Teaching About Tongues." https://jimmyinman.com/topical-studies/the-biblical-teaching-about-tongues/.

Irwin, Véronique, et al. "National Center for Education Statistics Report on the Condition of Education 2021: Public High School Graduation Rates for the 2018–2019 School Year." https://nces.ed.gov/programs/coe/pdf/2021/coi_508c.pdf.

———. *Report on the Condition of Education 2021* (NCES 2021-144). Washington, DC: U.S. Department of Education, National Center for Education Statistics, May 2021.

Jeremias, Joachim. *The Parables of Jesus.* Rev. ed. Translated by S. H. Hooke. New York: Charles Scribner's Sons, 1963.

Johnson, Idella Lulamae. "Development of the African American Gospel Piano Style (1926-1960): A Socio-Musical Analysis of Arizona Dranes and Thomas A. Dorsey." PhD diss., University of Pittsburgh, October 1, 2009. http://d-scholarship.pitt.edu/9095/.

Johnson, Todd M., and Gina A. Zurlo. *Introducing Spirit-Empowered Christianity: The Global Pentecostal & Charismatic Movements in the 21st Century.* Tulsa, OK: Oral Roberts University Press, 2020.

Joint Center for Housing Studies of Harvard University. *The State of the Nation's Housing 2021.* Cambridge: President and Fellows of Harvard College, 2021. https://www.jchs.harvard.edu/state-nations-housing-2021.

Jones, E. Stanley. *The Christ of Every Road: A Study in Pentecost.* Nashville: Abingdon, 1930.

Juergensmeyer, Mark, ed. *Global Religions: An Introduction.* New York: Oxford University Press, 2003.

Kaiser, Walter C., Jr. *A History of Israel: From the Bronze Age through the Jewish Wars.* Nashville: Broadman & Holman, 1998.

Kalu, Ogbu. *African Pentecostalism: An Introduction.* Oxford: Oxford University Press, 2008.

Keller, Timothy. *Generous Justice: How God's Grace Makes Us Just.* New York: Riverhead, 2010.

Kelly, J. N. D. *Early Christian Doctrines.* Rev. ed. San Francisco: Harper & Row, 1978.

Kiyosaki, Robert T. *Rich Dad, Poor Dad: What the Rich Teach Their Kids About Money That the Poor and Middle Class Do Not!* New York: Warner Business, 2000.

Klein, Herbert S., and Ben Vinson III. *African Slavery in Latin America and the Caribbean.* 2nd ed. New York: Oxford University Press, 2007.

Kunter, Katharina, and Jens Holger Schjörring. *Changing Relations Between Churches in Europe and Africa: The Internationalization of Christianity and Politics in the 20th*

Century. https://researchportal.helsinki.fi/en/publications/changing-relations-between-churches-in-europe-and-africa-the-inte.

Kurtz, Paul. *The Courage to Become: The Virtues of Humanism.* Westport, CT: Praeger, 1997.

Kurtz, Paul, and Edwin H. Wilson, eds. *Humanist Manifesto II.* Buffalo, NY: Prometheus, 1973.

Labanca, Nicholas. "Blood of the Martyrs is Still Seed for the Church." *Ascension Press,* September 17, 2018. https://media.ascensionpress.com/2018/09/17/blood-of-the-martyrs-is-still-seed-for-the-church/.

Ladd, George Eldon. *The Blessed Hope: A Biblical Study of the Second Advent and the Rapture.* Grand Rapids: Eerdmans, 1956.

———. *Gospel of the Kingdom.* Grand Rapids: Eerdmans, 1959.

———. *The Presence of the Future: The Eschatology of Biblical Realism.* Grand Rapids: Eerdmans, 1974.

Land, Steven Jack. *Pentecostal Spirituality: A Passion for the Kingdom.* 2nd ed. Cleveland, TN: CPT, 2010.

Learning Policy Institute. *Pushed Out: Trends and Disparities in Out-of-School Suspensions.* Palo Alto: Learning Policy Institute, 2022.

Leke, Acha, Musta Chironga, and George Desvaux. *Africa's Business Revolution: How to Succeed in the World's Next Big Growth Market.* Cambridge: Harvard Business Press, 2018.

Lewis, William G. "The Lake Chapel at Somerset Plantation and Religious Instruction in the Antebellum South." MA Thesis, East Carolina University, 2016. https://thescholarship.ecu.edu/server/api/core/bitstreams/d68eed13–9ebd-4435-b8d2–5c90fa4c8f8c/content.

Lincoln, C. Eric. *The Black Church Since Frazier.* New York: Schocken, 1974.

———. *The Black Muslims in America.* 3rd ed. Grand Rapids: Eerdmans, 1994.

———. *Race, Religion, and the Continuing American Dilemma.* New York: Friendship, 1984.

Lincoln, C. Eric, and Lawrence H. Mamiya. *The Black Church in the African American Experience.* Durham, NC: Duke University Press, 1990.

Litwack, Leon F. *Been in the Storm So Long: The Aftermath of Slavery.* New York: Alfred A. Knopf, 1979.

Lovett, Leonard. "Black Origins of Pentecostalism." In *Aspects of Pentecostal-Charismatic Origins,* edited by Vinson Synan, 135–47. Plainfield, NJ: Logos International, 1975.

Manning, Patrick. *The African Diaspora: A History Through Culture.* New York: Columbia University Press, 2009.

Martin, David. *Tongues of Fire: The Explosion of Protestantism in Latin America.* Oxford: Blackwell, 1990.

Masci, David. "Black Americans Are More Likely Than Overall Public to Be Christian, Protestant." Pew Research Center, April 14, 2024. https://www.pewresearch.org/short-reads/2018/04/23/black-americans-are-more-likely-than-overall-public-to-be-christian-protestant/.

Mather, Cotton. *The Negro Christianized. An Essay to Excite and Assist That Good Work, the Instruction of Negro-Servants in Christianity.* Boston: B. Green, 1706.

Mbiti, John S. *African Religions and Philosophy.* London: Heinemann, 1969.

McFadden, John, et al. "2002 AAPP Monograph Series: African American Professors Program." Scholar Commons, January 1, 2002. https://scholarcommons.sc.edu/mcfadden_monographs/1/.

McMurry, Linda O. *George Washington Carver: Scientist and Symbol.* New York: Oxford University Press, 1981.

McVeigh, Malcolm J. *God in Africa: Conceptions of God in African Traditional Religion and Christianity.* Cape Cod: Claude Stark, 1974.

Mdingi, Hlulani Msimelelo. "The Revelation of God: Meditations of the Black Church in Existential Times." ThD Thesis, University of South Africa, 2017. https://uir.unisa.ac.za/bitstream/10500/25123/1/thesis_mdingi_hm.pdf.

Meier, August, and Elliott Rudwick. *From Plantation to Ghetto.* 3rd ed. New York: Hill and Wang, 1976.

———. *The Making of Black America: Essays in Negro Life and History.* New York: Atheneum, 1969.

Menzies, William. *Anointed to Serve: The Story of the Assemblies of God.* Springfield, MO: Gospel House, 1971.

Merriam-Webster Dictionary. "Wealth." https://www.merriam-webster.com/dictionary/wealth.

Miller, Donald E., and Tetsunao Yamamori. "Global Pentecostalism: The New Face of Christian Social Engagement." Choice Reviews Online 45, no. 07 (March 1, 2008). https://doi.org/10.5860/choice.45-3735.

Mitchem, Stephanie Y. *Introducing Womanist Theology.* Maryknoll, NY: Orbis, 2014.

Morris, Leon. *The Gospel According to John: The English Text with Introduction, Exposition and Notes.* New International Commentary on the New Testament. Grand Rapids: Eerdmans, 1971.

Muhammad, Elijah. *The Fall of America.* Chicago: Muhammad's Temple of Islam No. 2, 1973.

———. *Message to the Blackman in America.* Chicago: Muhammad's Temple of Islam No. 2, 1965.

The Multinational Monitor. "The Wealth Divide: The Growing Gap in the United States Between the Rich and the Rest: An Interview with Edward Wolff." *The Multinational Monitor* 24, no. 5 (2003). https://www.multinationalmonitor.org/mm2003/03may/may03interviewswolff.html.

Muzorewa, Gwinyai H. *The Origins and Development of African Theology.* Maryknoll, NY: Orbis, 1985.

Müller-Fahrenholz, Geiko. *God's Spirit: Transforming a World in Crisis.* Geneva and New York: WCC Publications/Continuum, 1995.

NAACP. *Criminal Justice Fact Sheet.* Baltimore: National Association for the Advancement of Colored People, 2023. https://naacp.org/resources/criminal-justice-fact-sheet.

National Center for Education Statistics. "High School Graduation Rates." 2021. https://nces.ed.gov/programs/coe/indicator/coi/high-school-graduation-rates.

———. Methodology Studies—Achievement Gaps | NAEP." https://nces.ed.gov/nationsreportcard/studies/gaps/.

———. "National Student Group Scores and Score Gaps." The Nation's Report Card, 2022. https://www.nationsreportcard.gov.

———. "On-Time Graduation." Equity in Education Dashboard US Department of Education, Institute of Education Sciences. https://nces.ed.gov/programs/equity/indicator_c6.asp.

National Center for Health Statistics. "Health, United States, 2020–2021: Annual Perspective" (DHHS Publication No. 2022–1232). Hyattsville, MD: U.S. Department of Health and Human Services, Centers for Disease Control and Prevention, 2022. https://www.cdc.gov/nchs/hus/index.htm.

Ndubuisi-Nwuzor, Dominic. "A Survey of African Christology." *Cuadernos Doctorales: Teología* no. 30 (January 1, 1997) 1–64. https://dadun.unav.edu/bitstream/10171/11331/1/CDT_XXX_01.pdf.

Nelsen, Hart M., and Anne Kusener Nelsen. *Black Church in the Sixties*. Lexington: University Press of Kentucky, 2021.

Nelson, C. Eric. *The Pentecostal Movement in the United States*. Washington, DC: National Catholic Welfare Conference, 1955.

Newbigin, Lesslie. *The Gospel in a Pluralist Society*. Grand Rapids: Eerdmans, 1989.

Nichols, James Hastings. *History of Christianity, 1650–1950: Secularization of the West*. New York: Harper & Brothers, 1956.

Nickel, Joshua Mark. "Pentecostalism's Unlikely Grandfather—John Wesley and the Organized Pursuit of More." February 2023. https://joshuamarknickel.com/2023/02/.F

Niebuhr, H. Richard. *Christ and Culture*. New York: Harper & Row, 1951.

Novakovic, Lidija. *John 1–10*. Catholic Commentary on Sacred Scripture. Grand Rapids: Baker Academic, 2022.

Oden, Thomas C. *Early Libyan Christianity: Uncovering a North African Tradition*. Downers Grove, IL: IVP Academic, 2011.

———. *How Africa Shaped the Christian Mind: Rediscovering the African Seedbed of Western Christianity*. Downers Grove, IL: InterVarsity, 2007.

Oduyoye, Mercy Amba. *Hearing and Knowing: Theological Reflections on Christianity in Africa*. Eugene, OR: Wipf and Stock, 1986.

Office of Minority Health. "Home Page—Office of Minority Health (OMH)." https://minorityhealth.hhs.gov/.

Olaleye, Isaac O. *The Crisis of Mission in the African American Church: Reflections of a Missiologist*. Garland, TX: ILO Productions, 1997.

"Out of Africa." *Ministry Today*, January 1, 2006. https://www.ministrytodaymag.com.

Owens, Jayani, and Hugh Wok. "Black Boys Face Double Jeopardy at School." Yale Insights, January 9, 2023, https://insights.som.yale.edu/insights/black-boys-face-double-jeopardy-at-school.

Parfitt, Tudor. *Journey to the Vanished City: The Search for a Lost Tribe of Israel*. New York: Vintage, 2000.

Paris, Peter J. *The Social Teaching of the Black Churches*. Philadelphia: Fortress, 1985.

Parrinder, Geoffrey. *African Traditional Religion*. Westport, CT: Greenwood, 1976.

Patheos. "Nonreligious Questions." http://www.patheos.com/blogs/crossexamined/2015/05/christianity-becomes-an-african-religion-islam-overtakes-christianity-and-other-upcoming-changes/.

———. "Pentecostal Ethics and Community." https://www.patheos.com/library/pentecostal/ethics-values/pentecostal-ethics-and-community.

Patterson, Orlando. *Slavery and Social Death: A Comparative Study*. Cambridge: Harvard University Press, 1982.

Pegram, Jeffrey Keefe. "Political Liberalism, Religion, and the Prophetic Tradition." PhD diss., University of Maryland, 2007. https://www.academia.edu/74675819/Political_Liberalism_Religion_and_the_Prophetic_Tradition.

Pentecost, Dwight J. *Things to Come: A Study in Biblical Eschatology.* Grand Rapids: Zondervan, 1958.

Pew Research Center. "Christian Movements and Denominations." April 14, 2024. https://www.pewresearch.org/religion/2011/12/19/global-christianity-movements-and-denominations/.

———. "Facts about the U.S. Black Population." https://www.pewresearch.org/race-and-ethnicity/fact-sheet/facts-about-the-us-black-population/.

———. *Faith Among Black Americans.* Washington, DC: Pew Research Center, 2018. https://www.pewresearch.org/religion/2021/02/16/faith-among-black-americans.

———. "Faith and Conflict: The Global Rise of Christianity." April 14, 2024. https://www.pewresearch.org/religion/2005/03/02/faith-and-conflict-the-global-rise-of-christianity/.

———. "The Future of World Religions: Population Growth Projections, 2010–2050." Pew Research Center, April 2, 2015. https://www.pewresearch.org/religion/2015/04/02/religious-projections-2010-2050/.

———. *Global Christianity: A Report on the Size and Distribution of the World's Christian Population.* Washington, DC: Pew Forum on Religion & Public Life, 2011.

———. "Historical Overview of Pentecostalism in Nigeria." April 14, 2024. https://www.pewresearch.org/religion/2006/10/05/historical-overview-of-pentecostalism-in-nigeria/.

———. *A Religious Portrait of African-Americans.* Washington, DC: Pew Research Center, 2009. https://www.pewresearch.org/religion/2009/01/30/a-religious-portrait-of-african-americans/.

———. *Spirit and Power: A 10-Country Survey of Pentecostals.* Washington, DC: Pew Research Center, 2006. https://www.pewresearch.org/religion/2006/10/05/spirit-and-power/.

Phillips, Ulrich Bonnell. *American Negro Slavery: A Survey of the Supply, Employment and Control of Negro Labor as Determined by the Plantation Regime.* New York: D. Appleton and Company, 1918.

Pillsbury, Parker. "The Church as It Is: The Forlorn Hope of Slavery (1847, 1885)." https://medicolegal.tripod.com/forlorn.htm.

Pinn, Anthony B. *The Black Church in the Post-Civil Rights Era.* Maryknoll, NY: Orbis, 2002.

Pococke, Edward. *A Commentary on the Prophecy of Micah.* Oxford: Sheldonian Theatre, 1677.

Pyon, Kevin. "From the Suffering (Black) Jesus to the Sacrilegious Yeezus: Representations of Christ in African-American Art and Religious Thought." NC Docks, January 1, 2015. https://libres.uncg.edu/ir/listing.aspx?id=18331.

Raboteau, Albert J. *Slave Religion: The "Invisible Institution" in the Antebellum South.* New York: Oxford University Press, 2004.

Rauschenbusch, Walter. *Christianity and the Social Crisis.* New York: Macmillan, 1907.

Revival Theology Resources. "New Haven Theology." http://www.revivaltheology.net/pages/defin.html.

Ridderbos, Herman. *The Coming of the Kingdom*. Philadelphia: Presbyterian and Reformed, 1962.

Robeck, Cecil M., Jr. *The Azusa Street Mission and Revival: The Birth of the Global Pentecostal Movement*. Nashville: Thomas Nelson, 2006.

Roberts, J. Deotis. *Liberation and Reconciliation: A Black Theology*. Philadelphia: Westminster, 1971.

Roberts, Wesley. "Rejecting the Negro Pew." *Christian History*, January 1995, 18–22.

Robinson, J. A. T. *Jesus and His Coming: The Emergence of a Doctrine*. London: SCM, 1957.

Robinson, Rich. *Hebrew Heritage Bible Newer Testament: A Hebrew Roots Translation*. Simi Valley, CA: Messianic Jewish Publishers, 1992.

Rodgers, Darrin. 2005. Review of Assemblies of God Heritage. Flower Pentecostal Heritage Center, October 1, 2005. https://ifphc.org/-/media/FPHC/Heritage-Magazine/2005_04.pdf.

Ross, Kyle, and Justin Dorazio. "The Latest Poverty, Income, and Food Insecurity Data Reveal Continuing Racial Disparities." Center for American Progress, December 21, 2022. https://www.americanprogress.org/article/the-latest-poverty-income-and-food-insecurity-data-reveal-continuing-racial-disparities/.

Ruether, Rosemary R. *Sexism and God Talk: Toward a Feminist Theology*. Boston: Beacon, 1993.

Rutherford, Jane. "Equality as the Primary Constitutional Value: The Case for Applying Employment Discrimination Laws to Religion." *Cornell Law Review/The Cornell Law Quarterly* 81, no. 5 (January 1, 1996). http://scholarship.law.cornell.edu/cgi/viewcontent.cgi?article=2603&context=clr.

Ryrie, Charles C. *Dispensationalism*. Chicago: Moody, 1995.

Salley, A. S., Jr., and John M. Behm. *Negro Suffrage in South Carolina*. Columbia: The Historical Commission of South Carolina, 1913.

Salley, Columbus, and Ronald Behm. *What Color Is Your God? Black Consciousness and the Christian Faith*. New York: Harper and Row, 1979.

Sanders, Cheryl J. *Empowerment Ethics for a Liberated People: A Path to African American Social Transformation*. Minneapolis: Fortress, 1995.

———. *Saints in Exile: The Holiness-Pentecostal Experience in African American Religion and Culture*. New York: Oxford University Press, 1996.

Sanders, E. P. *Judaism: Practice and Belief, 63 BCE–66 CE*. London: SCM, 1992.

Sanneh, Lamin. *Abolitionists Abroad: American Blacks and the Making of Modern West Africa*. Cambridge: Harvard University Press, 2009.

———. "Lifting the Curse of Babel." *The New York Times*, November 6, 1994. https://www.nytimes.com/1994/11/06/opinion/lifting-the-curse-of-babel.html.

———. *West African Christianity: The Religious Impact*. Maryknoll, NY: Orbis, 1983.

———. *Whose Religion Is Christianity? The Gospel Beyond the West*. Grand Rapids: Eerdmans, 2003.

Sawyerr, Harry. *Creative Evangelism: Towards a New Christian Encounter with Africa*. London: Lutterworth, 1968.

———. *God, Ancestor or Creator? Aspects of Traditional Belief in Ghana, Nigeria & Sierra Leone*. Longman Group, 1970.

Sawyerr, Harry, and John Parratt. *The Origins and Development of African Theology*. Maryknoll, NY: Orbis, 1987.

Schweitzer, Albert. *The Quest of the Historical Jesus*. Translated by W. Montgomery. London: A. & C. Black, 1910.

Scott-Clayton, Judith, and Jing Li. "Black-White Disparity in Student Loan Debt More than Triples After Graduation." Brookings Institute, October 20, 2016. https://www.brookings.edu/articles/black-white-disparity-in-student-loan-debt-more-than-triples-after-graduation/.

Sells, M. L., Ethan Blum, Geraldine S. Perry, Paul Eke, and Letitia Presley-Cantrell. "Excess Burden of Poverty and Hypertension, by Race and Ethnicity, on the Prevalence of Cardiovascular Disease." *Preventing Chronic Disease* 20, no. E109 (November 22, 2023). https://pmc.ncbi.nlm.nih.gov/articles/PMC10684284/.

Sernett, Milton C. *Black Religion and American Evangelicalism: White Protestants, Plantation Missions, and the Flowering of Negro Churches in the Postbellum South.* Metuchen, NJ: Scarecrow, 1975.

Setiloane, Gabriel M. *African Theology: An Introduction.* Pretoria: University of South Africa Press, 1987.

Seymour, William J., and Apostolic Faith Mission. "The Apostolic Faith." https://azusabooks.org/papers.shtml.

Sherwood, Harriet. "Church Attendance Has Been Propped Up by Immigrants, Says Study." *The Guardian*, June 3, 2014. http://www.theguardian.com/world/2014/jun/03/church-attendance-propped-immigrants-study.

Shikany, James M., Yu-Mei Schoenberger, Badrinath Konety, and Selwyn M. Vickers. "African American Men's Health." *American Journal of Men's Health* 12, no. 5 (2018) 1265–74.

Signé, Landry. "US Trade and Investment in Africa." Brookings, July 28, 2021. https://www.brookings.edu/articles/us-trade-and-investment-in-africa/.

Skinner, Tom. *Black and Free.* Grand Rapids: Zondervan, 1970.

Smith, Harold B., ed. *Pentecostals from the Inside Out.* Christianity Today Series. Wheaton, IL: Victor, 1990.

Smith, Ember, and Richard V. Reeves. "SAT Math Scores Mirror and Maintain Racial Inequity." Brookings, December 1, 2020. https://www.brookings.edu/articles/sat-math-scores-mirror-and-maintain-racial-inequity/.

Spotts, Christopher Taylor. "Rediscovering Sabbath: Hebrew Social Thought And Its Contribution To Black Theology\U27s Vision For America." 2013. https://core.ac.uk/download/67759662.pdf.

Stagg, Frank. *New Testament Theology.* Nashville: Broadman, 1962.

Storms, Sam. "History of the Pentecostal-Charismatic Movements." https://www.samstorms.org/all-articles/post/history-of-the-pentecostal-charismatic-movements.

Strachan, Charles Gordon. *The Pentecostal Theology of Edward Irving.* Peabody, MA: Hendrickson, 1973.

Strange, Thomas. "Teaching Christianity in the Face of Adversity: African American Religious Leaders in the Late Antebellum South." Thesis, The University of Manchester, 2011. https://ethos.bl.uk/OrderDetails.do?uin=uk.bl.ethos.542712.

Substance Abuse and Mental Health Services Administration. "National Survey on Drug Use and Health (NSDUH)." Rockville, MD: U.S. Department of Health and Human Services, Substance Abuse and Mental Health Services Administration, updated 2023. https://www.samhsa.gov/data/data-we-collect/nsduh-national-survey-drug-use-and-health.

———. "National Survey on Drug Use and Health." September 2020. https://www.samhsa.gov/data/sites/default/files/reports/rpt31099/2019NSDUH-AA/AfricanAmerican%202019%20NSDUH.pdf.

Synan, Vinson. *The Century of the Holy Spirit: 100 Years of Pentecostal and Charismatic Renewal, 1901–2001*. Nashville: Thomas Nelson, 2012.

———. "Christian History Timeline: The Rise of Pentecostalism." *Christian History* 58, vol. XVII, no. 2 (Spring 1998) 36–38.

———. *The Holiness-Pentecostal Tradition: Charismatic Movements in the Twentieth Century*. 2nd ed. Grand Rapids: Eerdmans, 1997.

Taylor, Charles. *A Secular Age*. Cambridge: Belknap Press of Harvard University Press, 2007.

Taylor, Robert Joseph, Linda M. Chatters, and James S. Levin. "Religious Participation Among African Americans: Influence of Organizational, Non-Organizational, and Subjective Religiosity." *Review of Religious Research* 55, no. 4 (2014) 397–421.

Thomas, Hugh. *The Slave Trade: The Story of the Atlantic Slave Trade, 1440–1870*. New York: Simon & Schuster, 1997.

Tillich, Paul. *A History of Christian Thought: From Its Judaic and Hellenistic Origins to Existentialism*. Edited by Carl E. Braaten. New York: Harper & Row, 1972.

Tinsley, Annie. "Towards a Re-reading of Colossians From an African American Postcolonial Perspective." PhD Thesis, University of Birmingham, 2010. http://etheses.bham.ac.uk/id/eprint/1192.

Toon, Peter, and J.D. Spiceland. *One God in Trinity*. London: Bagster, 1980.

Townes, Emilie Maureen. *A Troubling in My Soul: Womanist Perspectives on Evil and Suffering*. Maryknoll, NY: Orbis, 1993.

Trevor-Roper, Hugh. *The Rise of Christian Europe*. London: Thames and Hudson, 1964.

———. "The Rise of Christian Europe." BBC Third Programme lecture, 1963.

Turner, Richard Brent. *Islam in the African-American Experience*. Bloomington: Indiana University Press, 1997.

Twelftree, Graham H. *Jesus the Exorcist: A Contribution to the Study of the Historical Jesus*. Eugene, OR: Wipf and Stock, 1999.

United Nations Conference on Trade and Development (UNCTAD). *Creative Economy Outlook: Trends in International Trade in Creative Industries (2002–2015) and Country Profiles (2005–2014)*. Geneva: UNCTAD, 2018.

United States International Trade Commission. *U.S. Trade and Investment with Sub-Saharan Africa: Recent Developments*. Washington, DC: USITC, 2020.

United States Sentencing Commission. *Demographic Differences in Federal Sentencing: An Update for Fiscal Years 2017–2021*. Washington, DC: USSC, 2023. https://www.ussc.gov/research/research-reports/demographic-differences-federal-sentencing-update-fiscal-years-2017-2021.

U.S. Census Bureau. "Quarterly Residential Vacancies and Homeownership, First Quarter 2021." Washington, DC: U.S. Department of Commerce, April 27, 2021. https://www.census.gov/housing/hvs/files/currenthvspress.pdf.

U.S. Department of Health and Human Services. "Chronic Disease Indicators (CDI)." Atlanta, GA: Centers for Disease Control and Prevention, updated 2023. https://www.cdc.gov/cdi/.

U.S. Department of Labor. "The Employment Situation—August 2021." https://www.bls.gov/news.release/archives/empsit_09032021.pdf.

———. "Labor Force Characteristics by Race and Ethnicity, 2020." Bureau of Labor Statistics, November 2021. https://www.bls.gov/opub/reports/race-and-ethnicity/2020/home.htm.

U.S. Government Accountability Office. "K-12 Education: Discipline Disparities for Black Students, Boys, and Students With Disabilities," April 10, 2018. https://www.gao.gov/products/gao-18-258.

van Klinken, Adriaan. *Pentecostal Plurality and Sexual Politics in Africana Worlds.* London: Routledge, 2023.

Velazquez, Jose, Jr. "The Theological Basis of John Wesley's Social Concern." MDiv thesis, Asbury Theological Seminary, 1967. https://core.ac.uk/download/216986394.pdf.

Waidmann, Timothy A., Kristen Brown, Karishma Furtado, and Vincent Pancini. "State Variation in Black and White Life Expectancy and Evolving Disparities." Urban Institute, January 27, 2025. https:/www.urban.org/research/publication/state-variation-black-and-white-life-expectancy-and-evolving-disparities.

Wallace, Charles Allen. "Sarah's Song: How Folk Music Shattered Slaveholding Ideology in Antebellum Alabama." MA thesis, College of William and Mary, 2009. https://dx.doi.org/doi:10.21220/s2-02wj-yr71.

Wariboko, Nimi. *The Pentecostal Principle: Ethical Methodology in New Spirit.* Grand Rapids: Eerdmans, 2012.

Warrington, Keith. *Pentecostal Theology: A Theology of Encounter.* London: T&T Clark, 2008.

Weaver, Elton H. *Apostle of the Poor: The Life and Work of Missionary Bishop Charles Harrison Mason.* Lanham, MD: University Press of America, 2003.

Weber, Max. *The Protestant Ethic and the Spirit of Capitalism.* Translated by Talcott Parsons. New York: Charles Scribner's Sons, 1958.

Weiss, Johannes. *Jesus' Proclamation of the Kingdom of God.* Edited and translated by Richard Hyde. Philadelphia: Fortress, 1971.

Welchel, Tommy. *They Told Me Their Stories: The Youth and Children of Azusa Street Tell Their Stories.* Tulsa, OK: Dare2Dream, 2006.

Wesley, John. "Letter to William Wilberforce." The Works of John Wesley 13. Edited by Thomas Jackson. London: Wesleyan Methodist Book Room, 1872.

———. *Thoughts Upon Slavery.* London: R. Hawes, 1774.

"Wesley, Wilberforce and the Battle Against Slavery—the Methodist Church." https://www.methodist.org.uk/for-churches/resources/posts/wesley-wilberforce-and-the-battle-against-slavery/.

West, Cornel. *Prophesy Deliverance! An Afro-American Revolutionary Christianity.* Philadelphia: Westminster, 1982.

White, Deborah Gray. *Ar'n't I a Woman?: Female Slaves in the Plantation South.* New York: W. W. Norton, 1985.

———. "Reactions to Oppression: Jurisgenesis in the Jurispathic State." *The Yale Law Journal* 100, no. 8 (June 1, 1991) 2727–46. https://doi.org/10.2307/796910.

White, Peter. "Pentecostalism and Migration: A Contextual Study of the Migrant Ghanaian Classical Pentecostal Churches in South Africa." *HTS Theological Studies* 77, no. 4 (2021). https://doi.org/10.4102/hts.v77i4.6318.

Wikipedia. "Azusa Street Revival." https://en.wikipedia.org/wiki/Azusa_Street_Revival.

Wilcox, W. Bradford, and Nicholas H. Wolfinger. *Soul Mates: Religion, Sex, Love, and Marriage among African Americans and Latinos.* New York: Oxford University Press, 2016.

Williams, Chancellor. *The Destruction of Black Civilization: Great Issues of a Race From 4500 B.C. to 2000 A.D.* 3rd ed. Chicago: Third World, 1992.

Williams, Delores S. *Sisters in the Wilderness: The Challenge of Womanist God-Talk.* Maryknoll, NY: Orbis, 1993.

Wilmore, Gayraud S. *Black Religion and Black Radicalism: An Interpretation of the Religious History of Afro-American People.* Rev. ed. Maryknoll, NY: Orbis, 1983.

Wilson, Theodore Brantner. *The Black Codes of the South.* Tuscaloosa: University of Alabama Press, 1965.

Wilson, Valerie, and William Darity Jr. "Understanding Black-White Disparities in Labor Market Outcomes Requires Models that Account for Persistent Discrimination and Unequal Bargaining Power." Economic Policy Institute, March 25, 2022. https://www.epi.org/unequalpower/publications/understanding-black-white-disparities-in-labor-market-outcomes/.

Wilson-Hartgrove, Jonathan. *Reconstructing the Gospel: Finding Freedom from Slaveholder Religion.* Downers Grove, IL: InterVarsity, 2020.

Wolf, Eric R. *Europe and the People Without History.* Berkeley: University of California Press, 1982.

Woodson, Carter G. *The History of the Negro Church.* Washington, DC: Associated Publishers, 1921.

World Health Organization. *WHO Global Report on Traditional and Complementary Medicine 2019.* Geneva: WHO, 2019.

Wright, N. T. *Jesus and the Victory of God.* Minneapolis: Fortress, 1996.

———. *The Kingdom New Testament: A Contemporary Translation.* New York: HarperOne, 2011.

Yamauchi, Edwin. *Africa and the Bible.* Grand Rapids: Baker Academic, 2004.

Yong, Amos. *Beyond the Impasse: Toward a Pneumatological Theology of Religions.* Grand Rapids: Baker Academic, 2003.

———. *In the Days of Caesar: Pentecostalism and Political Theology.* Grand Rapids: Eerdmans, 2010.

———. *The Spirit Poured Out on All Flesh: Pentecostalism and the Possibility of Global Theology.* Grand Rapids: Baker Academic, 2005.

Yong, Amos, and Estrelda Y. Alexander, eds. *Afro-Pentecostalism: Black Pentecostal and Charismatic Christianity in History and Culture.* New York: New York University Press, 2011.

Young, Brad H. *Jesus the Jewish Theologian.* Grand Rapids: Baker, 1993.

www.ingramcontent.com/pod-product-compliance
Lightning Source LLC
LaVergne TN
LVHW100519110826
845146LV00002B/707

* 9 7 9 8 3 8 5 2 2 4 1 1 1 *